W9-CIO-503

Create
PowerPoint
Presentations

How to Order:

For information on quantity discounts, contact the publisher: Prima Publishing, P.O. Box 1260BK, Rocklin, CA 95677-1260; (916) 632-4400. On your letterhead include information concerning the intended use of the books and the number of books you wish to purchase. For individual orders, turn to the back of this book for more information.

Create PowerPoint Presentations

BRIAN REILLY

PRIMA PUBLISHING

P is a registered trademark of Prima Publishing. In a Weekend is a trademark of Prima Publishing, a division of Prima Communications, Inc. Prima Publishing is a registered trademark of Prima Communications, Inc., Rocklin, California 95677.

©1997 by Brian Reilly. All rights reserved. No part of this book may be reproduced or transmitted in any form or by any means, electronic or mechanical, including photocopying, recording, or by any information storage or retrieval system without written permission from Prima Publishing, except for the inclusion of brief quotations in a review.

Publisher: Matthew H. Carleson
Managing Editor: Dan J. Foster
Acquisitions Editor: Deborah F. Abshier
Development Editor: Joyce Nielsen
Project Editor: Kevin Harreld
Technical Reviewer: Paul Marchesseault
Copy Editor: Susan Christophersen
Interior Layout: Marian Hartsough
Editorial Assistant: Kevin W. Ferns
Cover Design: Prima Design Team
Indexer: Katherine Stimson

Microsoft and Windows are registered trademarks of Microsoft Corporation.

IMPORTANT: If you have problems installing or running Microsoft PowerPoint 97, notify Microsoft Corporation at (206) 635-7056 or on the Web at www.microsoft.com. Prima Publishing cannot provide software support.

Prima Publishing and the author have attempted throughout this book to distinguish proprietary trademarks from descriptive terms by following the capitalization style used by the manufacturer.

Information contained in this book has been obtained by Prima Publishing from sources believed to be reliable. However, because of the possibility of human or mechanical error by our sources, Prima Publishing, or others, the Publisher does not guarantee the accuracy, adequacy, or completeness of any information and is not responsible for any errors or omissions or the results obtained from the use of such information. Readers should be particularly aware of the fact that the Internet is an ever-changing entity. Some facts may have changed since this book went to press.

ISBN: 0-7615-1294-2
Library of Congress Catalog Card Number: 97-69600
Printed in the United States of America

00 01 02 BB10 9 8 7 6 5 4 3 2

To Confidence,
my beloved, beautiful, and brilliant spouse.

CONTENTS AT A GLANCE

CONTENTS

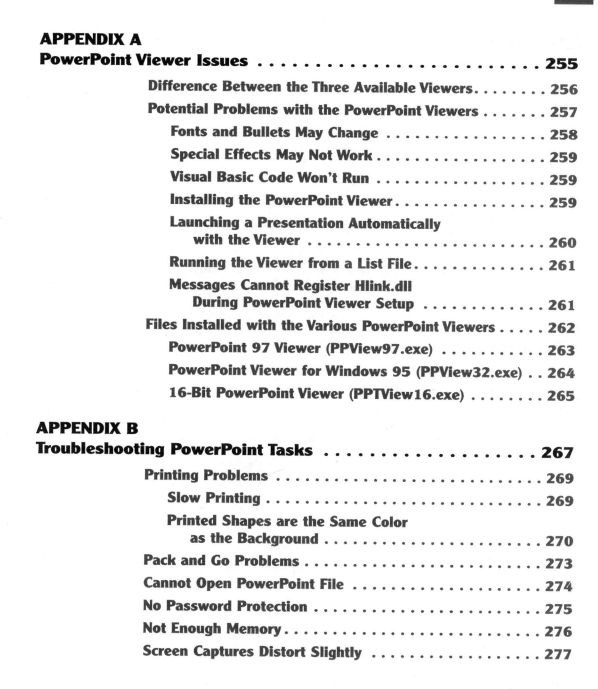

ACKNOWLEDGMENTS

Starting at the beginning of my career in computers, I'd like to thank the gentleman who took the fear of the chip out of my life. While spending a weekend at his home and using his special PC, pre-Windows, Tom Bagg let me do a simple tutorial in Lotus 1-2-3, and when I couldn't find my way out, he taught me the Baggian rule: "If the computer isn't doing what you think it should be doing, just hit the off switch." It took the mystery out of this mess, and I still say things like "Oh, I'll just do a Bagg" and pull the power cord. Thanks Tom. You have always had a simple way with words.

It takes a lot of people working together to make a book like this. I'd like to thank everyone who helped, especially the team at Prima Publishing, which does a lot of work and hides behind the scenes. A special thanks goes to Debbie Abshier, the Acquisitions Editor and lead hound dog. Debbie is blessed with the true talent of knowing that "author" is spelled l-a-t-e, and she still manages to make sure that things get done on time.

I also have to thank Joyce Nielsen and Paul Marchesseault for their tremendous help organizing my thoughts and for making sure everything was technically correct. And thanks also to Kevin Harreld, Kevin Ferns, and Susan Christophersen for their efforts.

Special mention has to go to my friends and fellow Microsoft MVP's, Cindy Meister, John Green, and Dian Chesney, who came to my assistance from all around the world (Switzerland, Australia, and Illinois) to straighten me out on some of the finer points of Word. And I can't forget MVP Steve Rindsberg, the true PowerPoint expert who taught me everything I know about formatting hard drives among other minor things.

Extra special recognition has to go to the real writer in the family, my wife, Confidence Stimpson, who always finds the right word or the shortest way to say something. She is my beloved, beautiful, and brilliant friend in this book, and in my life. Thank you Confidence. The book's done. Now, I'll cook dinner again.

The last contributor to the book was, of course, Cap'n the Cat, who often tried to help me by walking on the keyboard. Any typos are, of course, due to his attempts to reprogam my programmable keyboard. He's a whiz at C(at)++, as you might imagine, but not very good at VBA.

Finally, the real thanks go to you, the reader, for your interest in PowerPoint. I certainly hope this book helps you a great deal. Enjoy the learning experience and keep in touch.

ABOUT THE AUTHOR

Brian Reilly is the owner of Reilly & Associates, a computer consulting firm in New York that specializes in creating PowerPoint presentations and using VBA (Visual Basic for Applications programming) to integrate Excel spreadsheet data and charts into presentations. Brian is one of the few people who thinks of Excel as a graphics software program.

Brian is a frequent contributor to the online PowerPoint communities on the Microsoft newsgroups and the CompuServe forum. He is also a Microsoft MVP (Most Valuable Professional) and has written a variety of books on PowerPoint.

Brian can be reached directly by email at **Reilly_and_Associates@ compuserve.com** and is very receptive to hearing your comments on the book. You will also find him in the Microsoft newsgroup **microsoft. public.powerpoint** or in the CompuServe forum on PowerPoint, **Go: msdesktop**.

Introduction

Welcome to what is going to be a very rewarding experience! By Sunday afternoon, you will be an expert at creating your own multimedia presentations using the leading presentation software program—Microsoft PowerPoint. If you have experience using any other software package to write letters, calculate spreadsheets, or even balance your checkbook, then you are already on your way!

You can think of PowerPoint as a "word and picture processor" program just as Word is a "word processor" or Excel is a "number cruncher." PowerPoint makes organizing all of the critical elements of a presentation into a neat package easy for you. This book identifies and demystifies these elements and shows you how easy putting them all together can be.

What Is This Book About?

All presentations, no matter how sophisticated or complex, can be broken down into three key elements. This book will help you master each of them.

- How the presentation is shown
- How the presentation looks
- How the presentation reveals the content

This book shows you how to integrate pictures, sound, music, movies, and animation into your presentations. PowerPoint can help you look well-prepared during your presentation by providing access to all of the extra information you need to answer a question or further illustrate a point without shuffling through a stack of papers.

You will learn how to think of a presentation as a fixed number of manageable tasks, and discover the best ways to perform those tasks. If you follow the simple steps covered in this book, you can create dazzling and effective PowerPoint presentations with little effort.

Who Should Read This Book?

Anyone who makes presentations should read this book. Certainly, the typical businessperson who needs to effectively communicate ideas, whether it be to customers, clients, superiors, or existing staff, will benefit. But the book is also for people who have to give presentations in contexts other than business. Anybody who ever has to stand in front of a group of people and get a point across can benefit from this book. If you're a teacher, for example, you can imagine the difference that a good presentation makes in a classroom.

Public speaking has always ranked very high on the list of the most fearful experiences. Those good speakers who are not afraid of speaking in public are able to speak without fear because of a few simple things. Primarily, they know the subject matter, and more importantly, they know how their visual aids will help communicate the subject matter. Knowing how to create simple but effective visual aids in PowerPoint will help you with the second part of this equation. This book will not help you learn your subject matter, but it will teach you everything you need to know to visually communicate that subject matter in a simple and effective way.

Can You *Really* Learn the Essentials in Just a Weekend?

Yes! Here's how I've planned to help you do that. First, I identify the three key elements of any presentation. Then I show you how to prepare a simple presentation to see how easy it is. After that, I explore each of the three elements in more detail to help you learn the nuances of each.

You don't need to be a graphic designer to add pizzazz to your presentations. Although you can build a blank presentation from scratch, most people use PowerPoint's built-in presentation designs. These professionally designed templates give you a head start at creating your presentations.

What Do You Need to Begin?

You don't need the latest and greatest hardware available. In fact, the latest and greatest has likely changed by the time you're through reading this page. But certainly, the better your equipment, the more you can rest assured that your presentations will run as planned, without overtaxing the computer.

What the foregoing generally translates to is a Pentium-based processor. You can also probably manage with a 486-based processor. The operating system needs to be Windows 95 or Windows NT in order to use some of the elements of interactive presentations that I cover. As for RAM (Random Access Memory), the more the better. You should have at least 8MB of RAM to run PowerPoint under Windows 95, and at least 16MB of RAM to run PowerPoint under Windows NT. Your presentations may run much more smoothly if you can at least double these amounts, however.

In the PowerPoint Newsgroup and the CompuServe PowerPoint Forum, users frequently ask about the minimum amount of memory necessary to run PowerPoint presentations. The answer really depends on what is included in the presentation (for example, scanned pictures and movies), and what is in your budget. You can often get by with 8MB of memory, especially if you also have plenty of free space on the hard disk for Windows to use as Virtual Memory.

The reason behind this need for available memory is that PowerPoint actually uses twice the size of the active file to save the presentation, creating a temporary file of the presentation before saving the actual file in order to check for file corruption. So a presentation with a fair number of scanned pictures that is 15MB would need at least 30MB of free memory. And that is on top of the 8MB of memory that PowerPoint and Windows need just to be open.

Luckily, memory has become inexpensive (at least compared to what it used to cost!). So, if you plan to use a computer for several important presentations a year, you'll find adding an adequate amount of memory worthwhile. And like money and beauty, you can't have too much of it.

Last, and this is important, you need a copy of PowerPoint. Although this book uses PowerPoint 97 and explains many of the new features of this version of the software, many of the underlying principles still apply to PowerPoint 95 and PowerPoint Version 4. But to get the most benefit from this book, you should have PowerPoint 97 loaded on your hard drive. If you do not already have PowerPoint loaded, refer to the installation instructions in Appendix C of this book.

How Is This Book Organized?

This book includes six PowerPoint sessions designed around a weekend. You don't actually *have* to complete the sessions in a weekend, of course, but they are designed to build on each other and should be covered in order. Each session covers a few subjects that build upon what you have learned in the previous sessions. One session is scheduled for Friday evening. Then, three additional sessions are set for Saturday. The two concluding sessions on

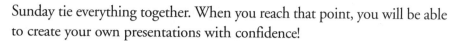

Sunday tie everything together. When you reach that point, you will be able to create your own presentations with confidence!

Here's what you'll learn during each of the PowerPoint sessions:

⚙ *Friday Evening:* You receive an introduction to the concept of the three key elements of a presentation, as follows:

How the presentation looks. This element involves the primary background, the typefaces and type size, the color scheme, the company logo, and so on.

How the presentation reveals the content. This element applies to the real content of the presentation, such as text pages, charts, pictures, movies, sound, and clip art.

How the presentation is shown. Is it on a disk? On the Internet? On a projector? Can you use animation or interactivity? What about slide transitions?

In this first session, you will create a simple ten-page presentation as I walk you through each of the three steps. This sample presentation will contain at least one example of every possible element that you will ever face in any presentation.

Friday evening also covers in detail the first of the three key elements of a presentation: *How it looks.* You'll learn how to use typefaces to make your words readable to large or small groups of people, how to make the logo pop, and how to use colors to enhance your message.

⚙ *Saturday Morning and Afternoon:* These two sessions cover in detail the second of the three key elements: *How it reveals the content.* I explore the ten key pieces of content that might be included in a presentation. You will learn everything about entering text, creating charts or tables, adding clip art or pictures, adding movies, playing sound in presentations, and even creating your own drawings. By the end of the afternoon, you will have learned everything about the content of the presentation.

✪ *Saturday Evening:* In this session, I move into an equally important part of the presentation: *How it is shown.* This session covers what happens on the screen with all of the pieces of content that you have put together. You will learn how to add animation to specific objects to help make your communication effective.

✪ *Sunday Morning:* This session continues the exciting parts of *How it is shown.* You will learn how to add transitions to slides to help emphasize your points. The most exciting part of PowerPoint presentations is covered in the session on adding interactivity. You can actually build presentations that are no longer sequential but let you control what you want to show next.

✪ *Sunday Afternoon:* To complete your knowledge of how to show the presentation, I cover the issues of physically distributing the presentation, either by taking it on the road to a hotel meeting room, showing it in your own conference room, mailing it out on disks, or placing it on the Internet for viewing.

By Sunday evening, you will be a PowerPoint presentation expert!

How do I define *PowerPoint expert?* I have seen and created a lot of presentations in PowerPoint and many other presentation programs and have been able to judge by the audience's reaction what works and what doesn't work for them. I have approximated an estimate of the number of presentations that use the available tools to help make a fantastic presentation. Given how easily it is to use all of the tools, scanned pictures, animation, sound, and video, it is surprising that about half of the PowerPoint presentations given don't really use any of these tools to help the presentation. And only about 30% of presentations use sound or video. It is very easy to use these tools and create a presentation that will put you at the top of the heap.

After a good night's sleep on Sunday night, you'll be able to run into the office on Monday morning and stun your coworkers by creating a professional-looking presentation with a minimum of effort.

Special Features in This Book

In this book, you'll notice special elements and text formatting that will help you make the most out of your PowerPoint sessions. For example, **bold** text indicates text that you should type. Also, new terms are identified with *italics* when first introduced.

You'll find the following special elements throughout this book:

NOTE Notes provide additional information or enhance a discussion in the text by emphasizing a particular point.

TIP Tips offer helpful hints, suggestions, or alternate methods for a procedure.

CAUTION Cautions warn you about mistakes and pitfalls that inexperienced users often fall into.

FIND IT ON ▶ This graphic appears next to paragraphs that contain a Web address that may be help-**THE WEB** ful to the discussion. The URLs referenced in the text appear in **bold** type.

The Three Key Elements of Any Presentation

- ✿ How the presentation is shown
- ✿ How the presentation looks
- ✿ How the presentation reveals the content
- ✿ Getting started with a simple presentation

TGIF! No work tonight. Now it's playtime. You've probably just finished a long hard week at work and would like to relax until Monday morning. But, you have committed yourself to mastering PowerPoint this weekend. Well, relax. You are going to both play and learn at the same time.

You are going to have some fun while learning how easy it is to create first-class presentations without a struggle. I promise it will be quite easy and enjoyable. By the end of the weekend, you will be able to create PowerPoint presentations like an expert. So sit down, relax, and get started.

The place to start thinking about presentations is not at the beginning, but at the end. That is the moment of truth—the point at which the presentation meets the audience.

How is your audience actually going to view your presentation? On a big screen at the front of a room full of people? On a laptop screen viewed from over your shoulder as you fumble for the mouse to point out some detail? Or on the screen of a PC, alone at a desk?

If the audience is large and in a conference room, can the people in the back actually read the words on the screen? If the audience is small and is viewing the presentation on a laptop, can everyone see the screen from where he or she is standing? If the audience is one person viewing the presentation on his or her own computer, does that person have the same font type that you used? Is that person's computer fast enough to display all of the pictures that you used without slowing to a crawl? You must start at the end in order to answer all of these questions at the beginning.

Every presentation can be broken down into three key elements:

- *How the presentation is shown*
- *How the presentation looks*
- *How the presentation reveals the content*

Take a monthly budget review. The three key elements might be the following:

- *It is shown* on an overhead projector against the conference room wall.
- *It looks like* black type and black lines on a clear background.
- *It reveals the content with* words, numbers, charts, and tables.

Take something more complex: a new product introduction at a national sales meeting. You could describe the three key elements for this presentation as follows:

- *It is shown* on multiple screens with a big sound system in a big fancy hotel ballroom.
- *It looks like* a lot of colors, logos, product shots, different typefaces and sizes, still and moving photographs and drawings, live actors and props—lots of stuff happening all of the time.
- *It reveals content with* words, tables, charts, pictures (lots and lots of pictures), music, and videos.

All of these presentations have elements in common. But these elements must be handled differently. For instance, both presentations use words, charts and tables. After you learn how to create words, charts, and tables, you can apply this skill to either presentation.

To create the charts for the monthly budget review, you need to know what the charts will look like when printed on a black-and-white printer. For the national sales meeting, you have color. You'll want to follow a consistent color scheme and design throughout the presentation, so you need to know how to change the default colors for the charts.

This book is designed to teach you all of those things and more in just a few short sessions. In fact, you will go to bed tonight having completed a presentation that has at least one of each of the elements common to every presentation. Tomorrow and Sunday you will explore each of these common elements in more detail. You'll move from general subjects to more specific topics, learning how to modify the elements of a presentation to make them work perfectly for your particular needs.

Now it's time to take a closer look at each of the three key elements of any presentation.

How the Presentation Is Shown

The whole purpose of any presentation is to communicate. If the communication is not effective, it is a poor presentation no matter how fancy or cool the techniques are.

TIP ■
I can't say this enough: In order to make sure that your presentation communicates what you intend to communicate, always start the process by asking this question, "How is this presentation going to be shown?"
■ ■

Here's an example of how important the answer to this question can be. A common disaster that occurs is when words can be read just fine on a printed page but appear in type too small to be read on a screen at the presentation. Not only does the presentation fail to communicate what's in that illegible type, but also the illegible type serves as a distraction from the rest of the message. Thus, *nothing* is communicated.

Is the presentation going to be shown on a printed page? Or is it being shown on a screen? And, if it's on a screen, how big is the screen? For information that needs to be read and understood quickly *on a printed page,* you can use type as small as 12 points. (Don't use anything smaller or the type won't be readable.)

If you plan to project this presentation onto a screen from your laptop in a conference room, however, the type needs to be at least 20 points or larger so that the people in the back of the room can read it. If you try to explain a complex flow diagram with type that is less than 20 points in this environment, you will not communicate. You will, however, give your audience eyestrain. If you don't have room for 20-point type, break the message into multiple pieces and put it in type big enough to be read—20 points or larger.

A frequent question is, "What do I do if I have to present the presentation in both of the aforementioned situations: 1) on a projected screen from a laptop, and 2) as handouts that will also go to others who didn't attend the presentation?" The answer is in one of Reilly's Laws (actually I stole this one from an ancient Greek philosopher, or maybe it was a fortune cookie): "Expect the worst, and you'll never be disappointed." You have to execute this presentation anticipating the worst-case scenario. Use nothing less than 20-point type. The reader of the screen version will be happy, and the reader of the paper version will be able to read it without glasses.

A host of other disasters are possible as a consequence of a lack of foresight. As an example, the colors shown at the presentation don't look anything like they did back in the office. Or the computer takes thirty seconds to finally make it to the next page. Or a few of the numbers in the presentation change at the last minute, affecting a lot more of the numbers in the presentation (it is one of the fundamental Laws of Life—more common than Murphy's Law—that this will happen) and there isn't enough time to change all of the pages to reflect that change. The list can go on and on.

All I can say is, "Been there, done that." If you read this book, you will learn to anticipate these problems and plan ways to avoid them. The first step in avoiding these problems is to observe another one of Reilly's Laws: "The last step is the first step."

In addition to overhead projectors and 35mm slides, you can now project your presentation directly from your laptop to that of another single person, or connect your laptop directly to a projector that will project the presentation onto a wall or screen. Or you may even mail out your presentation to potential customers on a floppy disk or CD and let them view it on their own computer without your presence.

The method of showing your presentation is very much determined by the specific situation you are faced with. Each method comes with its own set of restrictions and opportunities—opportunities for failure as well as for success. I'll examine each of these methods of showing a presentation and outline some guidelines for each method. You'll learn more specifics about each of these methods in the Sunday Afternoon session, "How It Is Shown: Finishing Touches and Distribution."

Screen Shows

Screen shows are becoming more and more prevalent as laptops become more commonplace and the presentation goes mobile. Not all screen shows are created equal, however. Following are some differences between the hardware commonly used to display screen shows:

- ✪ **Laptop Monitors.** There is a bigger difference between laptops and desktop computers than just the size of the screen. Until recently, most laptops could not display as many colors as desktop computers. Although most desktop computers can display up to 16 million different colors, frequently referred to as True Color, laptops either displayed no more than 65,000 colors and frequently as few as 256 colors. In some situations, laptops displayed only 16 colors. Many a presentation, beautiful when previewed in the office, looked ugly as sin on a laptop in the field because the laptop displayed the images using a limited number of colors.

  Another major issue with laptop monitors is the viewing angle of the display. The highest-priced laptops have Active Matrix screens, but the merely expensive laptops may only have dual scan or

Passive Matrix screens. Looking at either monitor head-on as the sole user, you may not see much difference between these two screen types. The quality is very different when you view the display from off-center, however. If you have more than one person viewing a presentation directly on the laptop screen at a time, the results will be far superior if you are using the more expensive Active Matrix screen, because three or four people will be able to see the image on the screen simultaneously.

○ **Projectors.** Another popular way of showing a presentation from either a laptop or desktop computer is to connect the computer directly to a projector through a cable plugged into the parallel port on the back of the laptop. The parallel port is the place where you usually plug in your printer. The projector can then project the presentation onto a screen or a wall. A good-sized audience can view these presentations, much the same as they would 35mm slide presentations.

These projectors have various levels of quality, however. The newer ones can project at a higher quality than the earlier projectors that are being used by many people. The differences are in both the number of colors that can be projected and the actual resolution of the image. If you are planning to use a projector to present to an audience, this decision has significant impact on how you prepare the content of the presentation. Appendix D, "Other PowerPoint Resources," has a much more detailed discussion of projectors.

○ **Desktop Monitors.** Another way to show a presentation as a screen show is on a desktop monitor, either from another desktop computer or from a laptop. This is a very effective way to show presentations to relatively small groups of people. This is the way presentations are frequently shown in booths at trade shows.

Not everyone realizes that a desktop monitor can actually be plugged into a laptop simply by plugging the monitor plug into the laptop's plug labeled "Monitor." I have never seen a laptop that didn't have this capability. Actually, with just a little extra wiring, you could even connect your desktop or laptop to several monitors simultaneously and display your presentation on every monitor.

✿ **Customer's Computer.** A lot of people have expressed the desire to create presentations on either floppy disks or CD-ROMs. You could then mail these to customers or potential customers. Customers could view the presentation or catalog when it was convenient for them, with no further assistance from the presenter. In this kind of situation, because you have no control over the quality of the equipment that the presentation is viewed on, you have some extremely important decisions to make to be sure that the presentation is viewable on this unknown customer's unknown computer.

The Internet

You can even send a PowerPoint presentation to an Internet site and have that presentation viewable by anyone with a Web browser right on the Internet. The presentation can play just like any PowerPoint presentation does on your computer, and it will even show the same animation effects and hyperlinks you used on your own computer. This is a terrific application for placing a catalog on the Internet and allowing the viewer of the Web page to navigate through the catalog with hyperlinks. Because you can even play back animation and movies, you can easily create an impressive demonstration without knowing anything more than how to use PowerPoint.

35mm Slides

Yes, some people actually still do create 35mm slides. Oddly enough, the era of the laptop computer has not sounded the death knell for the 35mm slide business. Using PowerPoint, you can print your presentations directly to 35mm slides.

Paper Prints and Transparencies

The two biggest complaints about printing presentations to either a black-and-white or a color printer relate to the unpredictability of the colors and the amount of time printing takes. Both of these issues are manageable with a little planning.

How the Presentation Looks

Making a presentation look good is often the most daunting part of putting it together. Many presenters spend most of their preparation time on just this issue.

The overall look of a presentation should:

- Be appropriate to the subject matter
- Give the audience a favorable first impression
- Arouse the audience's interest in the subject matter
- Follow a principle of organization, thus making it easy for you to enter the content, and for your audience to understand the content quickly

The following examines the two previous example presentations in this context.

The staid financial reports should be just that: *staid*. The staidness works for you in creating an impression of sober fiscal responsibility. Delivering financial reports with songs and dances would make the viewer wonder whether they were anything close to accurate.

But at a national sales meeting, anything staid would make the sales force start looking for new jobs instead of getting excited about the opportunities at hand. The songs and dances give the audience an impression of excitement, energy, and enthusiasm for the product.

The overall look of a presentation consists of only four elements. PowerPoint lets you set those four elements once on what is called a *template* or *Master Slide*, and these elements are then automatically applied to each and every page, or slide, in your presentation. It doesn't matter whether the content of the slide is simple bullets or charts or tables or even a movie. The four elements of the template are applied.

NOTE PowerPoint uses the word *slide* to designate an individual page in a presentation. The terminology may be confusing, but *slide* and *page* refer to exactly the same thing.

The four elements of the overall look are as follows:

✿ The font type, size, color, and position of the title of the slide

✿ The font type, size, color, and position of the main communication of the slide (bullets, charts, tables, or whatever)

✿ The background color and design

✿ Any other graphics that you want to place on every page of the presentation, such as a company logo

These four elements appear in Figure 1.1.

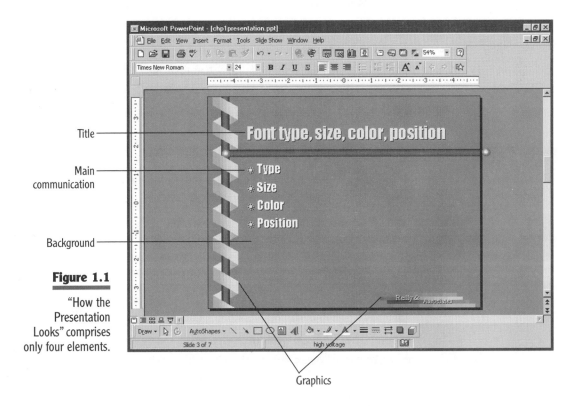

Title
Main communication
Background
Graphics

Figure 1.1

"How the Presentation Looks" comprises only four elements.

When you are able to isolate each of the four elements of "How the Presentation Looks," you can make some very quick decisions about the presentation.

TIP   Don't think you will have to live with these decisions forever. PowerPoint lets you change your mind later and update the presentation in one simple step. It also lets you deviate from this Slide Master on a selected page or series of selected pages. But you'll learn more about that later.

The core element of how a presentation looks is made easy in PowerPoint through the use of a template that applies common attributes to every page. Every presentation that is created in PowerPoint has an underlying template. After you have decided on a template, or created your own, you can focus on the content.

Don't worry that this will force you into what looks like canned presentations. Later, you'll learn how to change the attributes of a given part of the presentation so that it doesn't follow the template. For now, you need to focus on what the template is and how it will help you create presentations quickly.

The Template—The Glue That Holds a PowerPoint Presentation Together

Every PowerPoint presentation follows a template. PowerPoint includes a host of well-designed templates that you can use to help create presentations quickly.

All PowerPoint presentations have only one template. Each template includes a placeholder for the text of the title of the page, a placeholder for the main content of the page that you want to add, and a background color.

The templates that PowerPoint includes with every version of the program are located in a folder under the main PowerPoint folder. Appendix C, "Setup Issues," describes in more detail what files are installed with

PowerPoint and where they are located. In addition to the core templates that are supplied with PowerPoint, additional templates ship on the CD version of Office 97.

FIND IT ON ▶ THE WEB Additional PowerPoint templates are available for downloading. Point your browser to Microsoft's Web site for PowerPoint: **http://www.microsoft.com/powerpoint/**.

Templates are so easy to create that I prefer to spend a few minutes creating a custom template for major new presentations. By doing so, I avoid the possibility of someone in the audience recognizing one of the predefined Microsoft templates. When you see how easy it is to do, I think you'll probably agree. Nothing is wrong with using the predefined templates supplied by Microsoft, however, and I use some of them in this book as a way to help you understand how they have been put together.

How Does the Template Work?

The template actually consists of four different elements, as shown in Figure 1.2. You can set the attributes for these four elements and create any kind of presentation you like, no matter how it is to be shown or how many kinds of objects you plan to use when you enter content. The four elements of a template that control how a presentation looks are as follows:

- The Title Area for AutoLayouts placeholder
- The Object Area for AutoLayouts placeholder, which is for the main communication on a page
- The background
- Any other artwork that appears on every page, such as a logo

The template is applied to every slide that you create, and is applied regardless of whether you are creating a page with all bullets or a page with a title and a chart. The template, therefore, is more fundamental to your presentation than the AutoLayout that you choose to format a page. You will learn shortly how to set each of these placeholders to your specifications. For now, I focus on what each of them does for you.

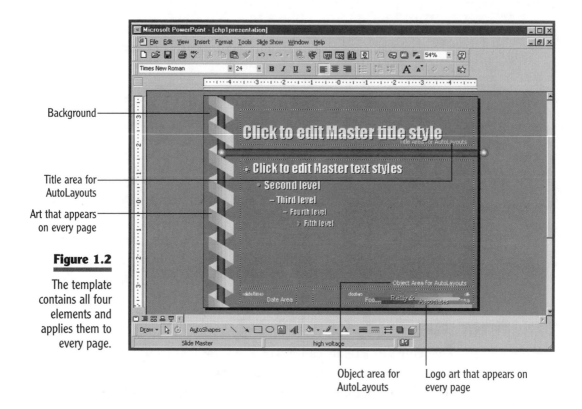

Background

Title area for
AutoLayouts

Art that appears
on every page

Figure 1.2

The template
contains all four
elements and
applies them to
every page.

Object area for
AutoLayouts

Logo art that appears on
every page

The Title Area for AutoLayouts Placeholder

The Slide Title placeholder is aptly named. Type any text into it and the text is automatically formatted as the title of the page. A traditionally designed slide has the title at the top of the page. You can set whether the text is left-aligned or centered within the placeholder. You also can set the size, color, and font style to be used.

The Object Area for AutoLayouts Placeholder

The Body Text placeholder is also known as the Object placeholder for AutoLayouts. This rectangle serves as a box to place whatever kind of object that you will use, such as text, a table, a chart, a media clip, or an organizational chart. Whatever kind of object you use to explain the main part of a given page, the AutoLayout that applies that object type (chart, table, and so on) places it inside this placeholder. The idea is that Power-Point will do all of the placement of any object type consistently for you throughout the entire presentation.

The Background

The background exists just as it is described, in the background behind the Title and Body Text placeholders. The background as a default is white and can easily be changed to any of 16 million colors, including gradations or shadings of colors. That may sound like a lot, but by itself even all of those variations may not give you all you need. You need to consider another aspect of the template—graphics that appear on every page.

Graphics That Appear on Every Page

You can also place any individual artwork on top of the background in the template. These objects will then show up on every page in the presentation. The simplest example of this is a company logo. Logos frequently find their way to the lower-right corner of a page (refer to Figure 1.2). But these graphic logos can also include drawn objects such as colored lines, filled shapes, or photographs. In essence, any type of the common objects already listed as normal objects for content can also be added to the template and will then appear on every page in the presentation. The only trick is to remember to place them on a lower layer than the two placeholders so that they don't cover up the content on the pages. By adding other drawn objects to the template, you can create any design that you might need for use in the template.

Now that you know about the template and how it will automatically apply formatting to any page you choose to create, you are ready to explore in a little more detail the types of content you can add to a Power-Point page to communicate your message.

How the Presentation Reveals Content

"How a Presentation Reveals Content" uses various tools such as: words, pictures, graphs, tables, and movie clips or sound recordings that you include. Most people spend most of their time working on creating these tools in a presentation because they reveal the message. PowerPoint lets you say anything you want. It lets you do this by having you make a selection from a very short list of choices. It offers six different ways to say something:

- Words
- Tables
- Charts
- Clip Art or Pictures
- Media Clips (Movies or Sound)
- Organization Charts

Everything that you have to say in a presentation can be said with one of these six object types. If you learn how to create or insert each of these six objects, you will be able to create your own presentations immediately. In fact, PowerPoint has a feature already defined for you to make adding any one of these six object types very easy.

Using just these six different object types, you can insert any content imaginable into your presentation. PowerPoint makes this easy for you with a special feature called *AutoLayouts*. AutoLayouts place the object types in position on the page, with all of the formatting options that you set in the template. This is a very handy feature because you can focus on what kind of object you want to use to communicate some specific content, such as a chart, and then just enter the data for the chart. Power-Point automatically creates the chart and places it into position for you.

The Slide Layout—Using AutoLayout

When you first open PowerPoint to create a new presentation, you are immediately presented with a dialog box giving you four choices, as

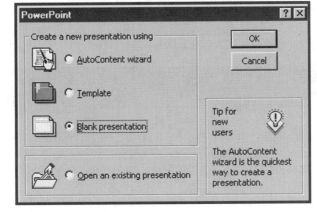

Figure 1.3

When you create a new presentation, you are given four choices.

shown in Figure 1.3. You will focus on the AutoLayout in any presentation, so follow these steps to get past this dialog box for the time being:

1. From the Windows menu, choose Start, Programs, Microsoft PowerPoint.

2. Select Blank presentation and click OK.

If you already have PowerPoint open:

1. Choose File, New.

2. Select the General tab, and then select Blank presentation.

3. Click OK.

Both methods of opening a blank presentation template will still lead you to the AutoLayout dialog box. You then choose which AutoLayout you want for your first page. For the current example, choose the second AutoLayout because there is something special about the Title page Auto-Layout, which you will learn later.

The instructions for using AutoLayouts to add objects to each placeholder are fundamentally the same. Just create a new page (or *slide*) by choosing Insert, New Slide from the main PowerPoint menu, or use the keyboard shortcut Ctrl + M. You are automatically presented with Power-Point's choice of 24 AutoLayouts (see Figure 1.4). Remember, you have to scroll through the dialog box to see the second twelve AutoLayouts.

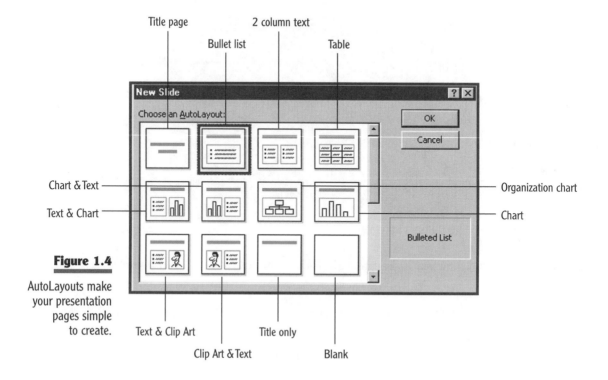

Figure 1.4

AutoLayouts make your presentation pages simple to create.

The principle behind this is that when you select an AutoLayout, Power-Point knows what object type you want to insert and guides you through the appropriate steps to add that object.

Covering Most Needs with Ten Predefined Layouts

Although PowerPoint does give you 24 different AutoLayouts from which to choose, ten of these AutoLayouts will probably suffice for most presentations. The remaining choices are purely additional ways to combine the basic object types. The twelfth AutoLayout (fourth one from left in third row) is for a blank slide with no predefined objects on the page. Of course, the template still is applied for that page, so a page with no object placeholders will still have the background and any other art that was placed on the background in the template.

Getting Started with a Simple Presentation

I have created a sample presentation, which is shown in Figure 1.5. It consists of the key elements of any presentation. You should now take some time and re-create this presentation following the steps in the rest of this section. At that point, you will have successfully created a Power-Point presentation that encompasses every object type that you might run into in any presentation.

I suggest that you perform the next section at your computer and follow the steps one by one. I use this technique frequently in the book to take you very carefully through each of the steps related to learning the process behind creating any page in PowerPoint. My objective is to use examples that illustrate what you need to look for when creating your own presentations. This way, when you receive presentations that are not perfectly laid out, you can immediately create the page anyway.

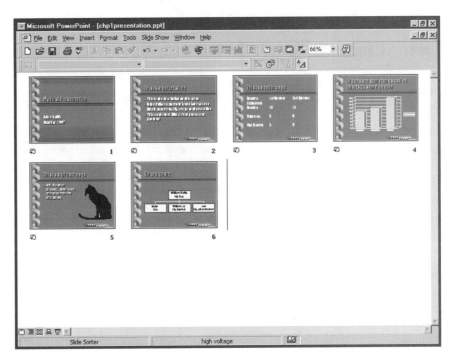

Figure 1.5

You can create this sample presentation.

This exercise is meant to walk you step by step through the actual creation of each kind of slide that you might run into in a typical presentation. It will not address every possible situation you may encounter. Those situations will be addressed on Saturday and Sunday as I basically repeat the creation of this presentation in much more detail. If for some reason you find yourself lost and not able to complete a specific slide, just skip it and continue with the rest of the presentation. For example, one of the pages asks you to insert a Sound file that I anticipate will be on your computer. If you weren't really careful installing Windows, you may not find that file or one like it. So, you should feel free to skip that page if necessary.

Take a Break

You might want to take a short break here and go outside, look at the stars, and then come back in; then, fasten your seat belt and start pumping those pixels.

Choosing a Template

Remember: last thing's first. How is the presentation shown? This sample presentation is designed for you to show on your computer monitor, visible to you and one other person at a time.

Now that you have done the first step of defining how the presentation will be shown, it is time to open a new file and define what the presentation will look like. You will actually use one of PowerPoint's predefined templates and make a minor modification to it, because one of its templates has a very complex structure. I come back to that on Saturday evening when I guide you through the real details of creating special animation effects on templates.

So now, open PowerPoint 97. Click the Start menu, move up to the Programs command, and then click on Microsoft PowerPoint in the resulting menu. PowerPoint presents you with an opening dialog box that

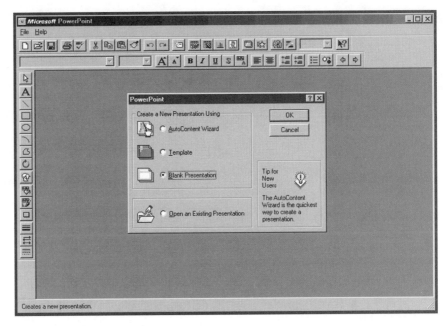

Figure 1.6

When you first open PowerPoint you can choose four ways to proceed.

gives you four options, as shown in Figure 1.6. Choose Template and click on OK.

PowerPoint immediately presents you with another dialog box that has five tabs for various template designs. You will explore each of these in detail tomorrow. For now, click on the Presentation Designs tab, as shown in Figure 1.7, select the *high voltage* icon, and click on OK.

Creating a Title Page

After selecting the presentation design, the New Slide dialog box appears. This dialog box gives you the choice of the 24 AutoLayouts to choose from for this slide (refer to Figure 1.4). I told you this was going to be easy! If you select the Title Slide AutoLayout in the upper-left corner and click on OK, you will be presented with the predefined template for *high voltage*. Two placeholders are used in this slide: one for the title and another for a subtitle.

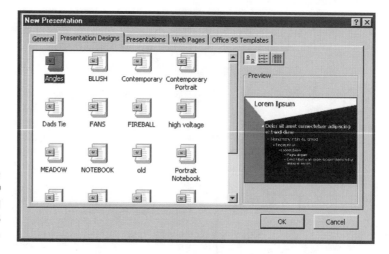

Figure 1.7

Choose an existing
template, such as
high voltage.

  PowerPoint uses a slightly different template for the title page. It works the same way
as a normal template, except that it usually has a slightly different look than the template used for the other AutoLayouts.

For the time being, ignore the difference and just type the title of the presentation. Click on the Title placeholder to select it, and then type **My
First Presentation**. Then, click on the Object placeholder (which says
"Click to sub-title") and type your own name. Press Enter to advance to
the next line, and type this month's date.

That's all there is to creating your first slide. Now you move on to another easy slide, one with bullets.

Adding Bulleted Points

Choose Insert, New Slide from the main PowerPoint menu, or press
Ctrl + M. You will see the familiar New Slide dialog box with the 24
AutoLayouts. The second AutoLayout in the first row looks like a typical
page with a title and bullets. Double-click on that icon and you will see
an image similar to the one shown in Figure 1.8.

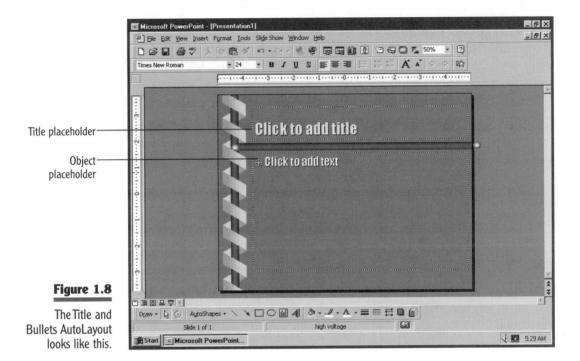

Title placeholder

Object placeholder

Figure 1.8

The Title and Bullets AutoLayout looks like this.

Type the title of this slide in the Title placeholder. Type **This is a bullet slide**. When you are done with that, you can click on the Object placeholder, the second placeholder that says "Click to add text." Type the following three bullets. Be sure to press Enter at the end of each bullet statement.

- This is the first bullet on this page
- If the bullet statement is too long for one line, it automatically wraps to the next line
- This works just like a word processor program

You should be getting the hang of creating a new slide by now and typing the slide title, so now you can move on and start with some of the other object types. Don't worry if you have identified a few minor issues that haven't been addressed just yet. I plan to cover each of these slide types in a lot more detail in individual sessions on Saturday and Sunday.

Adding a Table

Adding a table is very much like adding bullets, except that the table is actually created using Microsoft Word, which PowerPoint starts for you automatically. Add a new slide by choosing Insert, New Slide. The fourth icon from the left in the top row of the New Slide dialog box looks like a table. Double-click on this icon. You will see something very similar to Figure 1.9. Add the title by clicking on the Title placeholder and typing **This is a table page** in the Title placeholder. Now you can add the table and enter the contents.

Double-click on the Object placeholder that says "Double click to add table." The Insert Word Table dialog box appears. This dialog box enables you to specify the number of rows and columns in your table. Don't worry if you are unsure how many columns and rows to specify when starting a new table. Although it helps to know roughly how many rows and columns you will create, you can always add or delete rows or columns later.

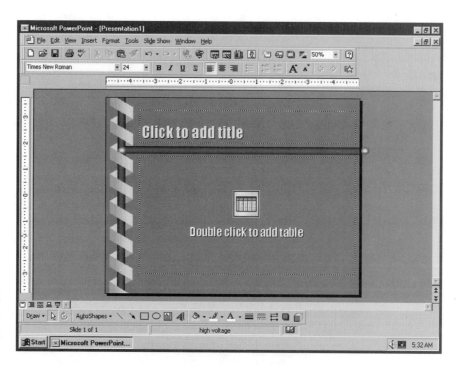

Figure 1.9

The Table AutoLayout looks like this.

In this case, you'll create a simple Income Statement for two quarters. The data for this table looks like the following:

Income Statement	1st Quarter	2nd Quarter
Income	10	15
Expenses	5	6
Net Income	5	9

Because this table has three columns and four rows, you'll fill in the Insert Word Table dialog box with the information shown in the preceding table; then, click on OK. PowerPoint automatically starts the Word program, and you see a predefined table that includes the number of rows and columns that you specified.

Simply type the data that is shown in the preceding table into the appropriate cell in the Word table on your screen. Do not use the Enter key to move to the next cell in a Word table. Use the Tab key or click on the appropriate cell. The Enter key is used to add another line to an existing cell.

 NOTE To see that you are in Word, click on the <u>H</u>elp menu. You will notice that <u>A</u>bout Microsoft Word appears as the last option on the menu. If you select that option, you will see what version of Word you are using to create this Word table.

Now that the text is entered into the Word table, you can return to PowerPoint. Whenever you are actually working in another program from within PowerPoint, such as Word, Excel, or Microsoft Graph, you simply click outside of that program window to return to PowerPoint and update the slide automatically. See Figure 1.10 for various locations showing where you can click to return and update PowerPoint. Click on one of those locations now to return to PowerPoint.

I chose to use this particular template for the sample presentation for some specific reasons. What you should see on the screen should be exactly what you created, that is, black text in a table from Word superimposed

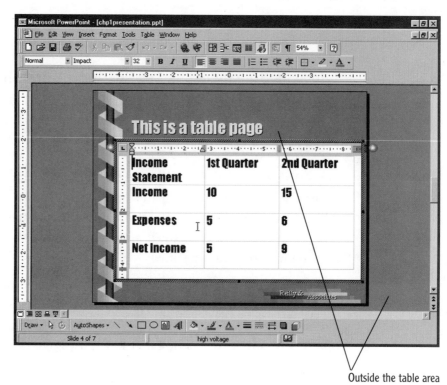

Figure 1.10

Click anywhere outside the table area to return to PowerPoint.

Outside the table area

on the dark-blue background in PowerPoint. This is poor design because you have dark text on a dark background. It will be very difficult to read. When you create tables in Word, it always defaults to black text on a white page. What is shown on the PowerPoint page is only the Word text, which is black, by default.

Several ways are available to fix this, all of which are discussed in great detail in the separate section on creating tables in Saturday morning's session. For now, you'll use a simple solution to recolor (change the color) of the Word table's text from black to white.

To change the text color in the table, select the Word table object by clicking on it once. (Here, a double-click would re-launch Word, which is not what you want to do in this particular case.) With the Word object selected, choose F<u>o</u>rmat, <u>O</u>bject from the menu. The Format Object dialog box appears, which has five tabs: Colors and Lines, Size, Position, Picture, and Text Box (the latter will be grayed out because this is not a text box object). Select the Picture tab and click on the R<u>e</u>color button.

You will see yet another dialog box to set the choices for Recolor Picture. This dialog box permits you to identify specific colors in a picture and change the color of every pixel on the screen using that exact color to a new color. For this example, you should perform the following steps:

1. Click on the check box in the column that says <u>O</u>riginal (that's the black color now).

2. Click on the drop-down arrow under the <u>N</u>ew column and you will be presented with a screen that looks like Figure 1.11. You will see the eight predefined colors for this template's color scheme. Choose the second color, which should be white.

New drop-drop list

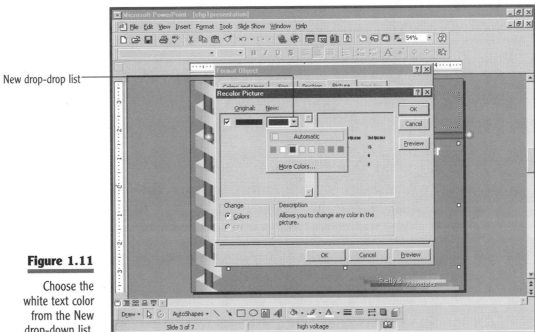

Figure 1.11

Choose the white text color from the New drop-down list.

3. Click on OK to close the Recolor Picture dialog box.

4. Click on OK again to close the Format Object dialog box. You return to PowerPoint, which now shows white text.

NOTE Word tables are a very strong asset to PowerPoint. They may appear challenging at first. They sure did confuse me when I started using them. I cover most of the rules and short-cuts to tables in a separate detailed section on Saturday morning, though, at which point they will become almost as simple as entering bullets. I also cover creating tables in Excel, which may be the easiest method for someone who works a great deal in Excel.

For now, you are done with your Word table in PowerPoint, and it's time to move on to the next slide type—Charts.

Adding a Chart

Adding a chart to a PowerPoint page is much like adding a table. Rather than fire up Word to enter the data, PowerPoint fires up another application: Microsoft Graph.

NOTE As mentioned earlier in the book, the words *graph* and *chart* mean exactly the same thing.

By now, you should know the simple two steps to add a new slide and choose the Chart type from the AutoLayouts. Choose Insert, New Slide from the menu (or press Ctrl+M). Then choose the AutoLayout that looks like a chart slide. It is the fourth icon in the second row. Double-click on that icon and your screen should look similar to Figure 1.12.

Type the title into the Title placeholder: **Graphs are sometimes called charts by some people.**

Now you can move right into the chart-making process. Double-click on the Object placeholder that tells you what to do: "Double-click here to add chart."

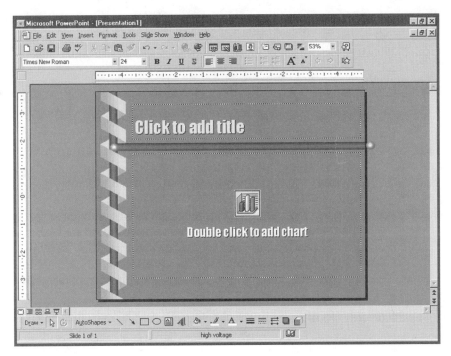

Figure 1.12

The AutoLayout
for charts

When you do this, PowerPoint starts Microsoft Graph and displays a datasheet (the grid that looks like a spreadsheet) with data already included, as well as a default 3-D column chart. You will soon come to dislike this default chart, but because you can't do anything about it, you will learn to ignore it. For now, use it as a guide as Microsoft intended.

Understanding the Chart Datasheet

The datasheet is just that: a grid in which you enter and store the data that creates the chart. Following are some simple rules that apply to the datasheet for any chart that you create:

✪ The datasheet is always rectangular. It doesn't matter whether it is wider than it is high or vice versa.

✪ The first cell in the datasheet is necessary for the chart. Anything typed in this cell never shows up in any chart, however. Usually, as in this case, it is empty. Its sole function is to make the datasheet rectangular.

⚙ You can enter the names such as East, West, and so on either in the first row or the first column of the datasheet. If you were to enter these names in the first column, you would enter the periods such as 1st Quarter, 2nd Quarter, and so on, in the first row of the datasheet (or vice versa).

⚙ You can create many different types of charts. In addition to the column chart, you can create a pie chart, a line chart, or even the new bubble charts that are new to PowerPoint 97. Several other chart types also exist, as you will learn in a later session.

These simple rules should make the chart-making process a lot faster for you. As long as you know what data you want to show, you can just enter the data in the datasheet, and then worry about formatting the chart later.

Creating the Chart

So, you're ready to create a chart. Here you'll create a simple chart of revenue by month for three months. Follow these steps:

1. Clear the entire datasheet that Microsoft provides by default. You do this by clicking anywhere in the datasheet and pressing Ctrl+A (for Select All). Then, press Del to delete all the underlying data and formatting. (This is different from selecting all the visible cells and pressing the Del key, which clears only the numerical and text values but leaves the formatting in place. You would end up, for example, with 0 values being plotted when you don't intend to do so.)

2. Now, with a clean datasheet, enter the data shown in the datasheet in Figure 1.13. Make absolutely certain that the top, leftmost cell in the rectangle is blank and is not filled with either January or Revenue. You will see the chart being drawn in the background

Don't add data
to this cell

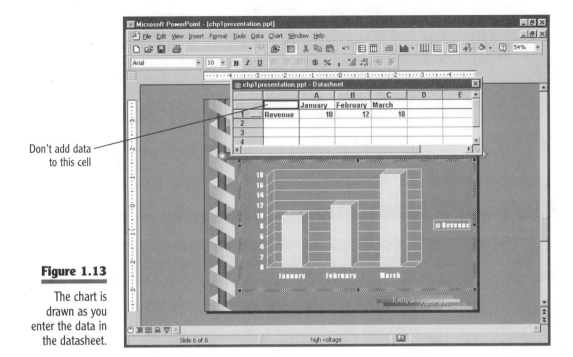

Figure 1.13

The chart is
drawn as you
enter the data in
the datasheet.

when you advance to the next cell. Note that you should use the
arrow keys to navigate because the Enter key may not take you to
the correct next cell.

3. Now that the datasheet is filled out, you are not likely to have to
deal with that again unless the data changes. In that case, there is
an easy way to get back to the datasheet, which I cover in the
Saturday Morning session. So, you have two options. The easiest is
to return directly to PowerPoint and have this chart show up there.
Or, you might want to make specific changes to the format of the
chart, such as the chart type or maybe a change to a color or font
size. Because this session is the summary session on charts, and I
repeat this in great detail during the Saturday morning session, you
should now return directly to PowerPoint by clicking outside of
both the datasheet and the drawn chart object.

TIP Many people think that selecting the data that is shown and using the Delete key will clear everything. If they did that in this case (clearing four data periods), and then typed in the data for just three data periods, they would still plot the fourth data period as a zero value, and the chart would look odd. The use of Ctrl+A to select all of the datasheet deletes everything and lets you start with an absolutely clean datasheet that will plot only the data that you enter.

Adding Pictures and Clip Art

Adding pictures and clip art is truly a wonderful way to add some style to your presentation, although it is not used as frequently as it should be. Adding the pictures or clip art is actually quite simple; the process is often misunderstood and creates undesired problems for people.

The more esoteric issues relating to file size management and file formats are covered in great detail on Saturday afternoon. There are some very simple rules to follow. If followed, these rules will never create any problems in your presentations—especially if you follow the basic Reilly's Law: "The last step is the first step."

You can think of clip art, pictures, sounds, and movies all in the same way. They can reside in a library on your hard disk in what PowerPoint refers to as a Gallery. Clip art is automatically installed into your library during program installation, if you chose to install the clip art at that time. You can also easily add pictures, sounds, and movies to your gallery.

NOTE Not everyone has installed PowerPoint with the clip art, and even if you have tried to install it, clip art is one of the frequent problems encountered with Office 97 installations. See Appendix C, "Installation Issues," for comments on how to re-install the clip art if you either don't have it installed or have had problems with this part of Setup.

I go into more detail on how to do this on Saturday afternoon, as well as how to add pictures, sound, or movies directly into your presentation without adding them to your Gallery. For now, I'll focus on adding clip art that should already appear in your Gallery.

I've chosen the black cat clip art image from the Gallery because it looks like the same black cat that keeps poking at my keyboard while I write this book. It doesn't seem to help that I've given him a mouse of his own. He wants to use the keyboard. You might notice the acknowledgement to him at the front of (t)his book.

Choose <u>I</u>nsert, <u>N</u>ew Slide. This is the first time that you don't actually have an AutoLayout just for an Object type. The choices in the third row of AutoLayouts are for a title and bullets on the left and a picture on the right, or a title with a picture on the left and bullets on the right. I guess Microsoft thinks that you'd probably want to use some words with any picture. So, pick either the first or the second icon in row three and click OK.

You already know how to add the title, so type **This is a clip art page.**

You also know how to add bullets. It's the same process as used for the bullet page that you created earlier tonight. Type **Add clip art or pictures, or even sound or movies from the Clip Gallery.**

Now the real point of this page is to add a clip art image. Double-click the "Double click to add clip art" icon. The Microsoft Clip Gallery dialog box appears; this is essentially a library of stored clip art, pictures, sounds, and videos.

Depending on how you installed PowerPoint, you will see a screen that looks somewhat like Figure 1.14. You may see different images on screen than those shown in this figure. Select the image that you are looking for (in my case it is the black cat) and click on <u>I</u>nsert (or double-click on the image).

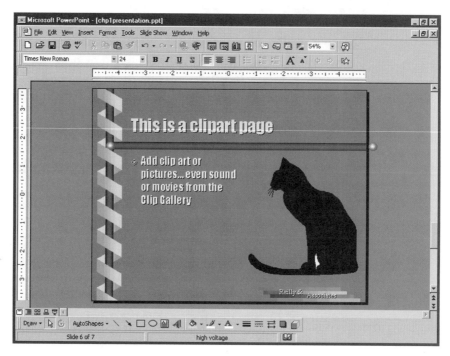

Figure 1.14

Clip art exists in the Microsoft Clip Gallery, along with pictures, sounds, and videos.

Adding an Organization Chart

Even organization charts can be added to a PowerPoint presentation using much the same methodology as tables and graphs. Microsoft Organization Chart is another program similar to Microsoft Graph that creates the organization chart for you, and then automatically places it into PowerPoint. The reality of Microsoft Organization Chart is, in the opinion of many users, that it is not a very good program and does not have much capability beyond the simplest org charts. Organization charts that are anything other than the simplest diagrams are difficult to create and not practical to resize.

For simple org charts, the Microsoft Organization Chart program can work well for you. The following paragraphs cover this area in more detail and identify alternative ways to create org charts if you need more complex charts that defy the simplicity of Microsoft Organization Chart.

THE GALLERY—ADDING PICTURES, SOUNDS, AND VIDEOS

You might think of the Gallery as a nice place to store frequently used clip art, pictures, sounds, and video clips. It is Microsoft's way of expanding the concept of clip art to include these three new object types and organize them in some manner. In fact, the Gallery is really just like a big card catalog in the library. The card catalog doesn't really contain the book that is in the library, but just contains a pointer, such as a Dewey decimal number, that points you to where the book actually exists. The pointer helps you to easily find the book. The Gallery does the same thing. It contains a pointer, such as *drive:\path\file,* so that if you want to insert this file, the Gallery knows where to go get it. If you want to delete the clip art pointer from the Gallery without affecting the source file, you can do so by selecting the thumbnail of the image in the Gallery and pressing Delete. It deletes the referenced pointer in the Gallery but not the original file.

It is quite easy to add any of these object types to your Gallery. Simply follow these steps:

1. Click on the "Double click to add clip art" icon in the slide and choose the tab for either Pictures, Sounds, or Videos, as appropriate.

2. Choose Import Clips and browse to find the file that you want to open.

3. Click on the filename to select it, and then click on Open.

4. A dialog box appears, enabling you to catalog this new file. To skip this step, click on OK. A preview of the file is displayed in the Gallery preview; that file can easily be inserted into new presentations quickly because there is now a pointer to its location.

Adding sound objects or video clips to the Gallery uses exactly the same process. Adding each of these object types to a presentation also follows exactly the same set of steps. You just choose the Sounds or Videos tab rather than the Clip Art or Pictures tab.

Add a new slide by choosing Insert, New Slide. The icon for Organization Chart is the third from the left on the second row of AutoLayouts. Double-click on that icon or click on OK; you see a familiar-looking blank page in front of you. Click in the Title placeholder and type the title, **This is a simple Org Chart.**

Then, double-click on the "Double click to add org chart" icon. What you see on your screen may be difficult to read, but it is a relatively typical org chart with three people reporting to one person. Each of the boxes represents one person, and you can enter four lines of text for any person:

✿ Type the person's name in the space that says "Type name here."

✿ Type the person's title in the space that says "Type title here."

✿ If you click the box again, you can type a comment in the optional Comment 1 and Comment 2 lines.

You should feel free to fill in the names and titles of the people you might work with to decide how well this works. To display the org chart that you create in PowerPoint, click outside of the org chart program.

Another weakness of the Microsoft Organization Chart program is that it doesn't follow the Presentation color scheme, so you will likely need to reformat the colors of the boxes and the type.

Enough said about organization charts at the moment. Later this weekend, you will discover ways to completely avoid this applet and create better org charts faster using PowerPoint's own drawing tools.

Viewing the Show

You have now completed a simple presentation that contains sample pages typical of many shows. In fact, this kind of slide show probably represents about 75 percent of PowerPoint shows. Saturday Morning's session goes into much more detail on each type of slide and its nuances. That session will give you the knowledge to prepare slide presentations that rival the top 25 percent of slide presentations. But before you hit the sack, take a minute and look at the end result—the slide show delivered on the screen.

To view the show, choose Slide Show, View Show. I think you'll be pleased. Press Enter to advance to the next page.

Adding a Special Effect

So, now you should be ready for a good night's sleep. But what would a good book be without a cliffhanger?

Would you like to spend just a few more minutes to quickly make this presentation even fancier and make it better than 75 percent of most presentations that are created? Sure you would. Here's how:

Choose View, Slide Sorter to view all of the pages onscreen simultaneously. Then, choose Edit, Select All or Ctrl+A from the keyboard to select all the pages.

Click on the arrow beside the drop-down list in the upper-left corner of the screen (see Figure 1.15). Select Wipe Right from the list to set this slide transition for all slides in the presentation.

Then, in the drop-down list just to the right of that, change No Effect to Dissolve (see Figure 1.15).

Now choose Slide Show, View Show again. Press Enter to advance the show and build the show element by element.

Don't forget to save the presentation. Choose File, Save As, enter the filename, and save the file as a PowerPoint presentation.

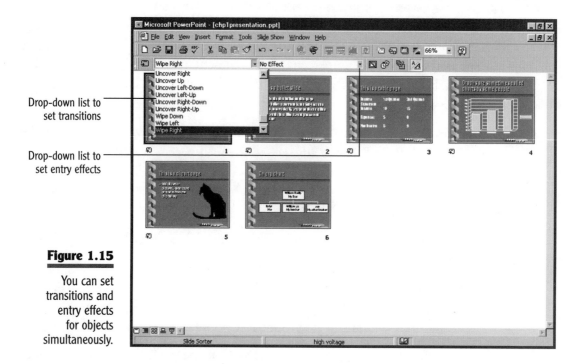

Drop-down list to set transitions

Drop-down list to set entry effects

Figure 1.15

You can set transitions and entry effects for objects simultaneously.

Wrapping Up

Congratulations on completing a very good presentation. But before you run off to bed, take a few minutes to review.

Slide presentations can be very simple if approached in the correct way. You should remember three key points to create any kind of presentation with PowerPoint: How it is shown, how it looks, and how it reveals the content.

Each of these key elements can then be broken down into their own simple lists of steps, which will help you build the entire presentation. As you've learned in this session, creating a PowerPoint presentation is really quite simple!

Well done. Have pleasant dreams—you've earned them. See you in the morning.

Creating the Presentation

- ✿ Planning the presentation color scheme
- ✿ Using the Slide Master
- ✿ Understanding AutoLayouts
- ✿ Working with text, tables, and charts

Congratulations on completing the Friday evening session. You have already learned enough about PowerPoint to go right out and create some very fine, though perhaps bland, presentations. But these will pale in comparison to those you will be able to create by Sunday afternoon!

The next sessions, three today and two tomorrow, are designed to give you a lot more detail on each of the key elements that you learned last night.

When you create PowerPoint presentations, you can accomplish each specific task in a number of ways. First, I show you the different options that are available to you. Then, I walk you through each of those options in detailed steps. At this point, you can choose the option that will get you where you want to go with the least amount of time spent banging your head against the wall.

Feel free to skim a section if you feel comfortable with the topic from prior experience. Now, if you've got the computer booted up, the coffee made, and the muffins warmed, jump right in.

Planning the Presentation

After you thoroughly understand the three key steps to your presentation, it is time to explore the best ways to go about creating the actual presentation.

PowerPoint offers a variety of techniques for entering data to create a presentation. You might receive nicely typed text from someone in a Word or other word processor file. You might have to enter the data yourself from handwritten notes that someone has made on the back of a napkin. You may want to sit down at the computer and write the presentation as you go. If you have multiple presenters, you might get input in a nonsequential order.

Whatever the manner in which you receive the input, you don't have to wait until you have all of it to begin working with the data. After you know how the presentation will be shown, you can begin entering the information even if you haven't settled on a design just yet. No matter what design you have chosen, or will choose later, after you enter the data into the AutoLayouts, you will not have to enter the data again.

Many professional creators of presentations really just try to get the actual data into the proper format as quickly as possible, without worrying too much at this point about the specific design of each page. Being finicky about how each page looks at this stage of preparation is often a waste of time.

The key questions to ask about each page as you prepare it are the following:

- What is the best way to communicate the content of this page: pure text, text and pictures, charts, movies, or a combination?

- Do you want to show all of the information simultaneously, or reveal it in a series of steps?

- Does everything you want to say on this page actually fit on one page? Or should you consider either dropping information or breaking it into more pages?

The answers to these questions will help you decide quickly which Auto-Layout to use. Choose an appropriate AutoLayout (keeping in mind that you can change it later) and enter the data.

If you are fortunate enough to be able to create the overall design of a presentation before you actually input the data, start by thinking in a sequential order about the things that will apply to every page in the presentation. They are as follows:

- The color scheme
- The Slide Master page
- The actual AutoLayouts that you choose

TIP Many people who make presentations have trouble visualizing what a page will look like without seeing it in front of them. By entering the data as it is submitted, you can make it a lot easier for the presenter to focus his or her own thoughts. So, get the data entered into PowerPoint and worry about the details later.

The Presentation Color Scheme

The presentation color scheme has to be one of the most ignored concepts in the world of PowerPoint. I am as guilty of this as anyone. Every presentation, whether you create it with an existing PowerPoint template, create your own template, or use the Blank Presentation, comes with a variety of color schemes. Maybe the multiplicity of these options has created *headache overload* with most of us, so we just tune the options out of our mind.

Let me try to explain this so that it might be helpful to you. Every PowerPoint presentation carries with it eight definable colors that set the default colors for various objects in your presentation. The idea is that you should be able to carry colors consistently throughout a presentation without having to set them manually on every page. PowerPoint thinks, "Okay, this guy wants blue text on a light-gray background. And the drop-shadow color should be light blue. Well, I'll do that for you on every page until you tell me not to do that on this one specific page." To view the color scheme of any presentation, use the Format, Slide Color Scheme command.

Viewing the Color Schemes

To start a new, blank presentation and view the available color schemes, follow these steps:

1. Choose File, New.

2. Click on the General tab in the New Presentation dialog box, select Blank Presentation, and click on OK.

3. In the New Slide dialog box, select any page layout from the AutoLayouts list, and click on OK.

4. Choose Format, Slide Color Scheme. The Color Scheme dialog box appears, as shown in Figure 2.1.

5. You will see seven different color schemes that are associated with the Blank Presentation template. To see the actual eight colors used in any of the Color Schemes, click on the thumbnail of the color scheme on the Standard tab, and then click on the Custom tab. You will now see the eight Scheme Colors, as shown in Figure 2.2. Click on Cancel to return to the presentation without making any changes.

Understanding what elements the colors apply to can be a bit confusing. Every palette in PowerPoint has eight predefined colors. Each color is used for specified elements in a presentation, as shown in Table 2.1.

PowerPoint not only gives you eight coordinated colors with every presentation, but also the option of many different color schemes with each predefined template. Why does PowerPoint give you all of these options?

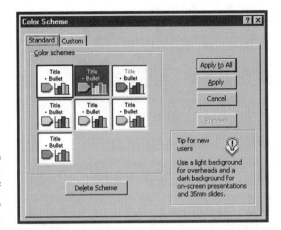

Figure 2.1

Each template can have a variety of color schemes associated with it.

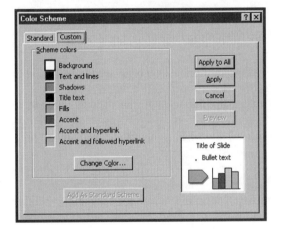

Figure 2.2

The eight scheme colors are viewable here.

Most people like to follow a unified color scheme throughout any presentation without reformatting every last parameter, such as font color. PowerPoint has created a wide variety of presentation templates that work with a number of colors for each of these object types. For the most part, they work quite nicely within the predefined PowerPoint templates. Sometimes they don't, or maybe you will be creating your own custom templates and will want to create your own custom palettes to go with these templates. The following section describes each of these

TABLE 2.1 SCHEME COLORS USED IN PRESENTATIONS

Scheme Color	Used in Chart Description	Series #
Background	The color of a background. Actually applies to only the first color of the background if a gradation is chosen.	N/A
Text and lines	The color of all text in placeholders and any lines in an AutoShape. Coordinates the text color in the Object placeholder with the line color of AutoShapes.	N/A
Shadows	The color that is applied to any object using the Shadow Color button on the Shadow Settings toolbar. This is a different button than the Shadow button located next to the Underline button on the Format toolbar.	5
Title text	The color that is used in the Title placeholder. You can use either the Shadow button in the Formatting toolbar to add a black shadow, or the Shadow Color button on the Shadow Settings toolbar to add or change a colored shadow.	6
Fills	The default color for any AutoShape. Text in a text box in an AutoShape will follow the Text and lines color. Used for the fill of the first data series in a chart.	1
Accent	Used for the fill in the second data series in a chart.	2
Accent and Hyperlink	Shows active hyperlinks during a screen show in this color.	3
Accent and Followed Hyperlink	Changes a hyperlink object to this color after it has been accessed.	N/A

key elements and shows you how to set up your own custom palette, as well as shows you how to add additional colors to the custom palette of a presentation.

Switching to Another Color Scheme

One benefit to switching the color scheme is for occasions when you are preparing a presentation for two different final outputs, such as a screen show and 35mm slide. Say, for example, that you have followed the color scheme and have used a light background and dark text for a screen show. You can change the entire presentation simultaneously to a dark background and light text for the 35mm slides, which makes reading the slides easier.

If you are not going to use a predefined template, creating your own color scheme is easy. The color scheme should work in concert with your overall Slide Master scheme. But you need to realize that every presentation has a color scheme attached. The text colors in the color scheme will be overlooked if you have made changes directly to the Slide Master, to the font colors of the Title placeholder, or to the Object Area placeholder.

Changing the colors in the color scheme is very much like setting a color for any other object in a software program. Just follow these steps:

1. Choose Format, Slide Color Scheme.

2. Click on the Custom tab.

3. Change a scheme color by selecting a colored box in the Scheme Colors area and then clicking on the Change Color button.

4. Select the color that you want to use from either the Standard tab or the Custom tab. Click on OK.

TIP If you want to save this new color scheme as a standard scheme that you can use repeatedly, click on the Add As Standard Scheme button on the Custom tab. The color scheme will be attached to whatever template you have saved this file as. A good time to do this is when you plan to use a template repeatedly and will want to output to more than one type of output, such as screen shows, color prints, or 35mm slides. You can save much reformatting time if you follow the existing color schemes, however.

5. Repeat steps 3 and 4 for as many of the eight scheme colors as you want to change.

6. Click on Apply to All.

How It Looks: The Slide Master

During the Friday evening session, you used a Slide Master page to add a logo and a rectangle to every page. Today you will learn how to completely modify the Slide Master page to change fonts, re-position type, and even add dates, page numbers, or even file locations to every page. You'll also learn about the master pages for speaker notes and how to customize that element for your special printing needs.

Remember that any changes made to Slide Master pages are made on every page in the presentation. This is the default setting, and unless you specify that a certain page not follow the Master, it will follow it religiously. If you do tell a page to not follow the Slide Master, you can later reapply the Slide Master to that page with a few mouse clicks.

Slide Master

The Slide Master controls the entire presentation, or at least it can if you let it. It will add consistency to your presentation with minimal effort on your part. It will make your life a lot easier.

Use the Slide Master to quickly enter data into your presentation. You can always take some extra time later and change individual pages if you see the need. But if you start by using an AutoLayout that uses the Slide Master, you can always reapply the Master if you don't like the changes that you have made. If you have not started with an AutoLayout, you will have a great deal more difficulty in making changes quickly.

Here's exactly how the Slide Master works. I think you will see why it generally makes the most sense to start with an AutoLayout, and then make changes, rather than create an individual page all on its own.

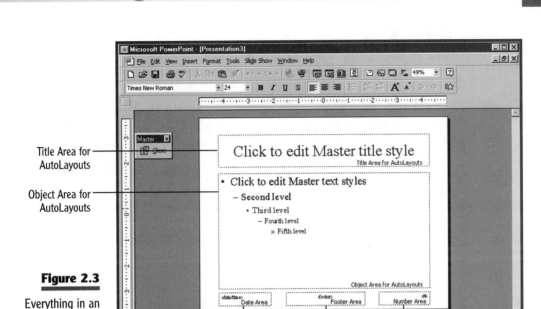

Figure 2.3

Everything in an AutoLayout is related to the placeholders.

As shown in Figure 2.3, the Slide Master consists of two placeholders—one for the Title and the second for all other general objects, such as text for bullets, charts, tables, pictures, and so on.

The Slide Title Placeholder

The first placeholder is for the Title of the page. This placeholder is pretty straightforward. A *typical* slide page contains a Title, which is the primary statement on the page. If this were advertising, this Title would be the headline of the ad. Although the Title doesn't have to be at the top of the page, it usually is. If you want to free your mind of this kind of thinking, you can actually just think of the Title placeholder as a fixed location on the page. It is always in the exact same position and contains the exact same attributes about the text, meaning font style, color, size, and alignment.

The Title placeholder is perfectly happy; it really doesn't have any emotions at all, and it just lives exactly where and how you place it. The only thing it does worry about is its own identity. It does have an identity, and there can only be one Title placeholder to a page. If you copy and paste the title to another location on the same page, that pasted image will be a clone of the Title placeholder. It will look and feel like the Title placeholder, but it is not the original and only Title placeholder on the page.

The point is that any changes that you make to the Title placeholder on the Slide Master page will apply only to that Title placeholder, and not to any other placeholders or copies of the Title placeholder. It's actually similar to the cloned sheep. If you sheared the original sheep, you wouldn't really expect the cloned sheep to suddenly have shorn coats, would you!

The Body Text Placeholder

The Body Text placeholder is actually called the Object Area for Auto-Layouts. Again, if this were advertising, the Object Area would be the main body of the ad. It might contain a picture and text or just text in its simplest form. Because this isn't advertising, the Object Area can also contain charts, tables, or any multimedia object.

There is a very strict concept that bears repeating about this Object placeholder. This Object placeholder occupies a fixed amount of geography on the page. If you have not made any modifications to the Object placeholder on a specific page, every page will strictly follow the Auto-Layout. If you have made changes on a specific page, those changes will override the AutoLayout. The geography of any AutoLayout is always a rectangle, even though it doesn't have to be wider than it is high.

But like the Title placeholder, the Object placeholder is unique and carries with it a fixed set of attributes, such as size of the geography. If it also contains a text placeholder, it will in turn also carry with it the fixed attributes of the text, such as font size, style, color, and so on. If it is another kind of object, that is, not text, it will not apply any of the default font styles to the object. So, a picture that is in this Object placeholder, and has text in the picture, will not apply this style to the text in the picture.

You can easily change the shape of either the Title placeholder or the Object placeholder by sizing the handles on the Slide Master page to suit your needs. For example, you might use a nontypical layout shown in Figure 2.4 for a catalogue. This figure shows a Title running down the left side of the page. The Object Area for AutoLayouts is to the right of the Title and extends to the right edge of the page. The Date Area and Footer Area placeholders have been moved to the bottom-left side of the page, and the Number Area has been moved to the top-right corner.

The Background

The background can be anything from a simple color supplied by PowerPoint to a combination of various colors, shadings, and shapes. Please don't use that corporate blue if you can help it! It is overused and therefore uninteresting to many audiences today. The blue background has been used often because it is a fairly dark color that provides a good level of contrast for text and pictures on 35mm slides. But, let me repeat,

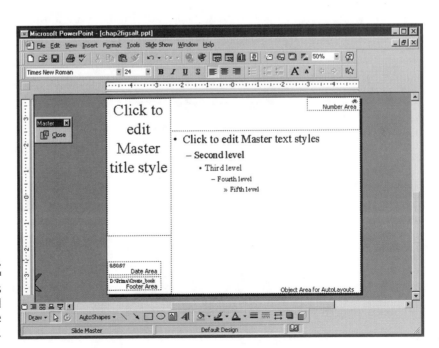

Figure 2.4

The placeholders can be moved and sized just like any object.

please don't use it ever again. It was effective in its day, just like propellers on big airplanes.

Rather than use a solid color background, you could use a gradation of colors, as shown in Figure 2.5. PowerPoint offers nine different gradations to choose from for this kind of background. These gradations add some more interest to backgrounds in many presentations, but can create a problem when you try to provide a high level of contrast to an entire page. Typically, the top of the page may be a dark color and the bottom of the page may be a light one. If you have an object that covers much of that page, the lack of a good level of contrast between the object and the background can make the object difficult to see.

Gradations in the backgrounds add another level of design complexity that a new designer should avoid. Yes, the gradations look good on the screen. But creating enough contrast to make the text readable on all parts of the gradation is difficult to do. Because PowerPoint really still thinks of it as a slide program, as in 35mm slides, the difficulty is even greater. PowerPoint tends to think that backgrounds should be dark and text should be light, which is basically the rule for 35mm slides. With screen shows, however, you are usually better off with light backgrounds and dark text.

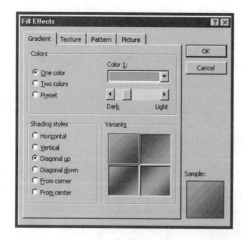

Figure 2.5

You can change gradations to many different patterns.

So, what should you do? Don't be frightened of gradations. You just have to learn to use them judiciously and correctly. If you are using gradations that don't have text to be read over them, you have free reign to do as you see fit. What I'm talking about here is when you expect to place text over a gradation. In order for the text to be readable, you must create enough contrast between whatever colors you are using behind the text and the text itself. The simple rule of thumb here is to choose a very light color that is close to the center of the Colors palette in PowerPoint (see Figure 2.6), and to choose white as the second color. This will give your pages an interesting look while also enabling them to be quite easy to read. If you choose exactly the opposite, dark colors gradated to light colors, you will have a beautiful background, but chances are that your audience will not be able to read your text on the screen.

Graphics to Appear on Every Page

Did someone say, "Put my company logo on every page?" Whether it's your own logo or your client's logo, you will most likely want to do this in any presentation. But the logo is not the only graphic that you will want to create for every page. You may want to design your own templates. How to design new templates is a frequently requested question in electronic forums.

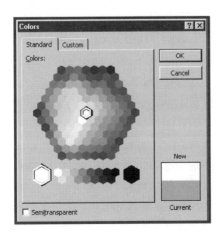

Figure 2.6

Lighter colors are in the center of the Colors grid; darker colors are on the outside.

Creating your own templates is such an easy thing to do that many of us who are PowerPoint professionals don't think of the idea of creating templates for other people as a worthwhile business proposition. If it just takes me a few minutes to create a template, why would people pay me a fair amount of money to do that? Creating templates is such an easy task. You only have a limited number of elements to deal with. The easiest element is the graphics that go on every page. Just plop the graphic down as you would with any object. Make sure that you plop it down on the Slide Master, and you are done. Triangles, squares, circles, pictures of the cat, the company logo, a client's logo, whatever. They are all the same. Place them on the Slide Master and they appear on every page in the presentation. Enough said on that subject? Well, for most presentations, the answer would be yes. But for this book, because you really want to become a PowerPoint expert by the end of this weekend, you should read the very next section.

Animations to Appear on Every Page

You can even add animations to every page in a presentation by adding animation to the Slide Master page. See "Saturday Evening, How the Presentation Is Shown: Animation Effects," for more specific details—but for now, the concept to understand is that any animation that you can add to a specific page in your PowerPoint presentation, you can now add to the Slide Master page. That animation will then show up on every page during the presentation, depending on the animation settings that you

CAUTION Although adding animation to every page is now very easy in PowerPoint, you should be very careful not to overdo this technique. It can grate on your audience quickly if you have not been especially careful. You might choose this technique at the start a presentation to slam home your main point, and then branch to another presentation (see the section on branching on Sunday morning) to go to a similar-looking presentation that does not use the animation on the Slide Master.

use. This is exactly what was done in the high voltage.pot template that you used Friday evening.

How It Looks: AutoLayouts

As you learned last night, the AutoLayout controls the fundamental way that a page actually looks, and keeps it consistent with the rest of the presentation. You should always use AutoLayouts for the first entry of data into a presentation. Then, if the AutoLayout doesn't work perfectly for your needs and you have to make changes, you can do so.

If you receive data as handwritten or typed text, you will probably do best if you type it into PowerPoint page by page and choose which Auto-Layout to use before starting the next page. If you receive a word processor file with the data already entered, however, you don't need to retype it. You can simply copy and paste the data quickly into the PowerPoint Outline, and then choose the AutoLayout after the fact. Doing so eliminates the need for you to enter the data yourself or proof your typing for errors that you may have made.

Either way, you end up with uniformly formatted pages that you can further modify if need be. Seeing how the submitted words fit, or don't, on a page will help everyone understand the limitations of the format.

Understanding AutoLayouts

Think of the AutoLayout as the geographical boundary for two different pieces of real estate on your page. The first piece of real estate is the Title placeholder. The second piece of real estate is generally the main point of the page, whether it be text, a chart, a picture, or even a movie. These two placeholders are just places to locate objects so that the objects look consistent. You don't need to fill a placeholder with anything, but if you do, you will not have to worry about formatting it to look consistent. The AutoLayout will do that for you.

Using the placeholders in the AutoLayout means that you worry about the formatting of a presentation only once. For example, say that you want the entire presentation to have the Title on every page appear in blue type in the Bodoni font, sized at 48 points and centered on the page. You can set all these parameters to these specifications once; henceforward, you need only type the words for the Title. Don't feel that doing so puts you in a straitjacket; changing the specifications for a given page is very easy. The AutoLayout just automates a lot of the repetitious tasks in creating presentations that look consistent.

Every AutoLayout is determined by the layout on the Slide Master page. This is a good time to look specifically at the Slide Master page and examine each of the elements that you can set there. To view the Slide Master page, choose View, Master, Slide Master.

The Slide Master page shown in Figure 2.3 actually shows five different placeholders:

- Click to edit Master title style
- Click to edit Master text styles
- Date Area
- Footer Area
- Number Area

Clearly, for most of us, the first two placeholders are fundamental to every presentation. For the sake of simplicity, consider it a given that every page has a title (Click to edit Master title style) and some key information (Click to edit Master text styles). Don't get thrown by the slight misnomer about text styles. This placeholder also goes by the name *Object Area for Auto-Layouts*. This placeholder even has this label attached to it (see the lower right corner of this placeholder in Figure 2.3). This box really means to say that this box contains either text, pictures, tables, charts, movies, or sound. (The way this box is put together makes you ponder how a communications program can communicate so poorly. It also makes you want to get up to refresh your cup of coffee.) So, do that, and then come back and read about the modifying AutoLayouts to specifically meet your needs.

Modifying Layouts to Suit Your Needs

The beauty of PowerPoint's AutoLayouts is that each element in an Auto-Layout has its own location on the page, making for an orderly way of life. Predictable and symmetrical. You may like predictable, but not symmetrical, though.

Don't panic. Life and PowerPoint don't have to be perfectly symmetrical. You can move each of these five placeholders to fit any rectangular shape and size on the page. And you can set any attributes of each of these shapes (for example, font size, font color, font style) to any specification. These attributes will then follow that specification throughout the presentation unless you change the specifications for a particular page.

Any changes that you make to the Slide Master will be reflected in every page of the presentation. To make this idea clear, take a few minutes now to make some modifications to the Master Slide page layout. Figure 2.7

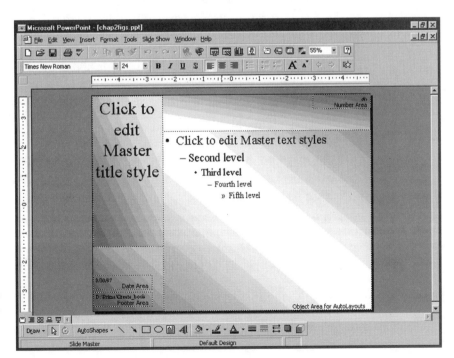

Figure 2.7

Every placeholder in this Slide Master has been resized and moved.

shows a modified Slide Master page illustrating the flexibility of the five placeholders on the Slide Master page.

You may not want the title of the page to run vertically and be limited to approximately 2.5 inches as this one is. Still, this approach would work for a catalog in which the Title is the name of the product and the Object placeholder is a picture or description of the product. The point here is to learn the flexibility and the rigidity of the AutoLayout. Each placeholder can be moved and formatted as you see fit. The attributes of each placeholder are then applied automatically to every new page that you create.

Changing the Attributes of Placeholders

Follow these steps to modify the attributes of a placeholder:

1. Open a new presentation using the Blank Presentation template by choosing File, New, and then double-clicking the Blank Presentation icon on the General tab.

2. Choose View, Master Slide Master to display the Slide Master page, which controls the AutoLayout.

3. Select the "Click to edit Master title style" placeholder box, and then drag it with the mouse to the left side of the page. Then size the placeholder to be approximately 2.5 inches wide by 4.75 inches high.

TIP Choose View, Ruler to display the Ruler, if it doesn't already appear on your screen.

4. Drag the Date Area placeholder to roughly the position shown in Figure 2.7. I'll show you how to format and align each placeholder later.

5. Drag the Footer Area placeholder so that it appears just under the Date Area placeholder.

6. Drag the Number Area placeholder to the top-right corner of the page.

7. Size the "Click to edit Master text styles" placeholder to fill most of the right side of the page.

8. To add the colored tiles for the background behind each of these placeholders, display the Drawing toolbar by choosing <u>V</u>iew, <u>T</u>ool-bars, Drawing.

9. Select the Rectangle toolbar button on the Drawing toolbar by clicking on it. Then, drag a rectangle around the "Click to edit Master title style" placeholder. You should see a colored rectangle covering what was the "Click to edit Master title style" placeholder. If you don't see the Drawing toolbar, choose View, Toolbars and select the Drawing option to make the toolbar visible.

10. If you have the filled rectangle showing on your screen, probably a green color, right-click on the rectangle and choose Format Aut<u>o</u>Shape from the shortcut menu.

11. Click on the Colors and Lines tab and choose a color from the Fill <u>C</u>olor drop-down list to fill the AutoShape. Try one of the lighter colors at the bottom of the list, and then click on <u>F</u>ill Effects (below the Fill <u>C</u>olor palette). The Fill Effects dialog box appears, as shown in Figure 2.8.

12. To make each of the rectangular fills that you use in this example stand out from each other, as shown in Figure 2.7, you should use different fill patterns. In the Shading Styles area, select Diagonal <u>D</u>own. Then, select the first of the four choices in Varian<u>t</u>s (in the upper-left corner).

13. Click on OK to apply that color.

14. Now, so the rectangle does not hide the placeholders, you need to place them on the bottom layer by sending them to the back. Choose D<u>r</u>aw, O<u>r</u>der and Send to Bac<u>k</u>, as shown in Figure 2.9.

15. Repeat Steps 9 through 13 for each of the other four placeholders in the AutoLayout.

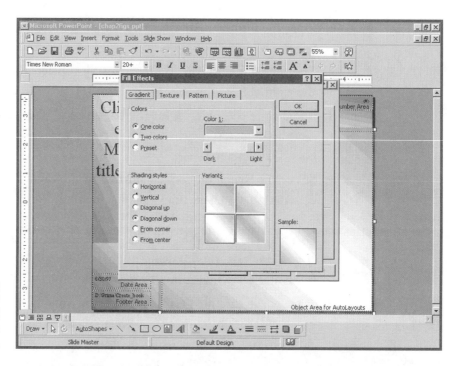

Figure 2.8

You can add
gradations to
any shape.

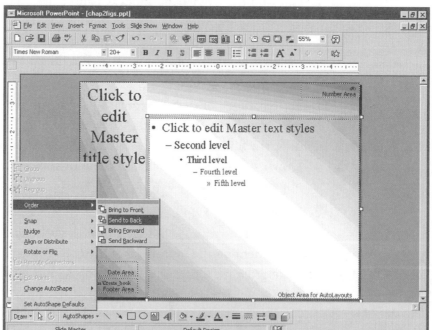

Figure 2.9

Put the
placeholders on
the bottom layer
by sending them
to the back.

The Drawing toolbar contains the command to Send to Back. If you followed these steps, you should have a slide that is similar to Figure 2.9. You will notice that every object resides in its own geography. PowerPoint organizes each element for you and sizes both the text in the bullets and the clip art to the same size rectangle. You can leave it that way, or you are free to make some changes to the AutoLayout if the AutoLayout does not take into account all of your needs.

Inserting Clip Art Outside of the AutoLayout

The next steps will show you how to create a simple typical slide, and then how to add an additional piece of clip art that is not allowed from within the Object Area for AutoLayout placeholder.

For an example of how you might do this, create the slide shown in Figure 2.10 by following these steps:

1. Choose Insert, New Slide (or press Ctrl+M).

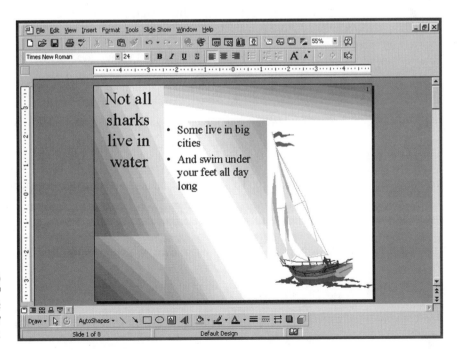

Figure 2.10

This complete slide uses every placeholder.

2. Select the second AutoLayout in the third row (the Clip Art & Text AutoLayout), and then click on OK.

3. Type the following text as the Title placeholder: **Not all sharks live in water**.

4. Type two bullet points in the "Click to add text" placeholder. For the first bullet, type **Some live in big cities**, and then press Enter to advance to the next bullet. Now type **And swim under your feet all day long**.

5. Next add the boat by double-clicking in the "Double click to add clip art" placeholder. Select the <u>C</u>lip Art tab and select the Transportation category. Select the boat image and choose <u>I</u>nsert.

The AutoLayout that you just applied takes into account only one clip art image, a boat sailing on the water. Say that you wanted to add another piece of clip art—a shark swimming under the boat. You cannot do that with the AutoLayout, but you can do it after the AutoLayout has been applied to a page.

1. Now you'll add that shark that isn't allowed by the AutoLayout. Choose <u>I</u>nsert, <u>P</u>icture <u>C</u>lip Art.

2. Click on the <u>C</u>lip Art tab and select the Animals category.

3. Select the shark image and click on <u>I</u>nsert (you could also just double-click on the shark's picture to insert the art).

4. The clip art is placed on the screen in the center of the screen and is not part of any of the AutoLayout placeholders (see Figure 2.11). It is a completely separate object that can be sized and moved as you see fit. To size the shark to be more in perspective with the size of the boat, use the sizing handle in any corner of the shark; the sizing handle is visible when the shark is selected.

Sizing any object in PowerPoint is easy, but the process has a few simple rules:

✪ Grabbing any of the four corners will resize the object and maintain the proportions so that the picture will not be distorted.

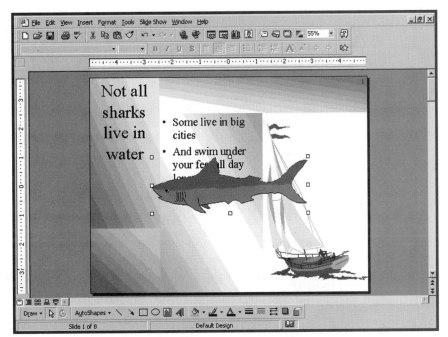

Figure 2.11

Use the object handles shown to resize an object.

✪ Grabbing any of the other four placeholders (see Figure 2.11) will change the proportions and is a common mistake. If you do this and didn't mean to, choose Edit, Undo (or press Ctrl+Z).

Now that you have the shark the right size relative to the boat, you need to move it into the water. Just select the shark, hold down the left mouse button and drag it into position under the boat. So, you have the shark in the water swimming under the boat. Now take one more look at the AutoLayout feature and what gets affected when you change things. You originally chose the Text & Clip Art AutoLayout. Switch this existing slide to the Clip Art & Text AutoLayout. Doing this should flip the text and the picture. Choose Format, Slide Layout, and then click on the second AutoLayout in the third row. Click on Apply. The text and the boat will change positions on the page, but the Title stays the same and the separate element, the shark, doesn't move.

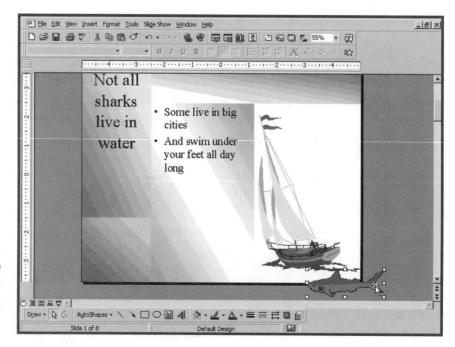

Figure 2.12

You can now
easily place
images partially
out of the frame.

Say that you don't want to show the entire shark on the screen, but just
part of it to make it more ominous. Isn't the image of just a shark's fin one
of the most ominous images in your mind? You can now drag the image
part of the way out of the screen and have only the fin show during a
screen show (see Figure 2.12).

Using Multiple Masters in the Same Presentation

You might be preparing a presentation for different departments of the
same company and want to have different Slide Masters for each department so that each of them had its own special look. The ability to have
more than one Slide Master in the same presentation is one of the still-
missing elements in PowerPoint. Possibly one of the future versions of

PowerPoint will give us that feature, but at the moment, there are two easy workarounds:

- One method is to create separate presentations using different templates, and then insert the additional presentations into the first presentation. This way, when you want to switch to the other template, you need only click on an object and it will launch the second or the third presentation.

- Another method, which is almost as quick, doesn't allow you to jump back to the previous presentation. This method involves creating multiple presentations using different Slide Masters; you save all but the first presentation as Windows Metafiles, and then insert each saved metafile as a Picture back into the first presentation.

Inserting a Presentation into Another Presentation

Inserting one presentation into another is easy. You do it with *hyperlinks*, which, if you don't already know, are simple little commands attached to an object. When you click on the object, you jump to another page, another file, or even to a Web site.

After you have created and saved both presentations, follow these steps:

1. Select an object on the last page of the first presentation to attach a hyperlink to.

2. Choose Insert, Hyperlink to see the Insert Hyperlink dialog box shown in Figure 2.13. If you are linking to another file, click on the Browse button; after selecting the file, click on OK.

3. You will then see the path to the file that you have established a hyperlink to. Click on OK.

Now, when you are showing the first presentation, you can just click on that object to open up the second presentation in Slide Show mode. When in Slide Show mode, the cursor changes to the hyperlink hand image, and

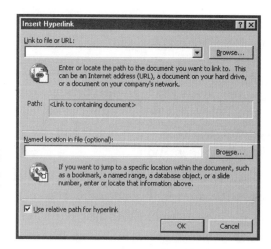

Figure 2.13

You can create hyperlinks to other presentations, slides, files, and even Web sites.

if you click it you will jump to the linked presentation. If you don't click the image right away, there will be a preview of the path and the file to which this object is linked, as shown in Figure 2.14. This is a very efficient way to mix presentations because all you have established is a pointer (the hyperlink) to the other presentation, so any changes made to that second presentation will still be reflected at future dates. The only drawback is a slight one: opening the second presentation creates a little lag time. The

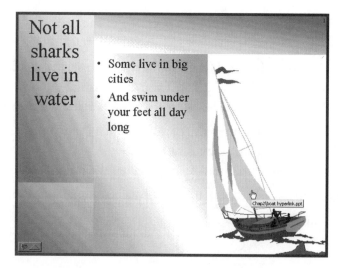

Figure 2.14

The hyperlinks are only active during Slide Show view.

lag time is not all that significant if you are opening another relatively small presentation on a reasonably powerful computer. But if that is not the case, you might want to try the other technique of inserting Windows Metafiles as pictures and having only one presentation.

Inserting Windows Metafiles into a Presentation

If you insert Windows Metafiles from one presentation into another presentation, you can also effectively simulate mixing two different Slide Masters in the same presentation. The benefit of using this method over using hyperlinks is the time that opening a tremendously big file during a presentation with a hyperlink takes. Use this method if you need to open one very large file before launching the presentation. The first step is to create both presentations and save them both. Then you need to create the Windows Metafiles. PowerPoint 97 now lets you export each page as a batch and will place each of the resulting Windows Metafiles in a new folder with the same name as the presentation. The files are numbered sequentially, starting with Slide1.wmf. Then you want to insert each file into the target presentation and size each one to the full page.

Here are the steps to accomplish the entire process:

1. Open the file that you want to save as a Windows Metafile, and choose File, Save As.

2. Select a folder to place the new folder into, and select Windows Metafile (*.wmf) from the Save as Type drop-down list.

3. Click on Save and choose Yes to export every slide as a Windows Metafile. If you click on No, you will export only the current slide.

4. Now open the target presentation and select the slide after which you want to insert the Windows Metafiles.

5. Choose Insert, New Slide (or press Ctrl+M) to add a new slide, and choose the Blank AutoLayout with no placeholders. Click on OK.

6. Choose Insert, Picture From File; select the correct folder and file, and then click on Insert.

TIP The inserted Windows Metafiles are still pictures, which means that they are not editable in PowerPoint. If you choose Draw, Ungroup, you will be warned about ungrouping. But, if you click on OK, you will have editable objects. Use this technique if you want to change some text after importing the Windows Metafile.

Now that I have covered everything you need to know about how to set up your presentation and how to change the appearance of every slide, it is time to shift gears and learn about things that affect only individual slides. This is the start of the nuts-and-bolts discussion of how to enter every imaginable kind of data into a presentation, whether it be text, charts, tables, movie clips, or a combination of these elements on a single page.

Take a Break

Before I get started with text, tables, and charts, it might be a good idea for you to take a short break. The next session this morning covers many different ways to perform these procedures, and I don't want you to miss any gems.

How it Reveals the Content: Text, Tables, and Charts

Text is probably the most common element in any presentation. Because we write and talk with words, we use words to express most of our ideas. This section covers a variety of ways to enter text into PowerPoint so that you can achieve the best possible communication of your words. You will learn a host of tricks for placing text into PowerPoint and making it all look uniform quickly and effortlessly. I also cover tables and charts, which are really just other ways to easily turn words and numbers into communication.

Text and Text Boxes

You have already learned about typing bulleted points into placeholders. What if no placeholder fits the layout that you want for a set of words? Well, there are also a few other ways to get text onto a PowerPoint page. The most common is to use a text box. A *text box* is simply what its name says, just a placeholder that doesn't apply to the Slide Master. It can contain text or numbers, and can even show or not show bullets. A text box can communicate words inside of an AutoShape or be placed over a photograph. The text box object is just another container that can be placed anywhere on the page and not be governed by the restrictions of the Slide Master.

Text boxes are the simplest means to add a small amount of text to a page that you do not want to follow the Slide Master. To add text, make sure that the Drawing toolbar is visible (choose View, Toolbars, Drawing), and click on the Text Box button.

Then, click anywhere on the page and start typing. You can add bullets or resize the text box shape or font size or color. After typing the text that you want, you can change the other attributes by choosing Format, Text Box. Click on the Text Box tab. You will then see a dialog box similar to the one shown in Figure 2.15.

Figure 2.15

Text boxes can be formatted just like paragraphs.

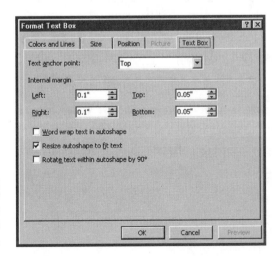

Take a look at each of the text box options. The first enables you to anchor the text to the text box. After selecting the Text <u>A</u>nchor Point drop-down list, you can anchor the text to either the top, the middle, or the bottom of the text box. Those first three selections leave the text aligned flush left. The next three selections center the text horizontally in the text box. The three text alignment toolbar buttons on the Formatting toolbar also change the alignment, however.

The settings in the Internal Margin area enable you to precisely position the text within the text box by setting <u>L</u>eft, <u>R</u>ight, <u>T</u>op, or <u>B</u>ottom margins.

The last three settings for a text box are the following check boxes:

- ✪ *<u>W</u>ord Wrap Text in AutoShape*: Lets you keep all the text inside of the AutoShape if it fits.

- ✪ *Resize AutoShape to <u>F</u>it Text*: Increases or decreases the size of the AutoShape to fit just around the entire text. This option is selected by default.

- ✪ *Rotat<u>e</u> Text within AutoShape by 90 Degrees*: Turns the entire text object 1/4 turn to the right so that the top of the words in the text box are facing the right side of the page.

TIP A very common use of text boxes is to add words inside AutoShapes. Draw the AutoShape, and then click on the Text Box button. Then, click inside the AutoShape and begin typing; the text starts at the vertical center of the AutoShape. Further refinements can be made as stated previously.

Adding bullets, changing font sizes, font styles, or colors to text in text boxes is done the same as with any selected text. Select the text or text box and change the font size, shape, color, and so on by using the F<u>o</u>rmat, <u>F</u>ont command.

TEXT BOX TRICKS

You may want to add several text boxes inside of an AutoShape that all look exactly alike in size, shape, and color, such as a flow chart on a project schedule. The easiest way to do this is to pick the biggest object that you will encounter. Then, spend the time correctly formatting that one so that you can copy and paste copies of that object as many times as you need, and they will all fit on the page.

If you want four ellipses, for example, as Figure 2.16 shows, you would create the one for the Second Object first because that would have the most letters. Copy and paste that three more times and roughly arrange the objects on the page. Then, select all four objects and choose Draw, Align or Distribute, Distribute Horizontally. Choose Draw, Align or Distribute, Distribute Vertically to align all the objects. All you have to do to finish is to select the text in the remaining objects and change the text in the text box. Because you created all of the objects with the longest text first, you can set the font size for that to as big as the font will go and still fit inside the object. Then, when you copy that object and change the text for the other objects, the font size remains the same and everything is exactly the same size.

Figure 2.16

Copy the shape and paste it to make sure that the multiple copies are sized identically.

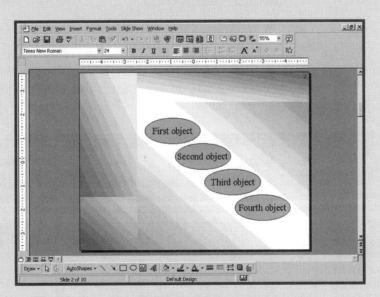

Modifying Bullets

You may want to change the size, shape, or color of bullets. Now, you'll learn how to change bullet settings. Specifically, I cover adding or deleting bullets and changing the size or shape of a bullet or collection of bullets. These instructions apply equally to using bullets in Slide Master placeholders or in text boxes.

In working with bullets, the key thing to keep in mind is what text you have selected. If you are in a text box and have selected just two of four sentences separated by a hard return (using the Enter key), the changes that you make will apply only to those two bulleted points. If you select all the text in the text box either by dragging from top to bottom with the mouse or by clicking on the text box, your changes will apply to the entire text box. If you are working with the Object Area for AutoLayouts placeholder text, the same logic applies.

Adding or subtracting bullets is quite easy. Select the text within which you want to add or subtract a bullet, and follow these steps:

1. Choose Format, Bullet.

2. You will see a dialog box similar to Figure 2.17, where you can change five different settings for the bullets in the selected text.

3. Select the Use a Bullet check box if you want to show bullets, or deselect it if you do not want to show bullets.

Figure 2.17

All settings for bullets are available in this dialog box.

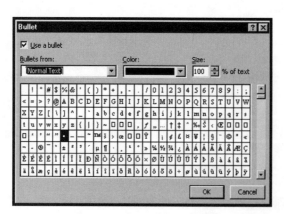

4. If you selected the Use a Bullet check box, you should now set the other four options. In the Bullets From drop-down list, select the font that you want your bullets to use.

5. In the Color drop-down list, select the color for the bullet.

6. In the Size text box, specify the size (as a percentage of the text).

7. The last choice, the shape of the bullet, depends on which font you have chosen. Selecting a shape with a single mouse click will show you an enlarged image of the shape being selected. Choose the one that you want to use and click on OK.

Typing Text in the Outline Page

There is even another way to get text into PowerPoint. That way is to use the Outline page. This is especially useful for situations in which the presenter has carefully approved all of the words to be used before creating the presentation in PowerPoint. In many cases, you might receive approved copy in a Microsoft Word file. Rather than retype each of the pages, you should first copy the text from the Word file into the Power-Point outline page (see Figure 2.18).

The Outline page in PowerPoint, which appears when you choose View, Outline, contains all of the text in the Title placeholder and the bullet points in the "Click to add text" placeholders. If you simply copy and paste the text from Word to the Outline page, you will be able to capture most of the text with minimal re-keying. It's not a perfect system by any means, but if you can import 60 pages of text and fix up the formatting for most of it fairly quickly, this is a better solution than retyping the entire 60 pages.

Importing Text from Word Outlines

The correct way to receive text from a Word document is to have the Word user prepare the Word file in outline form. Then, things work fairly well. This is not always the case because many people don't actually know how to use a Word outline and will hand you the document as text

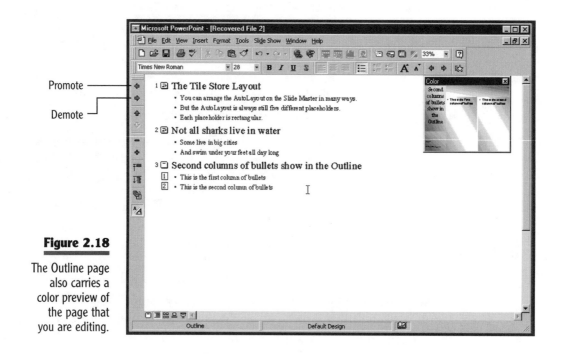

Promote

Demote

Figure 2.18

The Outline page also carries a color preview of the page that you are editing.

typed in a document. Whichever way you receive it, the text is probably easier to insert into the Outline and reformat there.

Follow these steps to import the text from a Word outline:

1. Open the PowerPoint file, and choose View, Outline.

2. Switch to Word and press Ctrl+A to select the entire Outline in Word.

3. Click on the Copy button (or press Ctrl+C) to copy the selection to the Clipboard.

4. Switch back to PowerPoint and click on the Paste button (or press Ctrl+V) to paste the Clipboard's contents into PowerPoint's Outline page.

You have now saved a great deal of time retyping all this text. But you still have to make sure that things are in the correct order. Another of Reilly's Rules is that not everything comes in perfectly, because various typists have different skill levels. But the good news is that almost everything is

easy to fix. And if a page isn't easy to fix in the outline, you will now have enough time to create it from scratch the correct way.

The Outline page lets you easily promote or demote a statement with the click of a button. Promote means make it more important, that is, a bullet point can be promoted into a new Slide and become a Slide Title. Demote goes the other way. A Slide Title can be demoted to a bullet under the previous bullet or previous slide title. Figure 2.18 shows an Outline page with callouts of the most important buttons on the page.

To use one of the buttons, such as Promote or Demote, just click once in the line that you want to promote or demote. The line is moved within the presentation and changes are reflected in the small color preview off the current slide in the preview box labeled Color.

Keep in mind that only the text in the Title placeholder and the "Click to add text" placeholder are reflected in the outline. No text that appears in pictures or in text boxes, tables, or charts will appear. The outline should really be thought of as a quick tool to getting a lot of text into PowerPoint before you finalize the layout of the slides.

TIP If you import text from a Word document that has not been formatted correctly, or doesn't paste correctly into PowerPoint, you can use any of the normal editing keys to edit text while you are still in Outline view. Press Enter if you want to force the remaining text in a sentence to a new level. Copy and paste works just as well.

WordArt Text

Yet another way to add text to PowerPoint slides is by using WordArt. You can think of WordArt as just another text box with some fancy graphics attached to it. The WordArt feature in Office 97 is a vastly improved tool. It comes with 30 predefined formats you can use to format text with any available font or font size. You can then change the colors used, the perspective of the type, and the shape that the text will fill. The result is that WordArt gives you thousands of ways to easily create *highly stylized* text.

Adding the WordArt is just about as simple as adding text in a text box:

1. Click on the Insert WordArt button (the tilted *A*) in the Drawing toolbar (see Figure 2.19).

2. Pick one of the thirty styles and click on OK. (Don't worry if you choose that horrid red/orange color in the last row—you'll be able to change that later.)

3. The Edit WordArt dialog box appears. You can set five different options for the WordArt. Try some text first. Where you see the words "Your Text Here," drag your mouse to highlight all of that text (if it isn't already selected). Then, just type the text that you want to display as WordArt.

4. Choose a font style from the <u>F</u>ont drop-down list.

5. Choose a font size from the <u>S</u>ize drop-down list.

6. If you do not click on either the B (for Bold) or I (for Italic), your

Insert
WordArt button

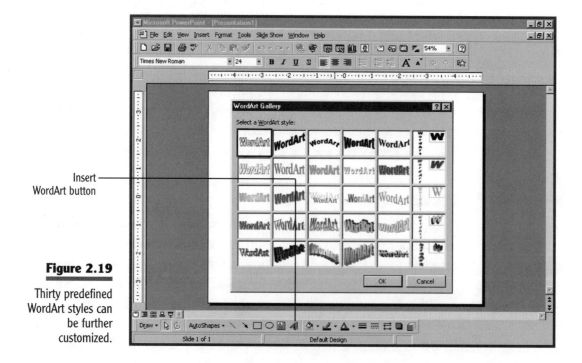

Figure 2.19

Thirty predefined
WordArt styles can
be further
customized.

Figure 2.20

You can use any font on your computer with WordArt.

text will appear in normal weight for the font that you chose. Click on OK; your WordArt appears in PowerPoint.

The WordArt object shown in Figure 2.20 is the finished WordArt. You can create many special effects with WordArt. In fact, you can create so many that covering even half of what is now available with the WordArt tool would be impossible. The best idea is to spend a little time experimenting by creating a new piece of WordArt, making sure that the WordArt toolbar is visible, and choosing each of the ten toolbar buttons to see what they do.

Tables

Another entirely different way to deal with text is so important on its own that PowerPoint has dedicated an entire AutoLayout to this technique: tables. Tables used to be the cause of many last minute heartaches because they would be prepared incorrectly, and when the inevitable text changes came just before a presentation, the changes would mess up the tables and make those pages look horrible. Generally, this happened because the original text was prepared using tabs and extra spaces in order to get the table to line up in columns. You should never use tabs in tables to line up columns anymore. In this session, before you get a chance for a lunch break, you will have tables simplified in such a way that you will use them for many things other than just text. I frequently use them to line up anything that is in columns or rows, even pictures.

PowerPoint doesn't really create its own tables. PowerPoint uses Microsoft Word to do this. It might appear a little complicated, but it's not. When you want to create a table in PowerPoint, you just use the Table Auto-Layout (fourth from the left in the top row of the AutoLayout dialog box). AutoLayout knows to fire up Word and give you a wizard to ask you how many rows and columns you want your table to be. You saw last night how easy it is to enter the text and numbers into a table. Today you learn how easy it is to quickly format a Word table exactly the way you want, and to have that formatting stay in place when the inevitable changes happen at the last minute.

Creating Tables in Word

Actually, tables are just rows and columns of words or numbers. You don't have to line up the columns because the columns in Word tables have boundaries. The trick is in understanding how Word manages the text and numbers inside the cells. Luckily, the understanding is almost intuitive and you can become *almost* an expert in tables without using any of the menus and simply by using only a handful of useful dragging commands.

Formatting a Word Table

Formatting Word tables—getting everything to line up and setting the column widths correctly—may appear to be complicated. Formatting is actually quite simple, though.

What would be a more appropriate way to explain a Word table than a table? There are only seven things to worry about when formatting most Word tables, as shown in Table 2.2. Six of these tools are slider tools that you can just drag into place and place visually without worrying about specific settings. Word sets the settings for you, which you can then

TABLE 2.2 FORMATTING WORD TABLES IN POWERPOINT	
Element Name	**Description**
First Line Indent	Sets the left margin for a column. It can be set by selecting a column or a cell and dragging left or right, and it can be aligned visually. In this case, the first line indent is set to the right of the rest of the cell.
Hanging Indent	Sets the left margin for text on the second and later lines. In this row of this table, both Hanging Indents are set two characters to the right of the First Line Indent.
Left Indent	Sets the left indent for a cell. This symbol will override the settings of First Line Indent and Hanging Indent if they are set to the left of this setting.
Right Indent	Sets the right indent for a column, in such a way that you can have different margins in each cell.
Move Table Column	Drag this to change the column width. Sets the column width if you need to resize columns. Note that all three columns are now different widths. Word wrap follows this column sizing and is a very nice feature.
Adjust Table Row	Same as Move Table Column except that this changes cell height, not width. This is handy if you want to mix column heights.
Tab	Sets tabs for left, right, center, and decimals. Use the decimal tabs to line up a column of decimal numbers of different lengths. Use the other tab settings sparingly. A better solution to the other tabs is to insert additional columns.

COMPARING TABLES IN WORD AND POWERPOINT

The blank table that Word opens within PowerPoint is a different default table than you would open if you were working directly in Word. Compare a typical 4x4 table in PowerPoint's version of Word to a typical 4x4 table that you would get by inserting a new table into Word directly from Word.

In the PowerPoint-generated table that works with the sample Sharks presentation, the cells are automatically fit to fill the AutoLayout geography on the page. That gives me columns that are just under two inches each, and row heights that are about 1.5 inches. The fonts default to 32 points, which make the text quite readable, but really only gives me just less than three lines of type before the cell reformats to a larger size. And I get only seven characters across at this size (see Figure 2.21).

If I were to open a new document in Word and insert a 4-row-by-4-column table, I get a table that also fits the page in width. It is a portrait page (only six inches wide), however, because of the default printer setup in Word. Also, the type size is

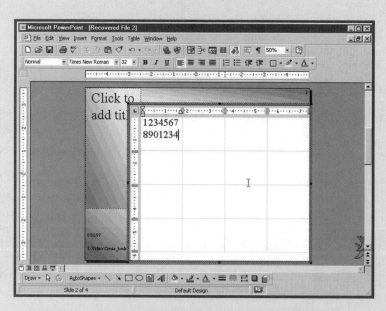

Figure 2.21

Font size is formatted for PowerPoint rather than for Word.

only 10 points, which is exactly 1/2 the size that, as I pointed out earlier, one can read in a screen show projected presentation. The row height is one character high, which is 10 points.

Clearly, I have two different things going on here, and depending on who prepares a table for PowerPoint, you are likely to get at least both, and probably more, variations on the table preparation. But in the words of my oft-quoted friend, "Don't panic." You will learn about all of the commonalties of preparing Word tables no matter how the operator starts. And you will be able to get perfect Word tables every time, if you just follow the guidelines.

change numerically, if you need very precise positioning, or you can also continue to slide the tool until you are happy. Figure 2.22 shows each of these tools with their results.

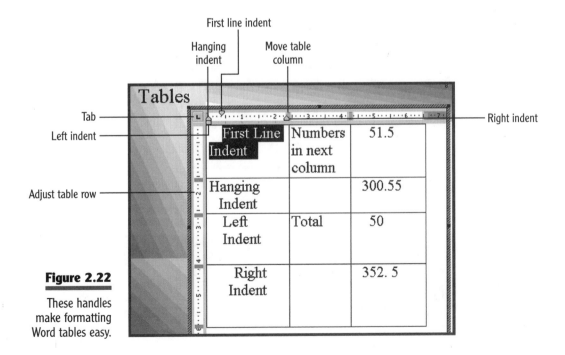

Figure 2.22

These handles make formatting Word tables easy.

NOTE   Each of these tools apply on a cell by cell basis. Figure 2.22 shows each of the callouts, but they are in position only for the first cell in this table. The position of each of these tools will vary by cell in this table, which is meant to point out the various formatting options in tables. They are shown in Figure 2.22.

You can use these handy slider tools to format your tables without having to worry about precise measuring in picas or inches. Just select the text that you want to format, carefully position your mouse right over one of the tools, and move the tool to the new position. The selected text will follow your directions. To use the decimal tab, click the tab icon until you toggle through to the decimal tab and click in the horizontal ruler guide, and the numbers in that column will align around the decimal point. The tool will be repositioned in the ruler guide (remember to turn the ruler guide on if it is turned off by choosing View, Ruler). Figures 2.23a, 2.23b, and 2.23c show the specific cell that has been highlighted in the table in Figure 2.22, and shows where the tools have moved to in the ruler.

Figures 2.23

Each cell can have its own formatting and the tool indicate where that formatting is located.

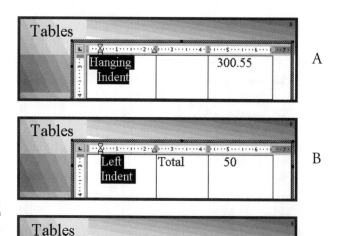

How do you select different pieces of text? This concept was somewhat perplexing for me when I first started working with tables, so let me tell you what I was told. Table 2.3 explains how to select the various items in a table.

TABLE 2.3 SELECTING ITEMS IN A TABLE	
To select this	**Do this**
Single cell	Drag your mouse, while holding down the left mouse button, from one end of the text to the other. If the text is several lines long, you can go from the start of the text and move straight down to the last line, and then all the way to the right in the last line.
Group of contiguous cells	Drag your mouse through the cells that you want to select.
An entire row	Click your mouse outside the table, to the left of the row that you want to select.
An entire column	Position your mouse pointer on the line at the top of the column that you want to select. When the mouse pointer's I-beam turns into a downward-pointing arrow, click and you will have selected the entire column.
A Move Table Column slider	You can resize columns in two ways: 1) select the entire column and you will see the Move Column Table slider in the Ruler Guide at the top of the page; or 2) position your mouse pointer over one of the vertical dotted lines in the table and the cursor will turn into two vertical parallel lines with arrows pointing left and right. You can then hold down the left mouse button and drag the column to a new width.
An Adjust Table Row slider	Works the same way as the Move Table Column slider except with rows.

Changing Font Colors in Word

Font colors in Word are restricted to only 16 colors. That's hardly acceptable for a PowerPoint presentation that can choose font colors from more than 16 million colors. When you complete the table in Word and click outside the table to return a picture of the table to PowerPoint, your fonts will be in one of the 16 colors of Word fonts. You may want to change those colors to match your own palette in PowerPoint. Here's how:

1. After clicking outside the Word table to return to PowerPoint, leave the Table object selected, or select it again with a single click. (Don't double-click on the table object; doing so will reactivate Word.)

2. From the PowerPoint menu, choose Format, Colors and Lines. Then, click on the Picture tab of the Format Object dialog box (see Figure 2.24).

3. Click on the Recolor button at the bottom of the dialog box.

4. You will see the Recolor Picture dialog box shown in Figure 2.25. Check boxes appear for each color that you have used in the Word table. If you want to change a color in the table, click in the check box next to the color under the first column, marked Original.

Figure 2.24

Recolor your tables from Word to match your color scheme.

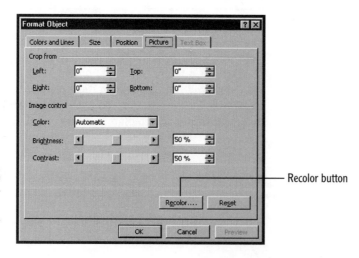

Recolor button

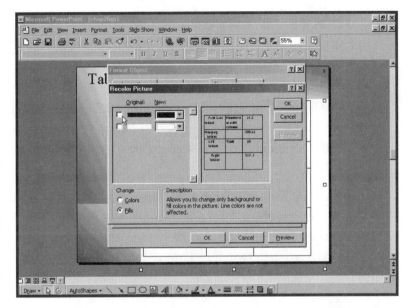

Figure 2.25

You can recolor any color by selecting it and changing the color.

5. Click on the <u>N</u>ew drop-down list and select a new color. You can exactly match any color in your presentation's palette, or choose <u>M</u>ore Colors to display the Colors dialog box and pick from the 16 million-plus colors available in PowerPoint.

6. After choosing a new color, click on OK twice to approve these choices.

TIP

If you create tables directly in Word and then copy and paste them into PowerPoint, you will not be able to resize the table in PowerPoint without the fonts becoming stretched out of proportion. If you create tables by using the Insert Word table feature from PowerPoint, you will not face this problem. However, when you paste the table into PowerPoint, you can make the fonts hold their integrity by choosing <u>E</u>dit, Paste <u>S</u>pecial, selecting Paste <u>L</u>ink, clicking on OK, and then resizing the table. If you don't want the link to remain, you can just break the link to the Word document by selecting <u>E</u>dit, <u>L</u>inks in PowerPoint. Then, select the link to the Word document from the list of links, click on the <u>B</u>reak Link button, and click on Close.

Creating Tables in Excel

Some of you may be more comfortable using Microsoft Excel than Word. Feel free to create tables in Excel and incorporate them into PowerPoint. It really won't make a difference to PowerPoint. The biggest differences between creating tables in Word and Excel is that Word gives you some more formatting power (hanging indents and decimal-aligned cells), whereas Excel gives you a great deal more control over arithmetic values.

To copy the table from Excel into PowerPoint is the same procedure as copying anything from one document to another. Simply select the appropriate range in Excel and copy it to the clipboard using Edit, Copy (or Ctrl+C). Then switch to PowerPoint and use Edit, Paste (or Ctrl+V).

TIP ■

Before you copy Excel spreadsheet ranges into PowerPoint, you may want to turn off the gridlines. In Excel, choose Tools, Options; then, click on the View tab and deselect the Gridlines check box.

■ ■

Creating Tables in PowerPoint with Text Boxes

You can also create some simple tables directly in PowerPoint by using multiple text boxes and aligning them horizontally in PowerPoint. These have the benefit of being very fast but will not have all the formatting capabilities of a real Word table.

The best way to use this method is to insert a text box and type the first column of text for the table. After you format the text box to fit in the space of the first column of your table, you can then copy that entire text box to the Clipboard and paste it back into PowerPoint as many times as you have columns. You should then arrange the number of columns to look like a table on the page and use the Draw, Align or Distribute, Distribute Horizontally and Draw, Align or Distribute, Distribute Vertically

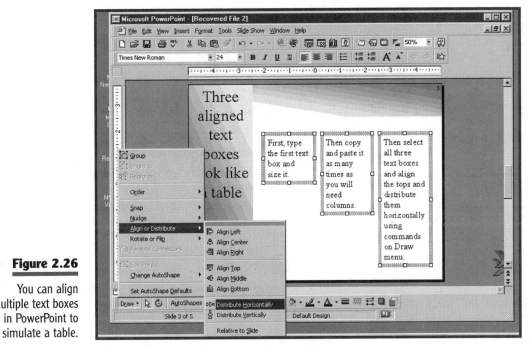

Figure 2.26

You can align multiple text boxes in PowerPoint to simulate a table.

commands to align each column. Then, just edit the text in the remaining columns. The result will look like a table, as shown in Figure 2.26.

TIP Whenever you create multiple objects that you want to keep together, you should first select all of the items by holding down the Shift key and clicking on each of the objects. Then choose Draw, Group to combine them into one object.

Advantages and Disadvantages of Each Method

With three different ways to create tables, you should consider the merits and drawbacks of each method before you decide which one is right for you. Many professional PowerPoint users use all three, depending on the situation. Here's a quick summary of when to choose one method over the other.

Method	Advantages
Word tables	Enable quicker and easier formatting control compared to text boxes.
	Enable decimal alignment of numbers.
	Make hanging indents easy.
	Enable OLE linking to the source document. If the source is likely to change, these changes will then be automatically updated in PowerPoint.
Excel tables	Enable better arithmetic and formula control than Word.
	Like Word, enable OLE linking to the source document. If that document is coming in the form of an Excel document, it is easier to leave it in Excel.
PowerPoint text boxes	Quick for very simple tables.

At this point, you have learned just about everything there is to know about how to work with text in PowerPoint. You should have a good way to place any text into PowerPoint and make it show up the way you want.

Now it's time to learn all there is to know about another major workhorse in PowerPoint—charts.

Charts

Charts are the first step toward using pictures to help communicate a message. Charts can help tell the story faster than all the information contained in the spreadsheet data that the chart represents. But charts can also make things more difficult to understand. In this section, I discuss how to create charts as well as how to avoid making charts hard to read or possibly misleading to the audience. I also show you how to use some of the new features of PowerPoint charts to drive home the point of the data.

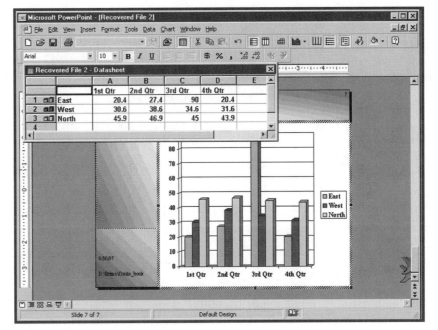

Figure 2.27

Microsoft Graph opens with a default filled-in chart and datasheet.

Charts in PowerPoint are actually created in a separate program that PowerPoint automatically opens for you. This program, Microsoft Graph, is automatically installed if you install PowerPoint. As you saw last night, when you chose the Chart AutoLayout, you were presented with a page that included a "Double click to add chart" placeholder. Double-clicking on that placeholder opens Microsoft Graph and presents you with a datasheet that includes sample data and a chart representing that sample data (see Figure 2.27).

Understanding the Datasheet in Microsoft Graph

The datasheet contains the actual data for the chart. This datasheet is one of the most important elements in the charting process. You cannot create a chart without a datasheet. If your datasheet is also incorrectly filled out, your resulting chart will look wrong.

The first thing to know about the datasheet is that you should *always* think of it as a rectangle. The next thing to know about the datasheet is that anything, a number or text, in the upper-left cell in the datasheet will never be plotted in the chart. That is truly an empty cell and serves only to make the data area a rectangle.

Take a few minutes and examine the datasheet in more detail, because understanding the datasheet in Microsoft Graph is absolutely critical. If you don't understand it, you can end up with a chart that looks wrong, and you won't know how to fix it.

First, I want to take the existing chart apart and examine what is and is not being plotted. The best way to learn about the datasheet is to open up the default chart on your computer and walk through this exercise step by step.

1. In PowerPoint, choose Insert, New Slide (or press Ctrl+M); then, select the AutoLayout for a single chart on the page.

2. Double-click on the "Double click to add chart" placeholder.

3. Use your mouse to resize the datasheet to make it wider and taller. You do this by grabbing the datasheet in the lower-right corner and stretching it until you can see column G and row 8 (see Figure 2.28).

4. If you look carefully at the gray boxes on the left and top edges of the datasheet, you should notice that all of the boxes above row 3 and left of column D have somewhat of a 3-D look to them, whereas all the other gray boxes on the sheet are 2-D. The 3-D edges tell you that the rectangle formed by these cells are what is plotted in the chart, shown in Figure 2.28.

5. To add some data for the South, type **South** in row 4, under the word **North**. Then, just make up some numbers for the data for the South. Typing **45** in cells A4 through D4 will do fine. Notice that those changes will immediately be reflected in the chart. Also notice that the gray cell in row 4 now looks three dimensional, indicating that it is being plotted on the chart.

6. Next, select the white-colored cells in column D that have data,

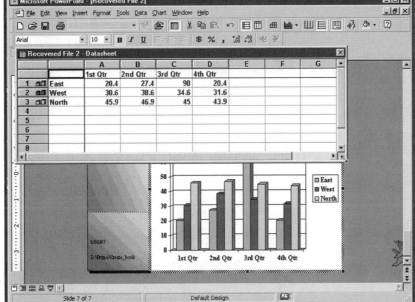

Figure 2.28

You can resize the datasheet to view more rows and columns.

and press Delete. The data in column D is actually still being plotted. That's indicated by the 3-D cell at the top of column D. But because no data is in the cells, everything is being plotted as a blank. Note that there is still a place for the 4th Quarter data on the right side of the chart.

7. Double-click the D column letter. Two things happen now: first, the D column letter turns to 2-D; second, the chart redraws to fill the chart with just the data for the first three quarters.

This process may seem tedious, but these steps should help you learn to make charts quickly and flawlessly in Microsoft Graph.

Creating a New Chart

Here, you will walk through the steps to make a new chart. You will then format it as a different chart type. Then, you will explore each of the elements of a chart and how to format them. It might be easiest to create a whole new page and start from scratch.

1. Choose Insert, New Slide (or press Ctrl+M) to insert a new page. Choose the AutoLayout for the single chart on a page.

2. Double-click on the "Double click to add chart" placeholder to display the datasheet.

3. To avoid any possibility of not clearing the plot area and ending up with a chart that is plotted incorrectly, you should clear and reset the entire datasheet. Microsoft Graph has no way to do this from the menu. As you saw, selecting the plotted range and pressing Delete cleared the data, but did not clear the underlying format of the chart.

    To clear the existing data in the datasheet, press Ctrl+A (for Select All), and then press the Del key. This clears the datasheet of all text and numbers. Or you can just press the uppermost left gray cell in the datasheet and press Delete. Either method will clear the datasheet of everything and prepare you for plotting charts of only the data you type into the datasheet.

4. Now you are ready to create a new chart for Sales, Expenses, and Net Income for the first three months of a year. Fill in the datasheet as shown in Figure 2.29. That will give you a column chart that compares each of the items by month. This may be what you want, but it is somewhat confusing to see the pattern. To fix this, you could retype all the data in a different order, but that wouldn't be much fun. It would be fun, though, to automatically replot this data to show the pattern better.

5. Choose Data, Series in Columns. Now the chart more readily shows that Sales have increased every month, whereas Expenses have been flat; therefore, the Net Income shows an increase every month as well (see Figure 2.30).

6. Now, make this a line chart because it might show the trend a little better. Choose Chart, Chart Type; then, click on the Line option in the Chart Type list and click on OK. Actually, the way the data is

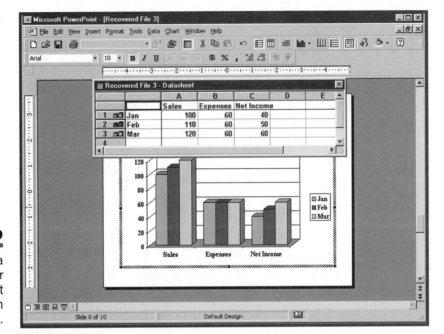

Figure 2.29

Typing the data into either rows or columns need not be a tough decision.

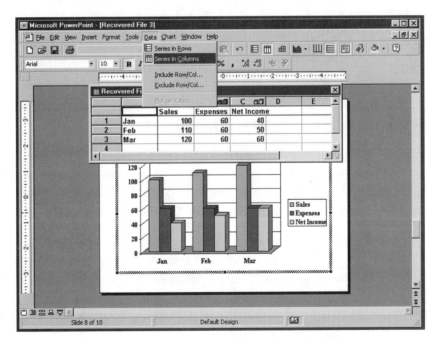

Figure 2.30

Switch the way the Series is plotted, in Rows or Columns.

now arranged makes it confusing again to see the pattern. Choose Data, Series in Rows, and the trend becomes quite obvious again.

You've now seen that data entered into the datasheet can be plotted in two different ways: with the series defined in the rows or the series defined in the columns. The main point is that you don't have to worry about which way your data is entered as long as you clear the datasheet format first. You can then just switch back and forth until you get the type of chart that communicates the point you are trying to make.

Before you close the datasheet and move forward with dissecting the chart and identifying each of the elements that you can format, you need to learn one last thing. Say that you don't want to show the Expenses line in the chart. You learned earlier that you could delete it, but if it is in the middle of the chart, you can simply double-click the gray box next to the Expenses text. Doing so will turn the gray box into a 2-D rectangle and not plot the data. You can do this with any row or column in the datasheet, as long as the remaining plot area is still rectangular.

This feature is especially helpful if your data is already in something like an Excel spreadsheet and you want to copy and paste the data directly to the datasheet. You can do it in one step, and then just hide the rows or columns that you don't want to plot.

Working with Chart Types

You have already seen that you can create a different kind of chart from the same underlying datasheet. Now that you are done with this datasheet, close it and read next about the various chart types that you can make with Microsoft Graph. You can make 14 different standard chart types and 20 custom types as well. I cover the standard types first.

The best way to look at these chart types is to scroll through the preview window in the Chart type dialog box, which shows a thumbnail image of each type and their subtypes. But before you do that, take a look at the useful information that you will see in the Chart Type dialog box. With a chart in Microsoft Graph selected, choose Chart, Chart Type to display

the Chart Type dialog box. Make sure that the Standard Types tab is selected, as shown in Figure 2.31.

This dialog box contains a lot of useful information to make your chart-making easier and faster. In the Chart Type list, you can scroll though the 14 different chart types. As you change the selection of the chart type, you will see the various chart subtypes that are available for that selection.

In the information box just below the Chart Sub-Type area, you can read a short description about each of the subtypes as you select each one. This can help you a lot in deciding just which chart type or subtype to use. If that is not good enough for you, the Press and Hold To View Sample button will give you a quick preview of the data in your datasheet, using that chart subtype.

The Chart Type dialog box also contains several other important settings that can make your chart-making faster. The Options area includes two check boxes. The first check box is probably grayed out because it is not available at the moment (because this dialog box is context sensitive and is based on the chart that you have in the active datasheet). If you select the Default Formatting check box, the chart will be automatically formatted with the default chart settings. In the next section, I'll discuss how

Figure 2.31

Use the Chart Type dialog box to switch to a different chart type.

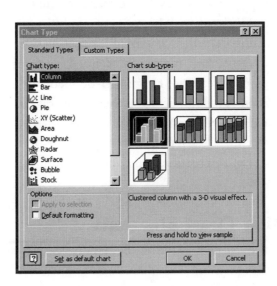

many settings you can change on a chart, and you will likely want to learn more about this setting because it will apply all those settings automatically. The first option, Apply To Selection, will reset any selected data series to the default settings.

The Set As Default Chart button is used to pick which chart type should be your default chart for any new chart. At the moment, in this book, and probably on your computer as well, the default chart has been the clustered column chart with a 3-D visual effect. If you wanted to change the default chart to any other chart subtype, you would select that chart subtype and click on the Set As Default Chart button. Then, any new charts will automatically default to that chart subtype.

I will leave the last helpful button for you to explore on your own. That button is the little question mark Help button that will let you have a conversation with the Paper Clip guy. If you click on the Example of the Selected Chart Type button, the Paper Clip guy will display a short set of examples of each chart type. It's worth the side trip if you are somewhat new to charting.

If you click on the Custom Types tab in the Chart Types dialog box, you will see 20 predefined custom subtypes of charts. Essentially, these are variations on specific subtypes of the Standard chart types. These charts have been preformatted by Microsoft to apply specific formatting to a specific chart subtype, and that special formatting was saved as a Built-in Custom Chart type. You may or may not like all of them, but more important, you can create your own user-defined custom chart types and save them. When you do that, if you then apply that user-defined style to any chart, the chart will automatically and instantly reflect the originally specified formatting. I cover how to save a user-defined Custom chart type a little later in this section, after you learn more about all of the ways to format a chart.

Formatting Chart Elements

When you have finished entering the data in the datasheet and selected the proper chart type for your data, it is time to format all of the other

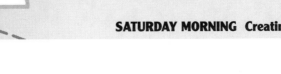
elements of the chart. The first step in formatting a chart is to set the titles and to determine whether to change settings for axes, gridlines, legends, labels, or even a data table. Unlike the Chart Wizard in Excel (if you are familiar with that), you set many of these options directly within Microsoft Graph by choosing Chart, Chart Options. You can do this whether the datasheet is open or not. When you choose Chart, Chart Options, the Chart Options dialog box appears, which includes a separate tab for each of these options. You can set each option and preview the changes as you make them (see Figure 2.32).

For the rest of the elements of the chart that you can format, you also have additional options of selecting each key element and applying special formatting to that element. You can get at almost any element of the chart and apply formatting to it. Essentially, you do this by selecting the item, such as the y-axis, and choosing the Format command. The Format command is context sensitive, based on what element you have selected. Before I go into a few examples of how to change the formatting, I want to review the key elements of the chart. The best way to see each chart element (each element will be explained following these steps) that can be formatted is to follow these steps:

1. If you're in PowerPoint, as opposed to Microsoft Graph, double-click on the chart object on the page. This should be an actual chart rather than the "Click to add chart" placeholder.

Figure 2.32

Changes to the chart formatting are reflected in the preview image.

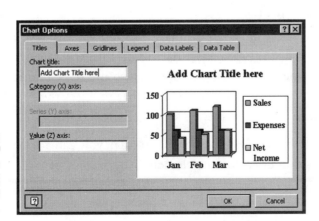

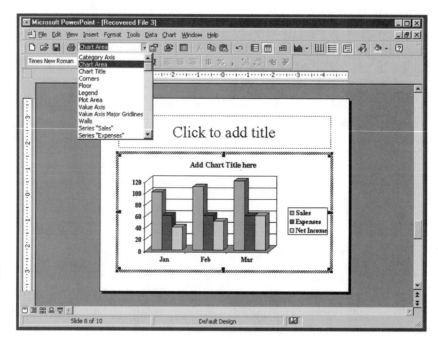

Figure 2.33

This is a list of the primary chart objects.

Microsoft Graph activates, as shown in Figure 2.33. Notice that the area that is selected is the entire chart object, which is known as the Chart Area. You can see the name **Chart Area** in the toolbar near the top of the screen. This Chart Objects drop-down list is located on the Standard toolbar in Microsoft Graph and should be visible by default.

2. To select the chart element that you want to format, you can use any of the arrow keys. As you do this, you will cycle through each element in the chart. You can also use the Chart Objects drop-down list in the Standard toolbar to select the specific chart object that you want to change (see Figure 2.33).

Table 2.4 lists the chart elements that you can format, and provides a description of each chart element.

TABLE 2.4 CHART ELEMENTS THAT CAN BE FORMATTED

Chart Element	Description	Items to Format
Chart Area	The overall size of the chart	Patterns and area, including fill colors and fill effects.
Plot Area	The overall size of the main part of the chart, excluding legends and titles	You can size this manually within the Chart Area without affecting the Chart Area. For example, you may want the legend to be larger and the Plot Area to be smaller.
Floor	The plane the data series sits on in a 3-D chart	2-D charts do not have floors. Floors can be filled with Borders and Area fills.
Walls	Like walls in a room, these are the planes that surround the data series in a 3-D chart	2-D charts do not have walls. Walls can be filled with Borders and Area fills.
Corners	Control the 3-D perspective in 3-D charts	Formatted by choosing Chart, 3-D View
Legend	The labels that the data series apply to	Borders and Area fills. Font size, style, and color. Placement in one of five different locations (Bottom, Corner, Top, Right, or Left).
Value Axis	The y-axis	This is how the numbers are measured. May actually look like an x-axis in some charts, also called the Value Axis. Patterns: Line styles and tick marks Scale: Set the scale manually if you don't like Excel's defaults Font: Typical font settings Number: Number formatting for the axis values Alignment: Text alignment from 90 to -90 degrees

TABLE 2.4 CHART ELEMENTS THAT CAN BE FORMATTED (CONTINUED)

Chart Element	Description	Items to Format
Series(1)	The first data series	In this case it is "Sales" Patterns: For Borders and Area fills
		Shape: For various shapes to portray the series
		Data Labels: Show labels or values or none
		Options: For setting 3-D effects of the various series
Series(2) etc.	Each of the remaining series in your active chart can be accessed	Same as Series(1)
Points	This option can only be selected with a mouse	Is each individual point of each series. E.g. Series "Sales" and Point "Jan." Useful in changing the formatting of a specific point to emphasize that specific point.

Combining Chart Types

Sometimes, you will want to combine two different chart types to make it clear which series you are talking about in a chart. In most cases, you can select an individual series, such as income in this case, and make that series follow a different chart type than the rest of the series.

To do this, first make sure you are in Microsoft graph by double-clicking the chart object in PowerPoint. Next, change the chart to a 2-D chart. Then, select the Income Series in the chart by clicking on one of the Income points in the chart. Any Income datapoint will do, and you will see all datapoints for Income selected. Then choose Chart, Chart Type,

and change the chart type to a line chart. You will now have a combination chart.

NOTE This can create unexpected results if you attempt to mix 3-D and 2-D chart types or even try to mix 3-D chart types. You are always best off saving the existing file before trying any of these options because some are reversible with Edit, Undo Chart Type. But some aren't.

Animating Charts for Screen Shows

When you finally get the chart completed, you also have additional options to help with the communication. You can now add animation builds to charts and the individual data series to reveal each series at a time. In many cases, this can help simplify complex charts. You will learn exactly how to do this in the section on animation effects in this evening's session.

Linking Chart Data to Excel Workbooks

Okay, you aren't any different from everyone else. The numbers in your charts are all going to change at the last minute when the final numbers are available. What can you do to avoid the last-minute time crunch of updating all of the revised numbers? Well, one more time: "Don't panic."

OLE is not foreign to Microsoft Graph. OLE (Object Linking and Embedding), lets you link your source data, probably Excel in this case, to your target data, Microsoft Graph's datasheet, so that when you have new numbers available the charts are instantly updated with no muss and no fuss.

You need to make just one minor change in the way that you enter the data into the datasheet. If your data is in an Excel spreadsheet, a Lotus 1-2-3 or a Quattro Pro spreadsheet, when you copy the data from the source spreadsheet, instead of pasting it directly into the datasheet, you should choose Edit, Paste Link, as shown in Figure 2.34. This will create the OLE link that you need on the actual underlying data that

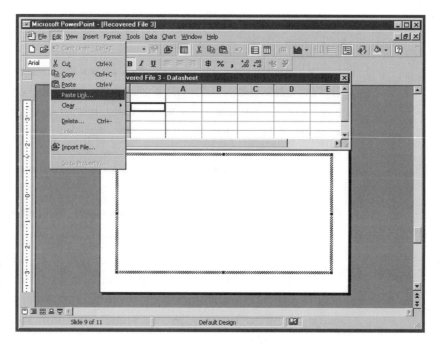

Figure 2.34

You can paste link data from Excel to the Microsoft Graph datasheet.

drives the chart. Then you can proceed with any chart formatting you see fit. That formatting will stay in place when you update the linked data with new data.

Creating Charts in Excel vs. Microsoft Graph

You may have noticed earlier in the book that I consider Word and Excel to be extremely valuable tools to anyone who is creating presentations in PowerPoint. For those of you who are skilled in Excel, you may want to create your charts in Excel and just copy and paste them into PowerPoint, bypassing Microsoft Graph altogether. I know many people who do this.

The advantages to creating charts in Excel are obvious if you already have your data in Excel. You may already have created the charts that you need for your presentation right in Excel.

You can continue to use your Excel charts in PowerPoint by using the Copy and Paste commands. Or, if you plan to use file linking, copy the Excel chart to the Clipboard, switch to PowerPoint, choose Edit, Paste Special, and select Paste Link.

◆ ◆

CAUTION If you link charts from Excel to PowerPoint, be aware that charts that are created on worksheets, rather than chart sheets, may resize unexpectedly if you do not save your Excel sheets at 100 percent zoom.

◆ ◆

Wrapping Up

Congratulations, you have made it through another session! If you have absorbed most of this information, you will now be able to create most presentations even better than the top 85 percent of presentations given with PowerPoint today.

Take a break for lunch, and then come back and spend the afternoon on the next session. When you finish this afternoon's session, you will be able to create presentations better than 90 percent of those that are out there. Stay with it—I cover some easier topics next time!

How It Reveals the Content:
Clip Art, Pictures, and Media Clips

- ✿ Inserting, modifying, and rotating clip art
- ✿ Taking advantage of drawing tools
- ✿ Scanning and linking to pictures
- ✿ Playing sounds and adding movies

Welcome back! You accomplished a great deal this morning and the hard part is behind you. Now you can move into the fun and easy part: using pictures and sound to help tell your story. You have now learned how to use all of the AutoLayouts for your slides. With what you already know, you can now create presentations that are at least as good, if not better, than about 90 percent of all PowerPoint presentations created today.

In this afternoon's session, you will learn all you need to know to customize the visual parts of one of the key AutoLayouts. You can also customize your presentations by adding visual elements such as pictures, (photographs, drawings, or clip art), sound, and video directly into your presentation.

In a broad sense, PowerPoint thinks of these three kinds of objects very much in the same way. They have some significant differences, but more similarities than differences. You have already learned how to insert a piece of clip art into a presentation, either directly into the AutoLayout placeholder or directly onto the slide page without using an AutoLayout placeholder, so you already know most of what you will need to know to add any of these other object types.

PowerPoint lets you insert any of these object types directly into a presentation. PowerPoint can help manage your clip art, pictures, and media clips for you in the Microsoft Clip Gallery 3.0. The Clip Gallery is essentially an organized library of these files.

Microsoft Clip Gallery 3.0

If you use the AutoLayout placeholder to insert an object (clip art, picture, sound, or video), the object must be located in the Clip Gallery. The default installation of PowerPoint installs only clip art and does not install any pictures, sounds, or videos. But installing these objects is easy. If you think you are going to be using these files repeatedly, installing them into the Clip Gallery makes sense.

The Clip Gallery will accept files in any of the file types that PowerPoint will accept. And it will automatically place the file in the correct location in the Gallery for you. You can import files into the Gallery in two different ways. The first way is to import a file directly from your own files. The second way is to use PowerPoint's own built-in hyperlink to Microsoft's Web site, where many more files are available in Microsoft's own clip gallery.

Adding Your Own Files to the Clip Gallery

The most obvious files that you might like to have in the Clip Gallery are frequently used files such as the company logo, employee pictures, common music recordings that you might use for walk-in music for meetings, or special videos that you might use to add humor to meetings. No matter what type of file you are inserting into the Clip Gallery, you use the same procedure. Follow these steps:

1. Because you are starting a new session, open a new presentation and select the AutoLayout for Text & Clip Art.

2. To access the Clip Gallery, double-click on a "Double click to add clip art" placeholder. You will see four tabs, one for each object type (see Figure 3.1). At this point, you will probably have preview images in the tab for Clip Art and none for Pictures, Sounds, or Videos. Proceed to add a picture to the Picture Gallery (don't worry about what it is; deleting it later is easy). Click on Import Clips.

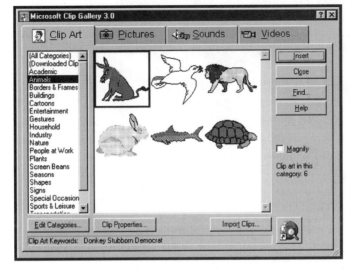

Figure 3.1

You can import clips from your hard drive or directly from Microsoft's clip gallery.

3. Use the Look In drop-down list to browse and find the file that you want to insert. If you use the Files of Type drop-down menu to filter the file types, you will see only certain file types in the browsing window (see Figure 3.2).

4. Select the file that you want to import and click on Open.

5. The Clip Gallery will then import the image and immediately present you with another dialog box to set the Clip Properties,

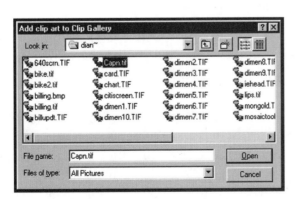

Figure 3.2

Just browse directly for the clip art that you want to import.

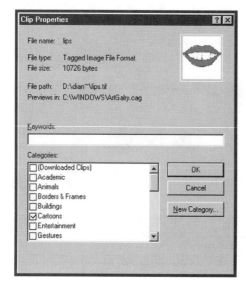

Figure 3.3

You can classify
new clips into
existing or new
categories.

such as in which category to place the image (see Figure 3.3). Place a check mark in the appropriate category or create a new category. Then, click on OK.

That's all there is to adding any object type to the Clip Gallery. If you make a mistake or want to remove the clip art at some later point, just select the clip art and press Del. You will see a warning that you are about to delete a picture permanently. Click on OK to delete it or click on Cancel if you change your mind.

When you add a clip to the Clip Gallery, you can index that image to several different categories, and you still have only one image occupying space on your hard drive. This can be extremely helpful if an image might mean different things to different people in your organization. For example, if you are a marketing company, you might have two custom categories called Brands and Packaging. A picture of the spaghetti sauce jar would make sense to place in both categories. That way, if you do a presentation on packaging developments, you could retrieve the image of the glass jar by looking in Packaging rather than have to guess how you classified it.

Adding New Clips from Microsoft to the Clip Gallery

When you installed Office 97, you had two different choices for installing clip art. Neither one is chosen by default, so you may actually have no clip art installed if you did not choose a custom install. See Appendix C, "Installation Issues," for information on installing or reinstalling Office 97. Additional clip art is available on the Office 97 CD-ROM. Also, a whole new resource exists for getting not only clip art but also pictures, sounds, and videos to add to your Clip Gallery. And it is free!

Microsoft has added a direct hyperlink to its own Clip Gallery, which contains a host of additional clips available for free downloading. If your Web browser is set up correctly, you can get to the Web site with two clicks of the mouse. The first click is on the Explorer icon in the lower-right corner of the Clip Gallery dialog box. This should directly open your dialup connection dialog box, and then connect you to the Web site shown in Figure 3.4. This site contains many clips available for

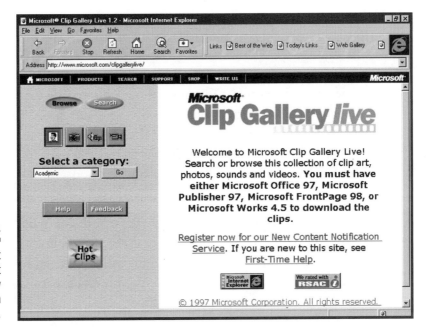

Figure 3.4

You'll find Microsoft Clip Gallery Live at **http://www .microsoft.com /clipgallerylive/**.

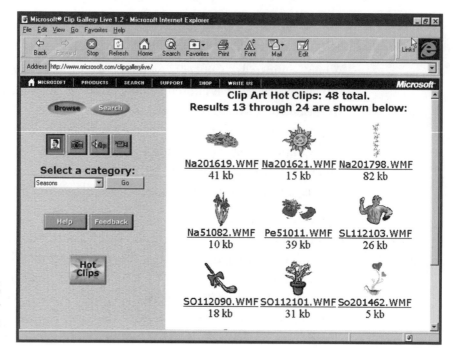

Figure 3.5

You can search or browse by clip type and by category.

download. After you accept the license agreement, you see the page shown in Figure 3.5, which is organized into two sections.

The left side of the page is used to Browse for images or to Search specifically for keywords. (You might find it interesting that a search for "happiness" turns up nothing!) Whether you search or browse, you have to select an image type from one of the four icons that resemble the icons in your own Clip Gallery—clip art, pictures, sounds, or videos. Select one of the object types and see what you can find.

When you have found an image that strikes your fancy, click on the filename (notice that the cursor changes from the pointer to the familiar hand). At this point, you can install the image directly on your computer by accepting the command to Open It, as shown in Figure 3.6. If you are on a network and don't have the necessary permissions to install the

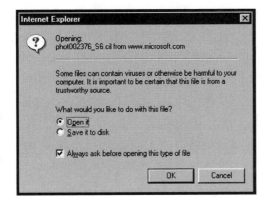

Figure 3.6

If you click on Open It, the clip will be directly installed for you.

file, you can download the file to your hard drive for later installation by the appropriate network police department. If that is the case, whoever installs the file need only double-click on it from Explorer. Doing so automatically opens PowerPoint, and the file will self-install, and then shut PowerPoint down when it is done in a few seconds. If PowerPoint is open, as is likely, the file just performs its self-install and is immediately available in PowerPoint. Nothing could be easier. All you need is the Web connection.

FIND IT ON ▶
THE WEB

You don't need to have the computer on which you are using PowerPoint connected to the Web to get to this site. Just type **http://www.microsoft.com/clipgallerylive/** as the URL address and go there on your own. Then, download the file for later installation.

The preceding pages should give you a good overview of using and building your Clip Gallery. But what if you want to use a picture just once and not install it into the Clip Gallery?

Bypassing the Clip Gallery

Although the Clip Gallery is a very nice feature for keeping files organized for multiple insertions into various PowerPoint files, you may want to use these special files only once. This is actually a very typical situation for most of us, and entering all these files into the Clip Gallery, only to turn around and delete them after the presentation, would be a ridiculous waste of time. Fortunately, you don't have to even know about the Clip Gallery to insert pictures, sounds, or movie clips into PowerPoint.

You can use the Insert, Picture, From File command to insert a picture (see Figure 3.7). You can insert Clip Art, AutoShapes, Organization Charts, WordArt, a picture directly from a Scanner, or a Word Table with the Insert, Picture menu option as well, as shown in the figure.

◆◆

 **CAUTION**   If you use any of these specific commands from the menu rather than go directly through the AutoLayouts, none of these objects will be affected globally if you make changes to the Slide Master page at a later date. Both techniques are valid—but they have different ramifications concerning how easily you can make changes.

◆◆

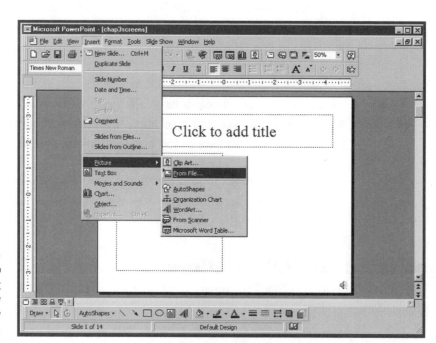

Figure 3.7

You can also insert a picture directly from a file on any of your drives.

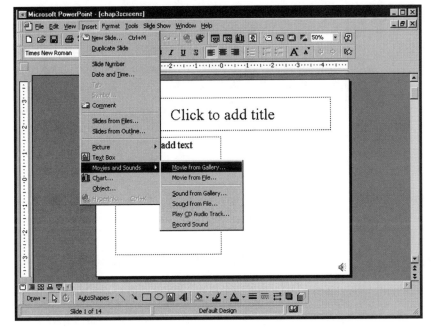

Figure 3.8

You can also insert movies and sound files directly from a file on your hard drive.

Also on this drop-down menu is the command From Scanner. If your computer is hooked up to a Twain-compliant scanner, PowerPoint will fire up the scanning software, let you scan a picture, and insert it directly into PowerPoint. I cover this command in much greater detail later in this chapter in the section "Scanning Pictures."

Besides the Clip Art and Pictures files, the Clip Gallery includes Movies and Sound files. You can also insert these types of files directly from the Insert, Movies and Sounds menu choices. You will have the same choices as those shown in Figure 3.8.

You've just completed a summary on how to get any of these objects into PowerPoint. As with text, you have more than one option; which one you choose depends on your specific needs. Next, I examine in detail each of these file types and identify the options that come with each of these object types to help you obtain the exact results that you need.

Clip Art

Clearly, adding graphics to any presentation can help to increase the interest level of any presentation. You already know how to add the clip art, but just adding clip art is not the only way to make your presentation more interesting. Finding the perfect piece of clip art to convey a specific thought is usually difficult. Well, don't panic. By the time you finish this section, you will be skilled at changing clip art images to suit your needs.

Modifying Clip Art

The key to understanding how to modify clip art is to understand how clip art is put together. Each clip art image that comes with PowerPoint (and most other kinds of commercially available clip art, for that matter) is generally a collection of separate pieces of art that are grouped together to give you an image. Take our friend the shark. Add him to a brand new page using Insert, Picture, Clip Art. Double-click on the shark image in the Animals category and he will appear on your page.

You can do two things with this image: recolor him just as you did with the Word Table text, or you can take the image apart and delete or change some of the pieces that make up the total image. If you don't quite remember how to use the recolor option, select Format, Colors and Lines and click on the Picture tab. Then, click the Recolor button. This will bring you to the same dialog box that you used to change the colors of the Word text into PowerPoint's 16-million-color palette.

NOTE Note in Figure 3.9 the two option buttons in the Change area. These buttons enable you to change the colors in Colors or in Fills. The difference between the colors and fills is not always obvious, and the explanation will vary from image to image. Experimentation is the best medicine here. Generally, in most clip art images, you have a limited number of colors to play with and can figure out which is a color and which is a fill fairly quickly.

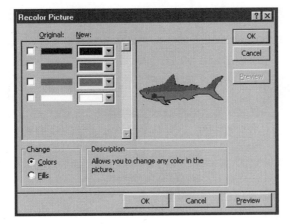

Figure 3.9

Recolor clip art just as you recolor Word table text.

Recoloring the image is a big help, but it isn't all you can do. You can take the image apart and make changes to part of the image. Now you'll take the shark apart to look at the separate pieces that compose the image. To get to the individual pieces, select the image, and then choose D<u>r</u>aw, <u>U</u>ngroup from the menu. The result is the warning message box shown in Figure 3.10. Don't be frightened by it. If you click on <u>Y</u>es, you won't do any damage to the poor shark. You will just convert the shark to separate pieces that can be moved, resized, or even removed.

This particular shark is made up of six distinct pieces. You can change each piece by either resizing or recoloring. If you wanted to make this shark even more ominous than you did in an earlier exercise, you could stretch his dorsal fin to be dramatically taller while leaving the rest of the body intact. Or, feel free to move his eye to his dorsal fin for a humorous effect.

TIP

Because most clip art is a collection of individual pieces, you can frequently get a good-looking, customized object with very little effort. Feel free to discard what you don't need or combine pieces from different clip art. Then, recolor the pieces to fit your color scheme. Although you don't have to regroup the object when you are done, doing so is wise.

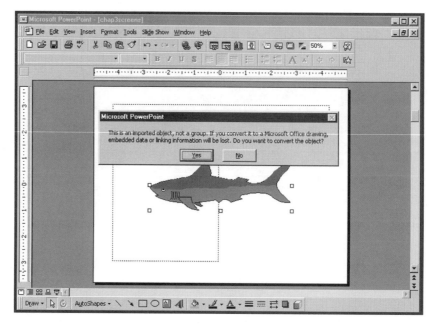

Figure 3.10

Don't worry about
ungrouping
clip art images.

Now that you are working with a collection of distinct objects, you can
also apply interesting animation effects to each piece to help make a
stronger impact. You'll learn about animation later today. For now,
understand that you can frequently ungroup clip art and recombine it to
fit your needs, even if you aren't a very good artist.

Rotating Clip Art

Clip art comes into PowerPoint in a fixed position, but it would be nice
to rotate it to help with the communication. For example, say that you
had two separate pieces of clip art, one showing a cat about to strike and
the other showing a dog. If they were both facing the same way, it would
not communicate the *fighting like cats and dogs* as well as if they were both
facing each other. Easy fix, you say—just rotate one of the pictures. Easy
it is—but not *that* easy.

PowerPoint, for some reason, does not let you rotate clip art unless it has
been ungrouped. So, you need to use the Draw, Ungroup technique that

you have learned; then, to keep the image intact, immediately choose Draw, Group to regroup it. Then, you can rotate the image(s) to your heart's content. You just need to remember to ungroup the object before attempting to rotate it.

Drawing Tools

Other graphical ways exist to enable you to add interest to your pages. PowerPoint 97 has added some very good drawing tools to let you quickly draw a host of shapes without needing the skills of an artist. The five most basic tools are all located on the Drawing toolbar (choose View, Toolbars, Drawing to display this toolbar, if necessary). The techniques for using the line drawing and the arrow tools are the same. Click on the Line or Arrow button on the toolbar. When your cursor is over the PowerPoint page, it will turn into a cross-shaped cursor, as shown in Figure 3.11. Simply hold down the mouse button at the start of the line and drag the line from start to finish to draw the line. When you are finished with the line, release the mouse button. When you are working with the arrow tool, the arrow head automatically rests at the end point of the line, so if you want to have an arrow pointing to the left, the easiest thing to do is to start the arrow at the right side and draw the line to the left.

You can always change the direction in which an arrow points after the fact. There are a variety of ways to do this. Here are a few things you can do if the arrow is already selected:

- Just select one end of the line so that your mouse cursor changes from the four-way arrow pointer to a two-way arrow pointer. Then, hold down the left mouse button and drag that end to re-position the end of the line where you release the mouse's left button. The other end of the line will stay anchored.

- From the Draw menu, choose Rotate or Flip and choose one of the options shown in Figure 3.12.

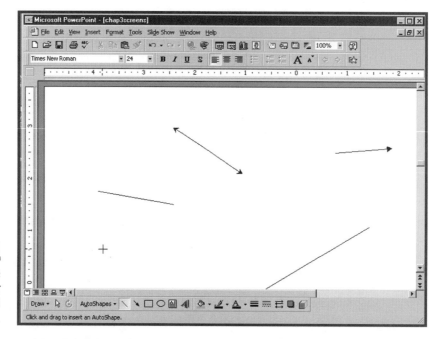

Figure 3.11

You can draw a line or arrow when your cursor has changed shape.

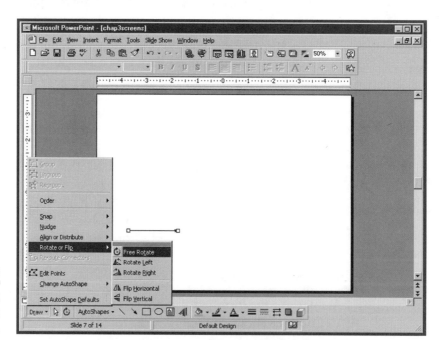

Figure 3.12

There are five ways to rotate or flip a drawn object.

✿ From the D<u>r</u>aw menu, choose <u>E</u>dit Points. Then, select one of the two points of the line (there is one at each end), hold down the left mouse button, and drag that point into place. More on this very powerful tool appears later in this chapter because this is a long-awaited feature for changing pre-drawn shapes in a precise, sophisticated way.

TIP When you draw straight lines either horizontally or vertically, start drawing the line, and then hold down the Shift key before you release the left mouse button. This will force the line to conform to a straight line that is either perfectly horizontal or perfectly vertical.

Another trick to use when you are working with lines that are meant to be perfectly parallel or of the same length is to draw the first line, and then use copy and paste to create the remaining lines. You can then use the D<u>r</u>aw, <u>A</u>lign or Distribute commands to place them perfectly on the page.

The other two common drawing tools are the Rectangle and the Oval tools. They are located next to the Line and Arrow toolbar buttons. Figure 3.13 shows the Drawing toolbar. The Rectangle and Oval shapes give you many of the most basic shapes that you will use. These two tools work similarly—you can use them to draw perfect rectangular boxes or ovals. Using some keyboard combinations with them will help you make perfect squares or perfect circles. Table 3.1 lists the keyboard shortcuts and explains the result that you will achieve when you use these keyboard shortcuts in combination with the toolbar button. To use the keystroke, just press the key before or after you start drawing the object.

Figure 3.13

The Drawing toolbar contains all the drawing tools.

Rectangle tool

Oval tool

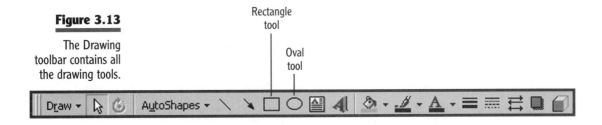

TABLE 3.1 KEYBOARD SHORTCUTS

Keystoke	Rectangle or Oval	Description
Shift key	Both	Constrains the shape to a perfect square or circle.
Ctrl key	Both	Constrains the shape's other boundary to be fixed. For example, if you have the width of a rectangle set, and if you then hold down the Ctrl key while stretching the height, the height will expand but the width will remain constant. The same concept applies to ovals.
Shift+Ctrl keys	Both	Draws a perfect square or circle outward from the starting point of the object. This is how you draw perfectly concentric circles or squares.

AutoShapes

Although the first four drawing tools are the workhorses of most drawings in PowerPoint, you also have well over 100 other drawing shapes to choose from in the AutoShapes menu on the Drawing toolbar. These AutoShapes work just like the four basic toolbar buttons that you have just learned to use. To use any shape, just select it from the AutoShapes cascading menus and draw the shape on the page. The same keyboard shortcuts listed in the preceding table also apply to AutoShapes.

The easiest way to explain all the AutoShapes is to show them in a table. You can choose from eight different groups of AutoShapes and each group has a submenu of choices.

AutoShape Group

Lines

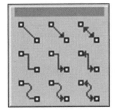

Connectors

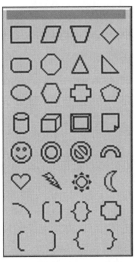

Basic Shapes

Block Arrows

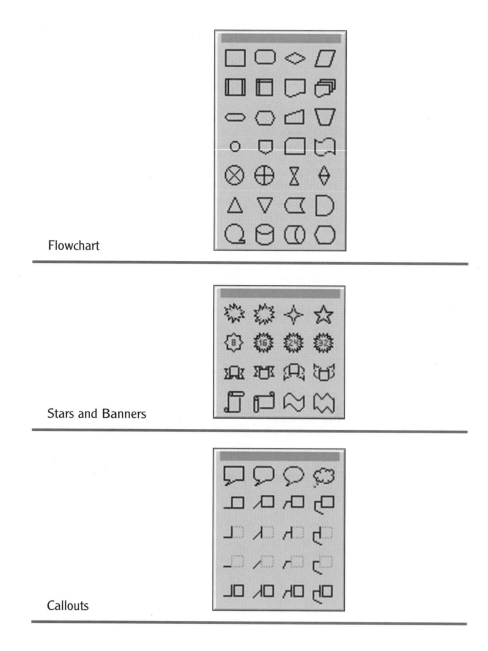

Flowchart

Stars and Banners

Callouts

Action Buttons

3-D Effects

Now you get to the really great thing about the new drawing tools in Office 97. You can instantly turn all of those AutoShapes into a variety of 3-D drawings at the click of a button. At the far right end of the Drawing toolbar is another cascading menu that will apply 20 different 3-D effects to any AutoShape. All you have to do is select the object—a simple circle, for example—and click and hold the 3-D toolbar button. Then, choose the appropriate 3-D setting (see Figure 3.14). This is an

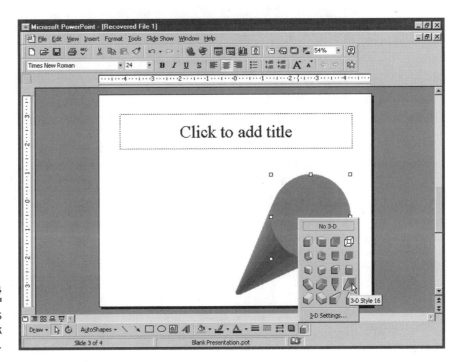

Figure 3.14

Change shapes to 3-D at the click of a button.

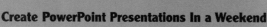

exciting addition to PowerPoint 97 because it enables you to add terrific effects to diagrams easily. After you have added those effects, you can create some very exciting animation effects to each object. This sure beats text slides.

Now try a short exercise to see exactly how to use the additional 3-D tools that you will need. They are not dissimilar to what you have already learned, but they *are* different. You will create the slide shown in Figure 3.15, walking through most of the techniques that you will use with 3-D effects. Remember to save this file when you are done because you will use it again this evening to illustrate how to add interesting animation effects to interesting graphics.

You'll use the same technique of creating all the objects from one original object so that all five objects start with the same sizing. You will then change the 3-D shape of four of the objects, followed by two brand new

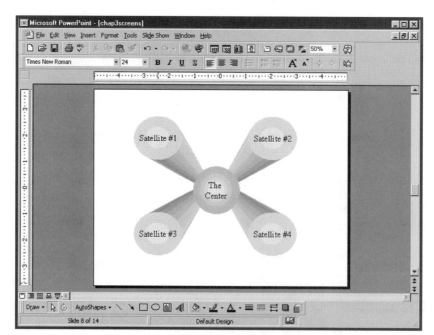

Figure 3.15

Complex-looking 3-D images take only a few steps to achieve.

things: changing the perspective of the object and the lighting effects on the object.

1. First, create a new page by pressing Ctrl+M (Insert, New Slide).

2. Using the Oval tool, draw a circle in the center of the page, (remember to hold down the Shift key).

3. Click on the Text Box tool, and then click your mouse inside of the circle and type **The Center**.

4. Change colors and lines to affect the colors used in the circle. Right-click on the circle and choose Format AutoShape. Select the Colors and Lines tab and click on Color in the Fill section of this dialog.

5. Because you have dark type in the AutoShape, you want a light fill color, so choose the Light Turquoise color (fifth from left in bottom row).

6. Click on Color again, and then click on Fill Effects to add a special gradient effect. Click on the Gradient tab if it is not already displayed.

7. In the Shading Styles area, choose the option From Center and the first of the two Variants (which should be selected by default).

8. Because you want a light color to give the dark text a high level of contrast with it, click on the Light on the Dark to Light slider bar three times to lighten the turquoise color even more.

9. Click on OK twice to apply that style to the circle.

10. Now, copy the first circle and paste it once; then, apply the 3-D style. Select the circle and use copy and paste (Ctrl+C to copy, Ctrl+V to paste) or (Edit, Copy and Edit, Paste from the menu).

11. To apply the 3-D effect, with the second circle selected, click and hold down the 3-D toolbar button, select 3-D Style 16, and release the mouse. There is your first 3-D shape, and it has all the same fill effects as the first circle.

12. Now you'll make the other four cone-shaped objects. Select the cone-shaped object and copy it to the Clipboard as you did with the circle and paste it back to the page three times.

13. At this point, you have all five elements. They are not arranged, however; the cones all point the same way. I bet you would think you can just rotate these cones (I thought so too, at first), but you can't. To arrange the shapes, you have to use the Direction button on the 3-D Settings toolbar, which is available only by selecting the 3-D toolbar button and clicking on 3-D Settings. You will then see the 3-D Settings toolbar. Figure 3.16 shows the 3-D Settings toolbar and identifies the Direction button that you are going to use next.

14. With the 3-D toolbar visible, first arrange the four cone shapes roughly in each quadrant of the page around the circle. Then, select the cone in the top-left corner, click on the Direction toolbar button, and click on the first button in the upper-left corner. See Figure 3.17 for the submenu under the Direction button. The cone

3-D Settings toolbar

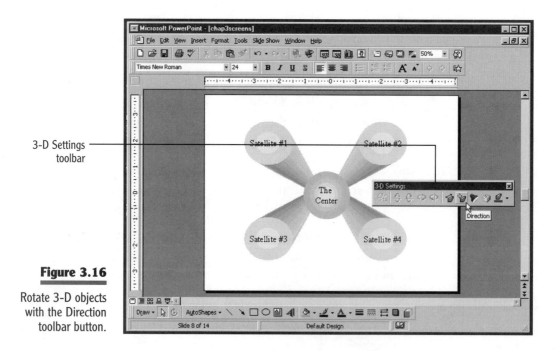

Figure 3.16

Rotate 3-D objects with the Direction toolbar button.

Figure 3.17

Rotate 3-D objects
to a variety of
perspectives.

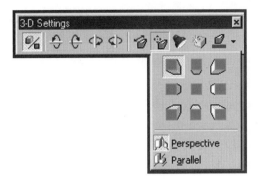

should now be the same size as it was before and should be pointing in the correct direction.

15. Select the cone in the lower-left quadrant and click on the Direction button; then, click on the button that has the callout to the
lower left, as shown in Figure 3.17.

16. Repeat the last step with the fourth cone and choose the appropriate button to make the shape switch directions.

You are done with the creation of the shapes, and now it's time to arrange
them on the page. It is a good technique when you are working with multiple shapes that should be the same size and color on the same page.

1. Before you actually arrange these shapes on the page, go back and
fill in the text boxes with the correct text for **Satellite #1, Satellite
#2, Satellite #3, and Satellite #4**, as shown in Figure 3.15.

2. Now arrange the five shapes on the page to match the sample at
the start of this exercise. You'll align these objects in separate steps
to align the top row, the bottom row, the left side, and then the
right side. First, select the Shapes at the top (Satellites #1 and #2)
by holding down the Shift key and clicking on each object. Then,
choose D̲raw, A̲lign or Distribute, Align T̲op.

3. Select the two satellites at the bottom of the page using the same
technique and align them using D̲raw, A̲lign or Distribute, Align
B̲ottom.

4. Select the two satellites on the left side of the page and align them with Draw, Align or Distribute, Align Left.

5. Select the two satellites on the right side of the page and align them with Draw, Align or Distribute, Align Right.

6. The last step is to select the circle and visually center it between the four cones, and then make sure that it is in front of all four cones by choosing Draw, Order, Bring to Front.

You are now done. Be sure to save the file because you will use it again tonight to show how these shapes can be animated to add further excitement to a potentially boring list of four satellite offices reporting to the Center office.

These 3-D effects are very easy to use when you know where to look for the menu options. Now you do. You can now add 3-D effects to your drawings quickly. But before you move on, you should briefly examine the 3-D Settings toolbar because this is where each of the 3-D effects is controlled. The following paragraphs cover the groups of commands that you can use to control the more important 3-D effects.

Tilt

The second, third, fourth, and fifth toolbar buttons on the 3-D Settings toolbar control the tilt of each object. If you select a 3-D object, you can control the tilt, forward or backward and to the left and right, in 10-degree increments. When you click on one of the directions, the selected object tilts in that direction 10 degrees at a time with each click of the toolbar button. This should give you complete control over any 3-D object to let you show it just the way you want.

Depth

Depth of an object can be set by selecting the object and picking one of the preset depths or by filling in the custom point size in the edit box (see Figure 3.18).

Figure 3.18

Depth is measured in points.

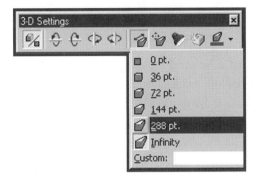

Lighting Effects

Lighting effects enable you to automatically change the angle of the shading in the object. If you have several different objects combined on the page, applying the same lighting style to each will make the shapes look more natural. Figure 3.19 shows the various lighting directions and intensities that you can apply.

Edit Points

Many pictures and clip art that you have used in this book have been resizable and changeable to some extent. You have already learned how to resize images so as not to distort their appearance. If you did want to distort them, you were limited to squeezing just one entire side of a picture

Figure 3.19

Lighting directions enable you to add various light effects easily.

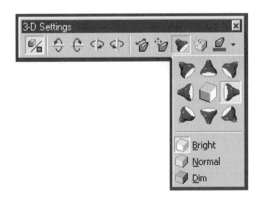

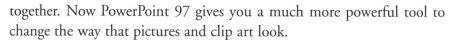

together. Now PowerPoint 97 gives you a much more powerful tool to change the way that pictures and clip art look.

This is a somewhat advanced technique, but it is so powerful that I decided to include it for the readers who will want to use it at some point. To use the Edit Points command, which is located on the Draw menu, revisit our friend the shark. Create a new page and insert the Shark clip art again. You should know how to do that by now. Then, Ungroup the clip art object again so that you can access each individual element. Now you'll walk through a series of steps to show you just how this tool works.

1. Because the shark has been ungrouped, it is a collection of separate elements. Select the top element, which is the darker purple piece. Choose Draw, Edit Points. You will see the outline of the dark purple piece of the shark identified by a series of closely spaced points. Each of these points is connected by a line to the next point, all the way around the dark purple shape, until the last point connects back to the first point and completes a continuous line (see Figure 3.20).

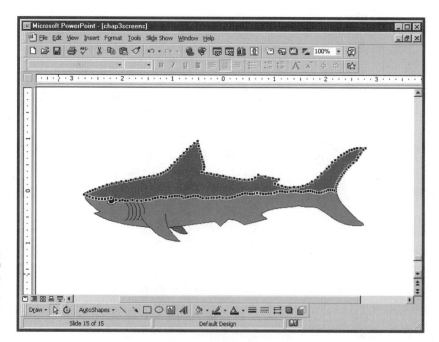

Figure 3.20

Shapes are usually just straight lines connected by lots of points.

2. You can drag any point to change the direction of the line between any two points and thereby change the underlying finished shape. Say that you want to disguise the shark's dorsal fin and make it look more like a periscope. Place your mouse over the top-most point (the cursor will change to a sort of square with four small arrows) and drag the point up about twice the height of the original fin. Notice how the shape changes because that point is still connected to the point before it and after it.

3. You can, if you have a little patience, drag several neighboring points one at a time and reshape this dorsal fin until it looks something like Figure 3.21 and disguises the ominous dorsal fin.

With this Edit Points tool, you can now take many objects (but not AutoShapes) and completely change the way they look. Because all objects are made up of lines connecting points, the closer together that you put the points, the smoother the curves you will get.

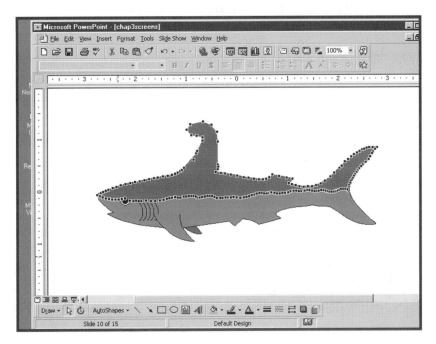

Figure 3.21

Move the points to redraw a shape.

Pictures

Although clip art is a terrific way to add graphics to a presentation, adding actual photographs can raise your presentation to a whole new level. Inserting pictures is as easy as inserting any object. You have already learned both ways of doing that earlier this afternoon.

Using pictures has always been an area that confuses a lot of people. Pictures can dramatically increase the file size of presentations, and if the picture files are not prepared correctly, you may experience tremendously large file sizes that could dramatically affect the delivery of your presentation as you wait for PowerPoint to load the next page. You should not encounter these problems if you prepare your pictures correctly. You can avoid all of the potential pitfalls if you follow some fairly straightforward guidelines.

The key issue with pictures messing up the presentation stems from people not following the first rule that I set up in this book: start at the end. You have to know how your presentation will be shown, and then get the photographs into the right file size for this end use. This section addresses the proper ways to prepare pictures for insertion into PowerPoint.

Scanning Pictures

How do photographs become digital files so that they can be inserted into PowerPoint? There are a couple of ways: they may be scanned using one of the many available scanners on the market today; or, they may be captured using one of the many new digital cameras available today. Either way that you capture the image, the rules are the same. And the rules should be followed to avoid any problems.

So, what are the rules? Well, that question sort of falls back into the first rule that I keep returning to. How is the show going to be presented? After you determine that, you then choose the highest resolution for how you'll be showing the presentation; or, if you don't have the computer resources to support the highest-use method, you create multiple sets of files for each method to be used for different versions of the presentation.

■ ■

Although any professional presentation preparers work with the best equipment available, not all presenters do. Certainly, not all my clients do. If I cannot convince a client to upgrade his or her equipment to meet the single file (meaning highest common denominator) for all of the kinds of output, I have to seriously consider the cost of carrying two sets of files at different resolutions for each of these resolution needs.

■ ■

But even considering good equipment, how do you really size pictures to be the correct size? How do you use the best file format for the picture? What is really going on here? These are the key questions that we are asked in the PowerPoint forums daily. Here are the rules that the real pros use daily without any problems.

The issue of how to figure out the way to make pictures the right size for inserting them into PowerPoint is in how to measure picture files. The real measure of a picture file should be measured only in the amount of geography it occupies. To most of us, that makes sense in inches, but it is a difficult concept to apply to scanning and photo-retouching programs because they usually don't talk the same language. Some programs talk in inches, some talk in pixels. Figuring out the translation is difficult. To make matters worse, PowerPoint talks only in inches, even though it does think internally in pixels.

So, how should you approach pictures? Certainly not with trepidation, but certainly by knowing how your presentation is going to be shown. This is the same issue that I referred to in the beginning session on Friday night. Different presentation outputs require different resolutions for pictures in order for the resolution of the pictures to be optimized. Keep in mind that you cannot run any presentation at a lower resolution than is required without losing quality. At the same time, you may not want to have 35mm Slide Quality Images in a laptop presentation. You may end up with beautiful presentations on the office machine where you are going to grab the files to send to the Service bureau for 35mm slides, but if you move this exact file to a 256 color-capable laptop, you

THINKING IN PIXELS

When starting to think about pixels, you have to start at the end. Every output device, whether it be a monitor or a laser printer or a 35mm slide camera, creates images with dots. The issue is how many dots the output device can print or display. This determines the resolution of the image.

You probably are familiar with the two most common resolutions of computer monitors: 640x480 and 800x600. In the first case, that monitor will show an image using 640 dots (pixels) wide X 480 dots (pixels) high. So pixels are just the measure of how fine a resolution that an output device can print/display.

So why worry about pixels? If you have a monitor that is displaying an image that measures 640x480 pixels and is going to show it at a 640x480 resolution, the computer sends the image to the video card and it converts each dot in the image into a pixel and paints that pixel with the correct color. The entire image looks fine. But if the monitor is going to display the image at 800x600 resolution, the video card has to figure out how to fill in the color values for the missing pixels. It generally doesn't do a very good job at this, and the resulting picture can be very disappointing.

Conversely, if the image started at a size of 800x600 pixels and the monitor was only going to display the image at the lower 640x480 resolution, the video card has to decide which of the extra pixels to throw away because it can't use them all. Again, the resulting image can be very disappointing.

That's why it is so important to match the pixel measurement of your images as closely as possible to the pixel measurement at which the image will be displayed or printed.

may be loading more file size than is necessary. As a result, you will still show the presentation only at the quality level that the laptop supports.

Why are color resolution and image size such a big deal? First, the page size between 35mm slides and a screen show is very different. A 35mm slide, as small as it is, is actually 4096x2732 pixels. A screen show at 800x600 is just that: 800x600 pixels, or about 1/5 the size measured in pixels. But the relationship of file sizes for these two outputs is more than 5:1. Take a look at Table 3.2, which shows the resulting file size for a 256 color image and the same image at true color (16 million colors) for various outputs.

Clearly, if you can get away with smaller file sizes without losing any quality, your shows will run faster.

Scanning Guidelines

How can you tell how many pixels are in your image? You will need a photo-editing program such as PhotoShop, PaintShop Pro, Corel Paint, or even Microsoft Photo Editor (which comes on the Office 97 CD-ROM). Open the image in one of these programs. Check the image size and make sure that it is shown in pixels as in Figure 3.22. If the image exceeds the measure that you need, use the photo-editing program to reduce the image to the correct size.

If you are using Microsoft Photo Editor, the command for checking image size is Image, Resize.

Here I want to take a minute and talk about the correct size for an image. If you are working in a screen show, you realize that an image should measure 800×600 pixels, but that is true if it occupies the entire screen

TABLE 3.2 FILE SIZES		
Output	16 million colors	256 colors
35mm slide	32mb	10mb
800 × 600	1.4mb	469k

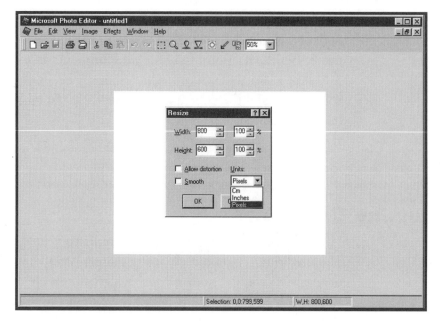

Figure 3.22

Always measure
scanned images
in pixels.

of your show. You can cut down the size of any image, as long as you measure in pixels, to the number of pixels it will occupy on the screen. For example, if you are only going to place an image in this screen show and not at a different size in another show, then the image can be further reduced to ½ of the 800×600 size or 400×300. That actually reduces this 1.4MB file to only 325K, about ¼ the size.

That means that if you managed your image size for a picture like this for a screen show that is 800×600, you could get four times as many pictures into the show without increasing your file size at all.

Scaling and DPI

Two other issues that deal with scanning often confuse people. They are scaling and DPI (Dots per Inch).

I have already said that the most important issue with image size is pixel measurement. Scaling comes into play when you scan your images. Say that you have two photographs that you want to place on a page, and each will occupy exactly half the page in an 800×600 screen show. Obviously, you want both images to end up sized at 400×300 pixels.

But one photograph is 2" × 2" and the other photograph is 4" × 4". If you scanned both photos at exactly the same scale, the larger photo would result in a file that is tremendously larger than the smaller file. Here's where scaling comes into play. To have the two photos end up with the same file size, you would scale the larger photo to 50 percent of the size of the smaller photo. The result would be identical files.

How do you set scaling? Generally, a good scanning program that comes with the better scanners will permit you to scale images, as well as to know ahead of time what size the image will be in pixels. I won't go into this in detail because there are many different scanning software packages. But if you are evaluating a new scanning software package, you should look for the ability to set scale and image size in pixels.

■ ■

TIP If your scanning software does not allow you to do this, you can still use your image-editing software to resize the image down to the pixel size that you want. Frequently, doing so can be faster than figuring out the scaling on multiple pictures ahead of time.

■ ■

DPI (Dots per Inch) is another issue that confuses people frequently about scanned images. The image is displayed in pixels (dots). How close together the dots are determines how smooth the picture looks. The fewer dots per inch, the more the picture looks like a collection of dots and less like a complete picture. The more dots per inch, the more realistic the picture looks.

You can forget about all the technical stuff behind DPI and just use two settings. Whether working in 35mm slides or with screen shows, if your image is only photographic, you can use a DPI setting of anything from 96 to 125, and the image will be perfectly fine. If your scanned image also contains type, as in scanning a page from a magazine ad with text in the

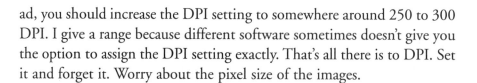

ad, you should increase the DPI setting to somewhere around 250 to 300 DPI. I give a range because different software sometimes doesn't give you the option to assign the DPI setting exactly. That's all there is to DPI. Set it and forget it. Worry about the pixel size of the images.

File Format Guidelines

What is the best file format to scan pictures into for use with PowerPoint? Well, it depends. PowerPoint comes with a variety of graphics filters for importing images into PowerPoint. When you install PowerPoint, you can choose what graphics filters to install. They are listed in Appendix C, "Installation Issues." So, which one should you use?

Various graphics file formats have significant differences that you need to understand before you choose any one file format for PowerPoint. GIF files are small but they are limited to 256 colors. JPG files are also small but the quality of the image might vary, depending on the software that you use to save the image to JPG. TIF files are good quality, but a new version of TIF files is incompatible with PowerPoint. Older versions of the TIF file work just fine. BMP files are the safest because you don't risk losing any image quality, but BMP files are stored in uncompressed form in PowerPoint and will give you larger PowerPoint files than if you use JPG files.

The two safest choices, but by no means the only valid choices, appear to be using either the BMP or JPG file formats. BMP files will always maintain their image quality. That is, they are non-lossy files. But BMP files are uncompressed files and will remain their full size on your hard disk. JPG files are in a lossy file format, and if you do not have the ability to save them at highest quality, you may suffer some degradation in image quality. If you can save the JPG files at highest quality, as you can with a good photo-editing software program, you will not lose any image quality and will have a substantially smaller PowerPoint file when you are done.

But there is one other wrinkle. When PowerPoint 97 stores a JPG file, it does so in the compressed JPG format, which is why the resulting file is smaller. But when you need to show that image in a PowerPoint screen

LOSSY AND NON-LOSSY

Both of these terms refer to file compression techniques when saving an image in a compressed file format. There is a significant difference in the two terms. A file that is compressed in a lossy format will indeed be the smallest file. But when that file is uncompressed to be viewed again, the quality of the image probably will have suffered because the lossy compression technique discards some of the actual data that tell the file how to display the image.

A non-lossy compression technique will yield a compressed file that is smaller than the original, but no actual data is discarded. When a non-lossy file is redisplayed in uncompressed format, it will be identical to the original.

show, PowerPoint needs to uncompress the file in order to show it. This can take a short but possibly noticeable amount of time while the decompression occurs. The time lag is probably not a big deal if you have only one half-screen image per page, but if you have pages and pages of montages, the time lag will probably be noticeable. In that case, you might want to use BMP files for the montages. You will have a more optimal screen show in PowerPoint. Feel free to mix file formats in PowerPoint—even on the same page. No additional complication or penalty occurs as a result of mixing file formats. It's up to you to decide what trade-off you are willing to make.

TIP

No matter what graphics file format you use in your presentations, your screen show will run more quickly if you page through the entire presentation in screen show view once before the actual show. PowerPoint seems to remember what is coming when you do this, and your pages will load faster than if you don't page through it once.

Linking to Pictures

A welcome new feature in PowerPoint 97 is the capability to link to graphics files without actually embedding the picture in PowerPoint. A wide variety of applications exist for which this is a valuable addition. Any image that you might update would not have to be re-embedded into PowerPoint. When PowerPoint wants to display that linked picture, it just opens up that linked file and shows it. But before you jump up and down with glee, you should know that PowerPoint has a bug in the way that it links to graphics files. The bug is still present in SR-1, the first service release to Office 97 to fix a variety of bugs. This one didn't get fixed.

● ●

NOTE When you link graphics files to PowerPoint 97, PowerPoint records the link with a hard-coded path to the file, such as d:\show\picture1.jpg. If you move the graphics file to another drive or folder, PowerPoint will not find the linked image and you will see an error message displayed.

Note that even if you place all of the graphics images in the same folder as the presentation and move the entire folder to a new location, PowerPoint will not find the link if the linked file is not still in the original location.

There are ways to fix the link using Visual Basic for Applications (VBA) code, but I don't recommend linking to graphics files if you are going to move the presentation to different computers.

● ●

Linking to picture files is available only by using the <u>I</u>nsert, <u>P</u>icture, <u>F</u>rom File technique of adding pictures. It is not available if your picture is in the Clip Gallery.

To insert a picture file with a link, be sure to check the Link to File check box, as shown in Figure 3.23.

If you don't plan to move presentations to new locations and want to use linking to graphics files, here are some applications for which doing so would be appropriate. The obvious occasions that come to mind are any

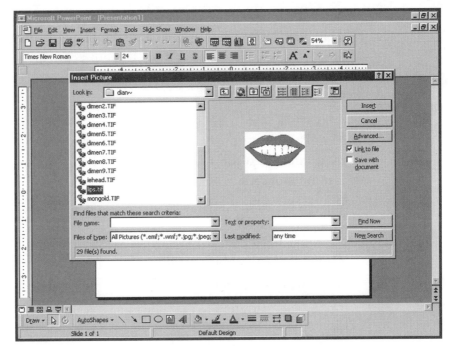

Figure 3.23

Be sure to click on Link to File if you do link.

situation in which pictures need to be placed in presentations before final artwork might be available. This is very similar to linking to Excel spreadsheets when the numbers may change at the last minute. Say that you are introducing a new product and need to create a presentation for a sales meeting but the packaging and selling materials are still being developed. You have a picture file named package.jpg, and you insert it with a link. When the final package file becomes available, you should name it package.jpg and place it in the same folder as the original file. PowerPoint will then show the updated file.

Another good application for linking graphics files would be if your company were running a PowerPoint presentation in the reception area every day. You could create a shell presentation with text links to Word or Excel that might change daily. You could also add graphics and link to those graphics files, changing them daily by moving the appropriately named files into the correct folder whenever you wanted to make changes.

Linking to graphics files is a big step forward for PowerPoint and will be a big blessing for many as soon as the linking gets updated to allow files to move to new locations as true OLE links currently do.

Sound

Most PowerPoint presentations do not currently use sound. It's really no more difficult to add sound to a presentation than it is to add a picture. Just think of sounds as another kind of object.

You can use sound in PowerPoint presentations in several ways:

- Adding a sound from the Clip Gallery
- Adding a sound from a file
- Playing a CD audio track
- Adding narration to each slide in a screen show

The first three of these options are very straightforward operations that work just like adding pictures to a file. If you are using an AutoLayout with a "Double click to add clip art" placeholder, you can just double-click on that placeholder and click on the Sound tab in the Clip Gallery. If you have no sound clips in the Clip Gallery, you can probably import some from your C:\Windows\Media folder or refer back to the section on Saturday morning about downloading Clip Gallery files from Microsoft's Web site.

If you want to insert the sound not from the Clip Gallery, but rather directly from a file, the process is still very familiar. But you will have to set the slide show settings for how to play the sound.

1. Choose Insert, Movies and Sounds, Sound from File.

2. Browse to locate the correct file. (Note that your Windows\Media\Office97 folder probably has sound files to practice with).

3. Select the file that you want to insert, and click on OK.

4. You will see a small icon on your screen that is supposed to look like a speaker. You will now need to tell PowerPoint how to play this sound during a slide show. Right-click the speaker object and choose <u>A</u>ction Settings. You have two choices: play it when you click on it with the mouse, or play it when you pass the mouse over it during the show. To set this option, choose Slide Show, <u>A</u>ction Settings and click on the Mouse Click or the Mouse Over tab.

5. Under the Object Action option, click on the Play option button. It is set to Play on Mouse Click by default. Or you can set it to None. Actually, because these option buttons are different tabs, you can set it to play on either a Mouse Click or a Mouse Over, if you choose.

6. Click on OK and you are done.

The problem with sound files is that most people don't have the equipment to record decent sound files. Additionally, recorded sound files are fairly large, depending on the quality at which you record the file. So, unless you do have these capabilities and plenty of disk space, you may be limited to the short sound files that come with Windows, and some sound clip collections. But you do have some other easy options for adding good quality sound files to your presentations if you have a CD-ROM in your computer. You can play sound tracks or parts of sound tracks directly from a CD-ROM just as you did in the last example.

Playing Sounds from CD's

When inserting a sound you will see the option, Play <u>C</u>D Audio Track. If you select that option, you will see the dialog box in Figure 3.24. This dialog box enables you to pick a starting and ending track on a CD. Each track represents an entire song in most cases. And you can set the timing to start at because each track is measured in time.

Figure 3.25 shows the settings that you would use to play the second track on a CD and stop at the end of the second track. This dialog box

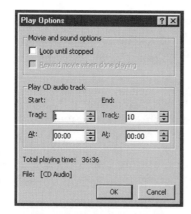

Figure 3.24

You can play CD tracks during your presentation.

Figure 3.25

Set the start and end times to play a CD track.

also shows that the track is 3:41 in length. When you click on OK, you see a little icon of a CD rather than the icon of the speaker. As with the sound object, you can assign the Play option properties to On Mouse Click or On Mouse Over.

Because both of these icons represent typical objects to PowerPoint, you can set them to be hidden objects so that only you know they are there. This is done in the Custom Animation settings of the Slide Show menu option. I'll show you how to do that shortly.

But first, you can also play this CD track (or tracks) continuously over many pages in a presentation, and even tell the CD to stop when you reach a specific page. So, if you want to have music playing during an entire segment of a presentation, doing so is now easy. Look at the following example to set both the <u>H</u>ide while not playing option and the Play across multiple slides in a show.

1. After you have told PowerPoint to Play the CD track either on a Mouse Over or on a Mouse Click, or both, choose Slide Show, Custo<u>m</u> Animation and click on the Timing tab.

2. On the Timing tab, make sure that you have selected the proper object, which is the CD. You will see it selected in the preview window. Click on <u>A</u>nimate.

3. Click on the Play Settings tab and place a check mark in the <u>H</u>ide while not playing box at the lower right.

4. Place a check in the Play using animation order check box and click on Continue slide show in the While playing option to keep all other animations operating while the CD is playing.

5. If you want to play the CD over multiple slides, you need to click the Stop playing Afte<u>r</u> option and change the slide number in the box.

You can also play prerecorded sounds and any sounds that have been added to your Clip Gallery during a transition from one slide to the next. I cover that topic in more detail in this evening's session when I discuss slide transitions in detail.

Adding Narration to Slides

In addition to prerecorded sounds and music, you can also add voice-over narration to a slide that will play during the slide show. And you don't have to necessarily use expensive studio recording equipment to do this. All you basically need is a sound card, a decent microphone, which is available inexpensively at any local electronics retailer, and someone to record the narration track. That can be you.

The narration that is recorded is saved with the show and will play when the slide show is presented based on the settings you set for the narration, just like you set custom settings for playing sound tracks from a CD. To record a narration for a slide show, be sure your microphone is hooked up to your sound card correctly, and also be sure that your sound card output plug is properly connected to a speaker. Then, from the menu:

1. Choose Slide Show, Record Narration.

2. You are presented with a dialog box as shown in Figure 3.26, in which you can set the recording quality of the sound. See the sidebar on Understanding Recording Quality at the end of this section. This dialog box shows you the Quality you are currently set to record at, the rate you will use up disk space in kb/second, the free disk space on the drive your presentation is saved on, and the maximum recording time you can record at this setting.

3. If this setting is not the level you want to record at, click on Settings to set the recording quality level. Then Click on OK to get back to the Record Narration dialog box you were just viewing in Step 2.

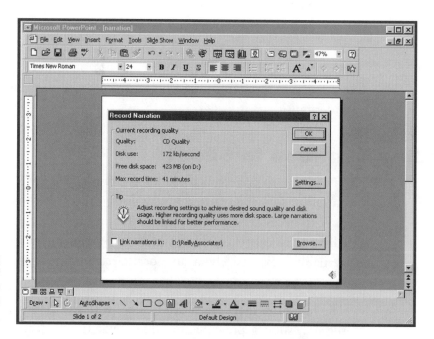

Figure 3.26

PowerPoint even tells you how long you can record.

UNDERSTANDING RECORDING QUALITY

Recording quality directly affects the quality of your sound, and the better the quality the bigger the file. Did you expect it to be any different? There are 15 levels at which you can record sound in PowerPoint. PowerPoint also has three of these levels predefined for you: CD Quality, Radio Quality, and Telephone Quality.

Each level results in a file size that is related to how long your sound narration is. The CD Quality level is 172 KBs per second, which is roughly a 1 megabyte file per 6 recorded seconds. Radio Quality is 22 KBs per second for 45 seconds of recorded time for that same 1 megabyte of space. Telephone quality is only 11 KBs per second for 90 seconds of sound per megabyte.

When you record sound, you should be concerned about available hard disk space and the quality of the speakers the sound will be played back on. High quality sound files still sound poor on poor speakers.

4. Get your microphone ready and script in hand and click OK to start the presentation in Slide Show view, and you can start recording your narration.

5. When the Show concludes, you see a message box telling you that your narrations have been saved with each slide, and it gives you the option of saving the slide advance timings as well. Click <u>Y</u>es to save the advance timings and <u>N</u>o not save the timings.

6. You then have another message box asking you if you want to review the slide timings in slide sorter view with <u>Y</u>es and <u>N</u>o options.

Movies

By now, you should be able to figure out how to add movie files to your presentation. That's right—you do it just as you add pictures or sound files. You can add them directly from the Clip Gallery if they are there. Or you can insert them directly from a file with the Insert, Movies and Sounds, Movie from File command.

Getting a good source of movie files is certainly a lot harder than inserting the files. Movies can be a variety of things. You may capture video from a VCR or directly from a TV, or you can create animations using an animation program. Either way, to create your own movie files, you need another software package. PowerPoint will only play the files; it will not create or edit these files.

If you do not have a good way to create your own movie files and need to do so, you might consider outsourcing that part of the presentation to a company that has the capabilities. It will probably be easier for you in the long run.

The issue of best file format always comes up when discussing movie clip file formats. The two default formats that can easily play in PowerPoint are .AVI and .MOV. If you are new to using movies in your presentations, you might be best off using .AVI files if you have the choice.

The .AVI file type is played back by Media Player, which is installed with Windows. The .MOV file type is a QuickTime movie format that requires QuickTime for Windows to play. It is not difficult to install QuickTime for Windows, and the software is available free for downloading at the Microsoft Web site. The issue becomes one of having an additional variable, and if you are likely to move the files to more than one computer, you will have to make sure that QuickTime for Windows is installed on those computers.

Wrapping Up

Well, that was a very full afternoon. You have now learned all of the tools necessary to plan your presentation, and how to add every kind of content to your presentation that you will ever run across. I hope you are seeing the similarities in the different kinds of content and now realize how simple this is all becoming.

Now you should feel very confident that you can add any object to your presentation. Take a break and have a nice dinner. Tonight will be an easy session, and you'll start to learn how to put the finishing touches on presentations by adding animation effects to individual objects on slides.

How It Is Shown:
Animation Effects

- ✿ Understanding the anatomy of an animation
- ✿ Using graphical builds
- ✿ Working with advanced animation techniques
- ✿ Publishing animation to the Web
- ✿ Animating charts

Welcome back. You have made a great deal of progress so far. I realize that today was a very busy day. Tonight's session is much simpler and shorter. It deals with only one subject, but it's one that will help you add a lot of excitement to your presentations. That subject is *animation*—which you can create easily within PowerPoint.

Not many people use animation effects in PowerPoint other than animating bullets. In fact, animated bullets is used in only about half of the presentations I have seen. Adding animation to presentations in PowerPoint is easy, and with a few simple effects you can dramatically help increase the impact of your presentation and become a leading PowerPoint presenter.

Animation in PowerPoint refers to a host of predefined effects that you can apply to any object in PowerPoint. Let me repeat that because it is very important—you can apply them to *any* object. Any object means just that—Title placeholders, 3-D shapes, chart series, scanned photographs, and so on. Think back to the presentation that you created Friday night with the predefined template high voltage.pot (see Figure 4.1). That Slide Master page had animation built into it so that a small, drawn object flew up the pole on the left side of the page, and then horizontally across the page. That is a very good example of how animation works in PowerPoint.

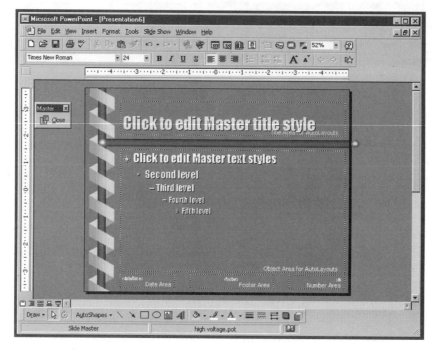

Figure 4.1

The high
voltage.pot
template has
two animation
objects on the
Slide Master.

The animation effect in the high voltage.pot template actually consists of two separate animation objects that combine to give you the one effect. The first animation effect was of a drawn object that entered the screen from the bottom, moved up the slide in a straight line, and then disappeared. The second animation effect was a copy (not the same object) of the drawn object; the copy entered the screen from the left and crossed the screen in a straight line to the right, after the first animation step was completed.

The following are the two most important concepts here:

❖ The object that was animated went in a straight line

❖ The objects that were animated executed their animation commands in sequence

Those two underlying principles govern animation in PowerPoint. You can add some terrific animation effects to help your communication. You won't easily get a special effect, however, unless you create it with either or both of the these two underlying principles, which also act as constraints.

The Anatomy of an Animation

The best way to learn the underlying principles of animation in Power-Point is to take apart an existing animation. I used the template high voltage.pot on Friday night to set the stage for this chapter, because animation in PowerPoint is explained so well by what is done on the Slide Master for this template. You'll use the same one tonight.

Keep in mind that although I dissect this animation on the Slide Master page, the exact same principles apply to any animation on any page. The only difference is that because these specific animation effects are applied on the Slide Master page in high voltage.pot, they run on every page.

So, why don't you get wired and jump right in? Open a new presentation using the high voltage.pot template. You should know how to do this by now, but if you need a little reminder, here are the steps:

1. Choose File, New and click on the Presentation Designs tab.
2. Double-click on the icon for high voltage.pot.
3. Choose any AutoLayout and double-click on it.

Good, I knew you wouldn't need to read those last steps. See how quickly you are catching on? Before jumping to the Slide Master page, take a few seconds to preview the screen show for this single blank slide by clicking on the Slide Show icon at the bottom-left corner of the screen (or choose View, Slide Show from the menu). Figure 4.1 shows the Slide Show icon.

You need to make sure that you know what is happening here. If you choose View, Slide Sorter, you will see the one slide in the new presenta-tion. (Although the animation issue is the main concern here, I want you to have five blank slides to view the same animation effect so that you will see what I am trying to demonstrate. The various slide views will espe-cially drive home some issues with PowerPoint animation and show you exactly how to extend the capabilities of animation in PowerPoint.) So, now that you are in Slide Sorter view, and have the first and only slide selected, copy that page to the Clipboard with Ctrl+C (you aren't using Edit, Copy from the menu any more, are you? Or those toolbar buttons for Copy and Paste?). Use Ctrl+V to paste that slide down as the second slide. See how easy it is to copy a slide? Now, press Ctrl+V three more times so that you have five copies of the same slide. Your screen should resemble Figure 4.2.

Select slide #1 on this page and click on the Slide Show button at the bottom-left corner of the page.

NOTE You can switch to Slide Show view from any of the other four different View levels: Slide, Outline, Slide Sorter, or Notes Page.

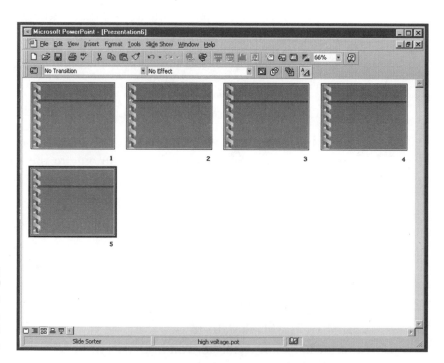

Figure 4.2

Slide Sorter lets you copy, delete, and move slides easily.

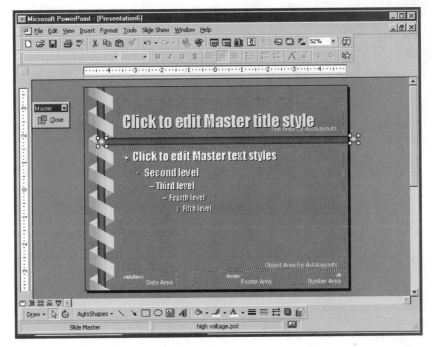

Figure 4.3

The first moving image starts from the bottom, and then disappears at the intersection point.

Press Enter to go to the next slide and look carefully at the intersection of the two dark blue tubular drawings on the page. You will notice that the first moving image starts from the bottom and then disappears at the intersection point (see Figure 4.3). Then, the second moving image starts to the left of that and goes off the screen to the right. It's almost as if the electricity short-circuited and started the wrong way, and then turned around and went the other way.

Now take a look at exactly how this was controlled by looking at the Slide Master page. Choose View, Master, Slide Master from the menu. The easiest way to cycle through each object on the Master Page is to use the Tab key, just as you used the arrow key with the chart objects. If you press the Tab key once, you will see the Title placeholder selected. Press Tab again and you will see the Object Area for AutoLayouts selected. Keep going with three more Tabs to select the Date Area, Footer Area, and Number

Area placeholders. After the Number Area placeholder, you will select a grouped set of shapes. Three more times of pressing the Tab key will likely get you to a selection of the first object that has animation commands attached to it. It is the small circle with the radial fill.

If you press the Tab key twice more, you will select the copy of the first circle. Actually, because the original of this circle was created with the Oval Drawing toolbar button, it will be called an oval. That's because you have confirmed all of the individual objects on the page and will now switch to the animation menu, which will let you program each individual object one at a time in sequential order. To do so, follow these steps:

1. Choose Slide Show, Custom Animation and click on the Timing tab. Please take a minute to examine the picture, as shown in Figure 4.4. It will show you the two items that have already been assigned animation commands. They are in the Animation Order

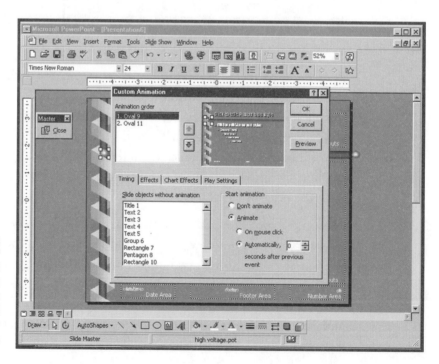

Figure 4.4

The Custom Animation dialog box is where you set Timing and Effects for animations

window. Also notice in this figure that the remaining objects on the page are available in the Slide Objects Without Animation window.

2. Take another moment to click slowly through each object in the Animation Order window, and then the Slide Objects Without Animation window, while noticing what is shown as a selection in the preview window and also noticing what option button is selected in the Start Animation area. You will see each of these change, depending on which object is selected on the left side of the dialog box.

3. Click on OK or Cancel to close the dialog box.

Note that all the objects on a page are available in one of the two windows: the Animation order window or the Slide objects without animation window. When you select an object and choose to animate or not to animate the object, the name of the object moves to the other window. This is a very helpful tool that will permit you to easily animate a large number of objects, which you will do later in this chapter in the section "Advanced Animation Techniques."

You should have noticed that there are two separate ovals: Oval 9 and Oval 11. Don't worry about the numbering at the moment. These two ovals are set to be animated in the Start Animation area and set to start automatically—immediately (0 seconds) after the previous event, which in this case is the start of the slide.

Now click on the Effects tab in the Custom Animation dialog box and make sure that Oval 9 is selected in the Animation Order window, as shown in Figure 4.5. This tab contains more animation settings for these two ovals. You will set two stages of the animation here: 1) what happens when the animation object enters the scene; and 2) what happens to the animation object after the animation event. Each of these settings is controlled through the drop-down list boxes that you see in Figure 4.5.

Take a quick look at each of these settings (I'll go into much more detail later).

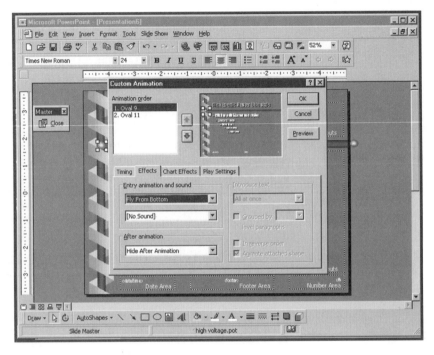

Figure 4.5

Make sure that Oval 9 is selected in the Animation order window.

The first option is <u>E</u>ntry Animation and Sound. If you click on the drop-down box, you will see a slider bar showing various transitions (see Figure 4.6). You have 56 animation effects from which to choose.

The next animation setting is the sound that you will use with the animation entry effect. You have the choice of no sound or 16 prerecorded sounds, as well as the opportunity to attach any sound file of your choice to an animation effect. In the case of this Slide Master, no sound effect is attached to these animations.

The third setting, <u>A</u>fter Animation, is what to do with the object after the animation effect has played. By default, the choice is Don't Dim, which just leaves the image visible on the screen. But you also can change the color of the object, hide the object, or leave it visible and hide it on the next mouse click.

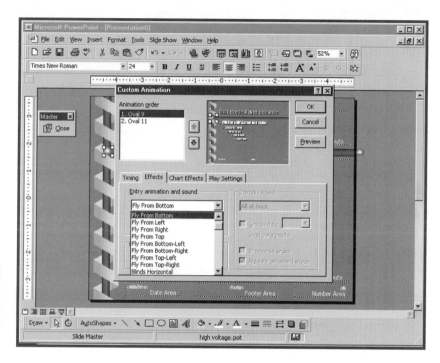

Figure 4.6

The animation
settings are all
available in
drop-down lists.

When you put all of these settings together for a series of objects, you can easily add a lot of activity to your screen.

NOTE Be careful not to fall into the trap of adding animation effects to every object just because you can. Too much animation in a presentation can be distracting and make your presentation look sophomoric.

Animation Effects

Now that you have seen how an existing animation has been built, it's time to create one yourself. Remember the shark and sailboat presentation that you were supposed to save this morning? It's time to open

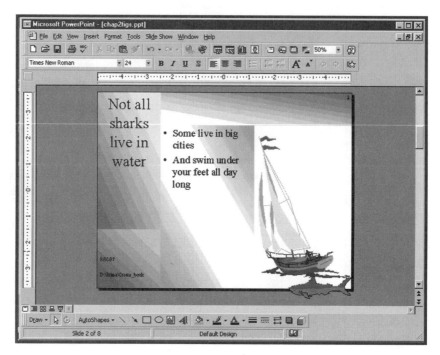

Figure 4.7

You'll add
animation effects
to the shark and
sailboat
presentation.

that file again so that you can add some simple animation effects to it.
Your file should look similar to Figure 4.7. If it doesn't look exactly like
that, the important things that you will be dealing with are the Title, the
bullet points, the clip art of the boat, and the clip art of the shark.

Create an animation effect for each of these elements—first, the Title.

1. Choose Slide Show, Custom Animation. Then, click on the Timing
   tab. Because you probably have not added any animation yet, your
   screen should look like Figure 4.8.

2. You have four objects to work with here. Click on each object in
   the Slide Objects Without Animation window and see which
   object your selection refers to in the preview window. Object 1 is
   the shark, Title 2 is the Title, Object 3 is the clip art of the boat,
   and Text 4 is the Object Area placeholder. Now click on Object 3
   and click on Animate.

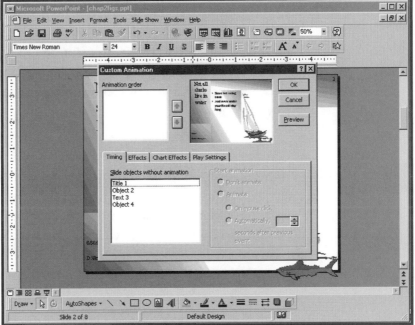

Figure 4.8

Nothing is selected
for an animation in
this figure.

3. You will notice that the Object 3 label now moves to the Animation Order window. Next, click on Title 2 and click on Animate. That label also moves to the Animation Order window.

4. Click on Text 4 and then click on Animate. Click on Object 1 and click on Animate. All four objects are now animated and the default animation effect will happen on mouse clicks, which were set by default.

5. Click on the Preview button now to see what has been set by default.

6. Oops, the boat and the shark are going backwards. You can fix that. Click on the Effects tab and select Object 3 (the boat). Notice that the Entry Animation effect is set to Fly From Left by default.

7. Change the Entry Animation to Fly From Right by clicking on the box that says Fly From Left. Scroll down one item and select Fly From Right.

8. Repeat the same steps for the shark (Object 1) to make it swim in from the right.

9. Now you'll fix the Title. Select Title 2 in the Animation Order window. You are likely seeing not only the Title fly in from the left but also the rectangle that you placed behind the placeholder. Separate the two by clicking on the box in the lower right of the screen—Animate Attached Shape. Then, select Swivel as the Entry Animation effect.

10. Click on Preview to see how you are doing. Good, you are almost there. Add some more emphasis to the title. Select Title 2 in the Animation Order window again and change the Introduce Text drop-down to By Word; then, click on Preview. Now, introducing the Title of the page takes longer, which sets up more suspense concerning this shark.

11. Select Text 4 and set the Entry Animation effect to Dissolve. Set the Introduce Text option to By Letter.

12. That should do it. Click on OK. Then, click on the Slide Show button in the bottom-left corner of the screen. Remember that all of the animation effects were set to advance on mouse clicks, so click your way through the page.

That's all there is to creating animation effects on a page. You simply select every item that you want to animate and set the effects that you want to occur.

Before I move on, you might be asking, "How about if I select the items and don't like the order?" Well, I should emphasize two more things here to make this absolutely clear.

When you select an item and attach animation effects to that object, you are attaching properties to the object, just as if you were attaching the property green to a circle. The attached properties stay attached until they are changed. If you change only one of the properties, such as the order, all of the other properties stay unchanged. I'll walk you through that issue.

1. Choose Slide Show, Custom Animation and select Title 2. Now click on the upward-pointing arrow to the right of the Animation Order window. Doing so changes the order of the animation. Click on OK.

2. Now, who has ever seen just one shark? They usually travel in schools, so I'll have you create a school of these fellas. Select the shark and copy it to the Clipboard with Ctrl+C. Now paste three of its friends back into the water by pressing Ctrl+V three times. Then, drag all four sharks to just off the left side of the page, as shown in Figure 4.9.

3. You can make all this happen automatically without mouse clicks. Choose Slide Show, Custom Animation again and select the Title 2 object in the Animation Order window.

4. Hold down the Shift key and click on the last object available to select all of the objects in the Animation Order window. They will

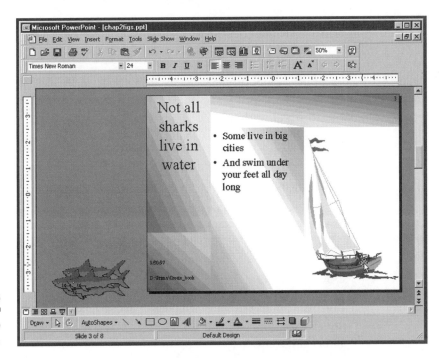

Figure 4.9

Sharks like to go to school.

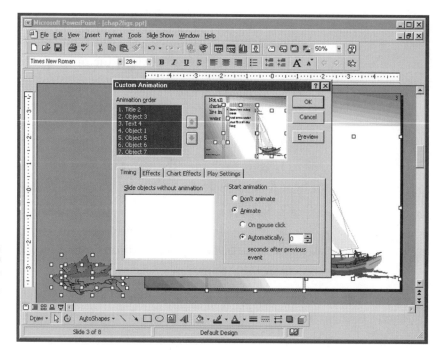

Figure 4.10

Use the Shift key
to select multiple
items in the
Animation
order window.

all be highlighted, as shown in Figure 4.10. Then, click on the Timing tab and select A̲utomatically. Leave the 0 in the timing box. Click on OK, and then click on the Slide Show button again to preview the slide.

That should be much better. You have now learned how to apply animation effects. Now you can move on and examine each of the animation effects in more detail.

Entry Animation Effects

The animation effects total 56 effects in all. They fall into the categories shown in Table 4.1.

The number of effects in each category vary and generally represent directional variations on the same effect, for example, wipe up, wipe down, wipe right, wipe left.

TABLE 4.1—ENTRY ANIMATION EFFECTS DESCRIPTIONS

Effect	Number of Effects	Description of the object's action
No Effect	N/A	No animation
Appear	1	Just appears on the screen
Fly From	8	Slides across the screen from out of the frame to the final location
Blinds	2	Simulates Venetian blinds
Box In/Out	2	Fills the screen to/from the center of the screen
Checkerboard	2	Reveals the screen in squares like a checker board
Crawl	4	Slowly slides into position
Dissolve	1	Appears in clusters of pixels
Flash	3	Appears and disappears
Peek From	4	Enters behind other objects from a direction
Random Bars	2	Similar to Venetian blinds but different-sized bars
Spiral	1	A combination of a zoom effect along a curved path
Split Horizontal/ Vertical	4	Splits the image in two and fills it in horizontally or vertically
Stretch	5	Fills in position
Strips	4	An uneven fill
Swivel	1	Appears to rotate on its center vertical axis

TABLE 4.1—ENTRY ANIMATION EFFECTS DESCRIPTIONS (CONTINUED)		
Effect	**Number of Effects**	**Description of the object's action**
Wipe	4	Reveals smoothly from a direction
Zoom	6	Object increases/decreases in size
Random Effects	1	Chooses randomly from the preceding effects

Mixing Entry Animation Effects

You can achieve some interesting effects by mixing animation effects on a page. In this afternoon's session, I asked you to save a file that had four different cones pointing into a circle. It looked like Figure 4.11.

You can only have one animation effect per object, but you can mix the animation effects of many objects to achieve an interesting effect that

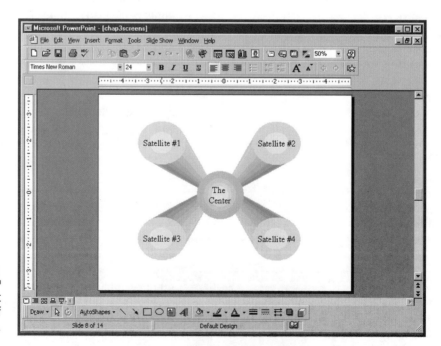

Figure 4.11

Satellites connect to the center of the universe.

helps reinforce your ideas. Although I have told you that the path for all PowerPoint animation effects is a straight line, there is one effect that is not. Used sparingly, it can add a special effect for just the right situation. A situation such as the satellite example demonstrates this idea very well.

Now, apply five different effects to each of the five objects on this page.

1. Open the Custom Animation dialog box by choosing Slide Show, Custom Animation. Select all of the objects in the Slide objects without animation window by holding down the Shift key while selecting the first and the last objects and clicking on Animate and Automatically, 0 seconds after previous event.

2. Change the 0 value to 2 to set the timing for each transition to two seconds each.

3. Move the Text 5 object, the circle, to the top of the list by using the arrow key.

4. Click on the Effects tab and select Spiral from the drop-down menu.

5. Select the cone in the top-left corner—you will know which one because it will be selected in the preview window—and select the effect Stretch Across. The object name will vary depending on the order the objects were created.

6. Select the cone on the lower right, and set the effect to Zoom in From Screen Center.

7. Select the two remaining cones, and select the effect Dissolve while saying "Beam me up, Scotty."

8. Press the Preview button to see what the effect looks like.

The point of this exercise is not to force you to like each of these transitions, but to point out that depending on your own special circumstances, you can use a variety of effects to achieve different effects.

The other point is to warn you that on some machines the spiral effect can sometimes be a little slow to load. You may or may not notice this depending on the quality of the computer you are using to work through this exercise.

Sound Effects

You can choose from 16 prerecorded sounds to attach to an animation effect. Additionally, you have the option of stopping a previous sound, and the option to attach any other sound that you can play on your system. You just have to select the sound file that you want to attach from the Effects tab of the Custom Animation dialog box. The 16 prerecorded sounds are very short and often not very good effects to attach. They are the following: applause, breaking glass, camera, cash register, chime, clapping, drive by, drum roll, explosion, gunshot, laser, ricochet, screeching brakes, slide projector, typewriter, whoosh, and an option to choose your own sounds through a dialog box when you choose other sounds.

Recording Your Own Sound Effects

The prerecorded sound effects mentioned in the previous section leave a lot to be desired. They are short and of not very good quality. You may want to record your own sounds or search for a source of other commercially available prerecorded sounds. You can use a variety of prerecorded sound clips to build your own collection of sound effects. The sounds that come with various Corel products come to mind. In products like this, you can get sound effects that are often 5-10 seconds, or even longer.

To add a custom sound from your hard drive to your presentation while you are in the Custom Animation dialog box:

1. Select the object in the Animation order window and apply an effect from the Entry animation and sound window. The option of No Effect will not let you apply a sound. You must apply some effect, even if it is just Appear.

2. Click the pull-down box that says [No Sound] and choose Other Sound at the bottom of the list.

3. You will be presented with the Add Sound dialog box, which is just like any of the dialog boxes you've seen for adding a picture or opening a file. Locate the correct folder of your special sound effect and select it. Then select OK.

4. Click OK to return to edit view in PowerPoint.

The sound is embedded in the presentation and is available to you if you choose the Other Sound option with another object later in the presentation. But that sound is not stored in PowerPoint itself, so it will not be available in your predefined list if you open a different presentation.

■ ■

If you plan to create your own custom sound effects and use them frequently, you should create a special folder for Sound Effects and store your favorites there. Then, it will be easy to find them in the future.

■ ■

If you don't have the time or the resources to purchase a library of sound effects, it is quite easy to create your own—either using your own voice, using sounds from an electronic keyboard, or by recording them directly from CD's or the radio. You have a decent tool for this built right into Windows 95 called Sound Recorder. Before you start, you should be sure that you have the input device, where you are getting the sound from, plugged into the Input plug on your sound card. Then, follow these steps:

1. Choose Start from the Windows menu, Programs, Accessories, Multimedia, and Sound Recorder to launch the Sound Recorder program.

2. In Sound Recorder, choose File, New.

3. When you are ready to record the sound effect, click on the Record button—the last button on the right. It is the one with the red circle. See Figure 4.12 to start recording.

4. You will see the timer clicking off the time of the recording. When you are done recording, click on the Stop button—the one with the black rectangle.

5. To play back the file you just recorded to be sure you like it, click on the Play button—the single black triangle.

6. If you are happy with the recording, save it to your Sound Effects folder by using File, Save As.

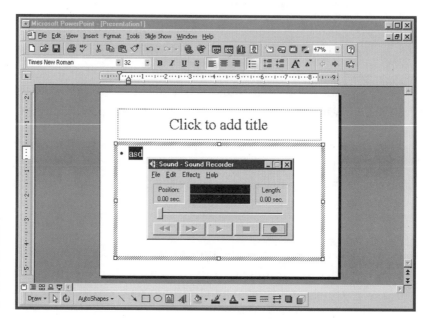

Figure 4.12

Use Sound
Recorder to
create your own
sound effects.

7. Exit Sound Recorder, and that sound file is now available for you to place into any PowerPoint presentation as a sound effect.

CAUTION Where you get your sounds from and how you use them can become a very serious copyright issue. I am certainly not encouraging you to break any copyright laws. Think before recording a sound from a public source such as a CD or a radio station and seek advice if you think you might be possibly breaking the law.

Graphical Builds

How can you use graphical builds? You can use them to reveal a complex message step by step. Or you can even use graphical builds to construct a whole story while reminding the audience of each key segment of the story. Or you can even use slide transitions to help you with graphical builds that you can put together in the normal manner. The following sections show some real world examples of these concepts.

The Tic-Tac-Toe Build

Assume that you have a series of pros and cons to reveal about a subject. You could use the popular tic-tac-toe game to help you do this graphically.

Take a look at Figure 4.13 for a finished copy of a slide that you know how to make now. It only consists of four lines, seven text boxes, and one arrow. The beauty of a slide like this is that it mixes simple graphics, text, transitions, and animation to create a very dramatic impact.

You should be able to create the slide without any trouble at this point in the weekend. So create the slide, and then I'll take you through the animation steps again. To create the slide:

1. Add the title to a new slide that uses the Title Only AutoLayout. The text of the Title is **The Tic Tac Toe Build.**

2. Create a vertical line and hold down the Shift key after you start drawing the line to constrain it to perfectly vertical. Copy the line

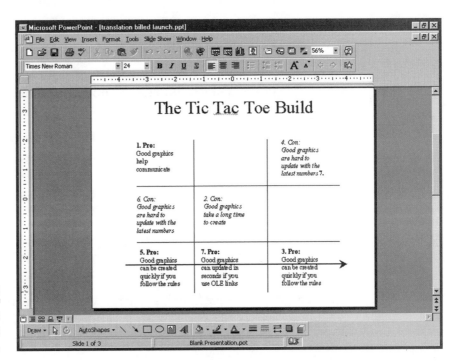

Figure 4.13

The tic-tac-toe build is simple but elegant.

and paste a copy to the page so that it is identical in length. Then arrange it as shown in Figure 4.13.

3. Create a horizontal line, and then copy it, paste, and arrange it similarly to the way you did in step 1.

4. Now click on the text box button, and then click the mouse in the upper-left tic-tac-toe corner box and type 1. **Pro: Good graphics help communicate**

5. Repeat step 3 and type the correct copy for each tic-tac-toe box in the corresponding location. I have included a number to help you keep track of the order that the text should be entered, which will make it easier to keep track of the animation order later. For the record, the text to type is:

   2. **Con: Good graphics take a long time to create**
   3. **Pro: Good graphics can be created quickly if you follow the rules**
   4. **Con: Good graphics need a talented artist to create**
   5. **Pro: Good graphics are built on simplicity**
   6. **Con: Good graphics are hard to update with the latest numbers**
   7. **Pro: Good graphics can be updated in minutes if you use OLE links**

6. Now you may notice a few things. The type may not fit in the boxes because the font size may be too large. Select all of the text boxes by holding down the Shift key and clicking inside each text box. When you have all of the text boxes selected, change the font to 20 point by dragging your mouse, with the left mouse button depressed, through the Font Size toolbar and pressing the Enter key. Or choose Format, Font from the menu and type 20 in the Size box and click on OK.

7. I chose an example like this to teach you another trick. The way to get the words *Good graphics* to start on a different line than the *Pro:*

or *Con:* is to place the mouse cursor just in front of the *G* in *Graphics* and press Enter. This forces a return between the two words so that there will always be a line break between them no matter what the width of the text box is. Do that now.

8. The last object to add to this page is the arrow in the bottom row. Select the Arrow button on the Drawing toolbar and draw the arrow from left side to the right side to be sure that the arrow will point the correct way.

That is a nice simple slide that addresses the pros and cons of good graphics. The slide is pretty boring at this point. The way to make this very simple slide communicate effectively is to add animation to the elements so that each element builds. You will apply an animation effect to each of the lines to set up the tic-tac-toe effect. That will be 13 animation effects for the entire slide.

1. Start by opening the Custom Animation dialog box by choosing Slide Show, Custom Animation.

2. Click the Timing tab and click in the Slide objects without animation window.

3. Select the first item, which should be Title 1. While holding down the Shift key, scroll down to the last item and select that item to select all of the objects in this slide.

4. Click on Animate in the Start animation group box, and also Click on Automatically and leave the timing at 0. That will apply the same animation setting to every object in this one step. You will notice that all of the objects move to the Animation order window.

5. Now click the Preview button to see what the animation effects look like. It is very likely that everything is set to Fly in from the left, which is not a very good effect for a tic-tac-toe game.

6. You'll now want to fix each of the animation settings. But you don't have to do it in 13 separate steps. The first thing to do is to change the order so that the Title 1 appears after the four lines. Scroll up

to the top in the Animation order window, select Title 1, and use the down arrow button to move it after Line 5. Then press Preview again to see the progress you've made.

7. The order is better, but the lines that make up the tic-tac-toe grid fly in from the left, and that is not the way to draw a tic-tac-toe game. You can change each of the line animation effects to fly in from a direction so that it looks like the grid for the game is being drawn on the screen. Change each of the settings for the four lines by selecting them individually and applying either Fly in From Top, or Fly in From Bottom for the two vertical lines. Then, change the setting on one of the horizontal lines to Fly in From the Right. You'll notice that as you select each line, the line is shown in the preview window. Use the Preview button to make sure that each of the lines flies in from a different direction.

8. Now you can deal with the Title and all of the Text items on the slide in one step. Select Title 1 in the Animation order window, and while holding down the Shift key, select the last Text item and change that animation effect to Dissolve. The animation effect for each of these objects will be set to Dissolve with these few keystrokes.

9. Because the arrow, which is the last animation object, is already set to Fly in From Left by the default setting, you can just leave it that way. Click OK to go back to PowerPoint slide edit view.

If you followed the steps precisely as they were given, you will now have an interesting slide that builds automatically in about five or six seconds depending on the machine on which you are running. If you didn't follow the steps precisely, you may have to move one or more of the objects up or down in the order in the Animation order window. Chances are you used animations with many different objects and are concerned about the exact order that each object enters the screen. No need to worry however, because you can just change the order of entry and the transition of any object. Animations with multiple objects are made easy by frequently previewing the animation as you build it in the Preview window in the dialog box.

The Transition Build

There is another kind of build that can help make a point, but it can't be accomplished with the normal animation tools in PowerPoint. At the beginning of this chapter, you learned that PowerPoint animation effects work in straight lines. Sometimes you may want to have an arrow point from one object to a second object, but the two objects may not be lined up on the page in a straight line. You can still accomplish this effect by creating two slides and using a slide transition to create the effect. Look at Figure 4.14 to see the kind of arrow that cannot be handled with animation effects, but only with slide transitions. The idea behind this build is that something happens to the First Object, such as an e-mail is sent, and that triggers an event at the Second Object, such as the e-mail is transmitted to the Second Object.

Here's how to create this effect:

1. Create a slide that shows the final result like Figure 4.14.

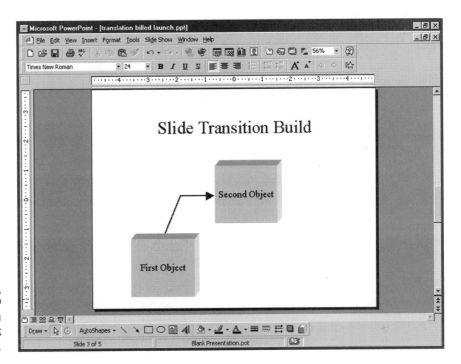

Figure 4.14

Slide transition effects can look like animation.

You already know how to create the two 3-D boxes and the text box labels in them. Go ahead and create them.

2. The line is actually two lines, one with an arrow. Create those two lines and make sure the two ends are carefully placed end to end so that the two lines appear as if they are one line.

3. Switch to Slide Sorter View by choosing View, Slide Sorter.

4. Copy this slide to the clipboard (Ctrl+C) and paste it into the presentation right after this slide.

5. Now you have two identical slides. Select the first slide, and then switch back to Slide edit view by selecting View, Slide. On the first slide, delete the two lines.

6. Switch to the next slide by pressing the Page Down key. Set this slide transition by choosing Slide Show, Slide Transition and set the Effect to Wipe Right. It doesn't matter what speed you set the advance for, or whether you set the Advance to happen On a mouse click or Automatically after a period of time. The effect will be the same. Press Apply to apply this transition to this slide only.

7. Choose Slide Show, View to review the slides. Advance if you need to use a mouse click and the arrow will draw perfectly from the First Object and point to the Second Object.

TIP

■ ■

Frequently you can achieve effects that are not built into PowerPoint by combining objects like the two lines, or by building the slide across multiple slides. The objects all stay fixed in place from one page to another, and when the screen repaints with the new slide, if the correct transition is used, the viewer cannot detect that they are looking at multiple slides. In the previous example, it would be easy to have this arrow continue to a third or fourth object and back to the first by applying the appropriate effect of wipe down, wipe left, or wipe right.

In other situations the effects of Appear, or Dissolve can frequently be used to achieve special effects that are not natively available through a traditional approach to PowerPoint.

■ ■

Advanced Animation Techniques

Animated objects in PowerPoint move along a straight line path from off the screen to their final location. There is no way to make an object have a starting point other than from outside of the viewable screen. But there are some examples, similar to the arrow in the Transition Build, when you would want the object to start from somewhere within the onscreen frame. You can accomplish this, and it is not that hard—it just takes a few more objects and careful placing of those objects on various layers by bringing them forward or sending them backward until you get the right effect. Figure 4.15 shows the completed slide, which has four arrows that fly in from under the circles that I have drawn.

You can now walk through these steps to re-create this image. I'll break it into two sections. The first will be to create the slide that contains the extra trick to make the arrows start from behind the circles. The second will be to animate the slide, which is quite straightforward.

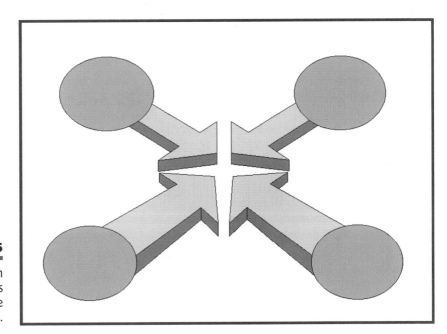

Figure 4.15

Use objects on different levels to achieve special effects.

1. To create the slide, first create a new page using the AutoLayout for a Blank page.

2. Add the arrow clip art (Insert, Picture, Clip Art), which is in the Shapes category of the Clip Gallery. You should select the four arrows that are straight and click on Insert.

3. Immediately ungroup the clip art to convert it to four separate PowerPoint objects by choosing Draw, Ungroup and clicking on Yes in the warning box.

4. Draw the four circles to cover the straight end of the arrow.

5. Now the trick. Using the rectangle toolbar button on the Drawing toolbar, draw four rectangles as shown in Figure 4.15 to create a mask to hide the arrows when they are actually flying in from off the screen.

6. Select all four rectangles by holding down the Shift key and clicking on each rectangle.

7. Right-click the mouse on one of the rectangles and choose Format AutoShape. You will then see the Format AutoShape dialog box.

8. Change the Fill Color to Background by clicking on the Color pull-down menu and clicking on Background.

9. In the Line section of this dialog box, click on the Color pull-down menu and click on No Line. Click OK.

10. Now, the last trick with layers. Select each of the four circles while holding down the Shift key and choose Draw, Order, Bring to Front. Your slide should look just like Figure 4.15.

Take a moment and think about what you have done. You have used an AutoShape and filled it with the background color to make a mask. A mask is simply a term, from the old days of creating artwork manually, to hide objects so that they could not be seen. Any AutoShape can be filled with the background color and be placed anywhere on the screen, and it will pick up the exact color attributes of the background right behind it. This technique even works with gradations so that you don't have to worry about precise color matching of masks against the background color. Now you can quickly finish up this example by adding the animation effect to each of the four arrows.

1. Go to the Custom Animation dialog box by choosing Sli<u>d</u>e Show, Custo<u>m</u> Animation.

2. Select each of the arrow objects by clicking on the Timing window and selecting all four of the arrows, which are called Group 1, Group 2, Group 3, and Group 4. You can do this by holding down the Shift key, as you have done many times today, and selecting the first and last of these objects in the <u>S</u>lide objects without animation window.

3. When all four are selected, Click on <u>A</u>nimate.

4. Now apply the correct animation effect to each arrow object by clicking on the Effects tab. Change the effect for the upper-left arrow to Fly From Top-Left.

5. Change the effect for the upper-right arrow to Fly From Top-Right.

6. Change the effect for the lower-left arrow to Fly From Bottom-Left.

7. Change the effect for the lower-right arrow to Fly From Bottom-Right.

8. To see what it will look like, click on the <u>P</u>review button.

That's all there is to tricking the animation in PowerPoint to do things it isn't completely designed to do. Most animation programs permit you to pick a position for an object to appear and a position for it to end. PowerPoint doesn't. Every object is actually entering from outside of the screen, but you can create layers of other objects to hide the animated object behind to get some interesting effects.

CAUTION Another interesting effect is to use actual objects that are not filled with the background, and by paying careful attention to which layer each object resides on, you can make animated objects pass in front of or behind objects. For example, you could have the school of sharks that were swimming near the sailboat actually pass both in front of and behind the sailboat.

Animation for the Web

An exciting feature of PowerPoint is that PowerPoint presentations can be saved in HTML format and published to your Web page with hyperlinks still active as JPEG or GIF files, the two most common Web file types. Both of those file types, however, are static captures of the page. The animations that you have learned are not replayed for someone when they look at your Web page when you save your files as these file types and publish them to the Web.

FIND IT ON ▶
THE WEB PowerPoint does have a feature for publishing PowerPoint animation files to the Web so that someone viewing your Web site can actually see all of the animation effects you have created in your PowerPoint presentation. You can see an example of a PowerPoint presentation that has been published to my Web site at **http://ourworld.compu-serve.com/homepages/Reilly_and_Associates/**.

Before I cover how to publish your own presentation—complete with all of its animation effects intact—to your Web site, let me explain a little background about PowerPoint animations on the Web.

PowerPoint uses a special player, the PowerPoint Animation Player, to compress the PowerPoint presentation into smaller files for faster transmission across the phone lines of the Internet. Then, when the file arrives on the computer of the person viewing the Web site, the PowerPoint Animation Player program that is available on that local computer decompresses the files on the fly and plays them just like they would look if you viewed them directly on the screen from your own hard drive.

The PowerPoint Animation Player is actually playing the presentation through the browser of the person viewing your site, so it is not necessary for that person to have either PowerPoint or the PowerPoint Viewer loaded on his or her computer. The browser in conjunction with the PowerPoint Animation Player is doing all of the work to display the presentation.

You might ask at this point, if the person visiting the site doesn't already have the PowerPoint Animation Player loaded on his or her machine, how does that person view the PowerPoint presentation on your Web site? That person can't without the Player loaded, but PowerPoint provides an option for that. If people try to view the presentation without the Player loaded, they are informed that they need to have the PowerPoint Animation Player loaded in order to view this Web page presentation, and then PowerPoint offers to automatically load the Player for them. If they choose to load it, and the load time is automatic and only takes a few minutes, they are immediately returned to your Web site, and the presentation starts running. It is really quite a painless experience.

To learn more about what is needed to publish your presentation with animation included, see the Sunday afternoon session in this book, which discusses publishing PowerPoint presentations to the Web in detail.

When you save a PowerPoint presentation for publishing on the Web using File, Save As HTML, you have the option of saving the graphic type as either a GIF, JPEG, or PowerPoint animation. If you save the file as a PowerPoint animation, animations will play back when the presentation is viewed on the Web. You need to use the PowerPoint Animation Player to play back PowerPoint animations on the Web.

FIND IT ON ▶
THE WEB
The PowerPoint Animation Player is available for download at Microsoft's Web site for PowerPoint at **http://www.microsoft.com/powerpoint/default.htm**.

Although saving the file as a PowerPoint animation is not difficult (the wizard does it for you), sometimes you may not see what you expect to see. Unfortunately, the current version of the Animation Player does not handle animation order in the same way that PowerPoint 97 does. So, the Web animation may not play back exactly as the PowerPoint 97 animation does.

What is the difference in how these programs handle the animation? The Animation Player is an older program than PowerPoint 97 and builds animations in layers, just as PowerPoint 95 does. So, you can pay careful attention to what layer an object is on relative to other objects to determine how the animation will play back in the Animation Player. You can use the Draw, Order commands from the menu to send objects forward or backward one level at a time when you try to build your animations for the Web.

Animating Charts

The overall chart object can be animated just as any object in PowerPoint can be animated. New to PowerPoint 97, however, is the capability to animate the objects within charts. You can build and animate the chart categories, series, and even each element within a series. This is different from animating the appearance of the overall chart, as I have been explaining with text and objects.

Animating a chart object will be easy for you because the process is very similar to what you have just learned. Create a new page in a presentation and choose the chart page AutoLayout. Double-click on the Chart placeholder, and then click back into PowerPoint to accept the default chart. Now you'll animate the objects within the chart. Keep in mind that the chart must be selected and you must be in PowerPoint, not Microsoft Graph.

Now you'll add animation to this chart. The animation controls are in the same Custom Animation dialog box, so after you select the chart in Power-Point, choose Slide Show, Custom Animation.

Chart animation effects are all set on their own tab page in this dialog box. Click on the Chart Effects tab. You will see a familiar but slightly different interface to set the animation effects. The Entry Animation and Sound and the After Animation drop-down list boxes are now on the right side of the dialog box. The setting for how to introduce the effects is now on the left side of the dialog box. It strikes me that two different programmers must have designed these two interfaces, one being left-eye dominant and one being right-eye dominant. Either way, it's basically the same interface, except that you may have different effects available depending on the options chosen. Another big difference is that depending on how you introduce the chart elements, the <u>E</u>ntry Animation options change. Perhaps that's why they changed order after all.

Now, to apply an animation effect to this default chart, click on the <u>I</u>ntroduce Chart Elements drop-down list and select By Series. Then, click on the <u>E</u>ntry Animation drop-down list and select Wipe Up.

Make sure that the Ani<u>m</u>ate Grid and Legend isn't selected, because you don't want too much happening here. Click on <u>P</u>review. Changing the settings in <u>I</u>ntroduce Chart Elements and previewing each setting to get a good idea of all the options here is a good idea.

Here are those options for future reference:

Introduce Chart Elements	Comments
All at once	Shows all series and categories simultaneously
by Series	Builds the chart by series across all categories
by Category	Builds the chart by category across all series
by Element in Series	Builds each element (data point) in each series across all categories one at a time
by Element in Category	Builds each data point in a category and then builds the next category

TIP There are a lot of variations in deciding how to build charts. You can click on the Preview button to get a quick example of what the current settings will show.

You are not done with this chart just yet. I said that all of the chart animation effects were set on the Chart Effects tab. That is true, but what about the timings of the effects? Just like any animation effect, the timings of the effects are controlled by the Timing tab of the Custom Animation dialog box. If you have a Title on this page and go to the Timing tab, you can set the order of the Title and the Chart just as you can for any object. When the chart animation effects play, they will play with the timings that are set for them on the Timing tab. See Figure 4.16 for an example of this tab, with both the Title and Chart animated.

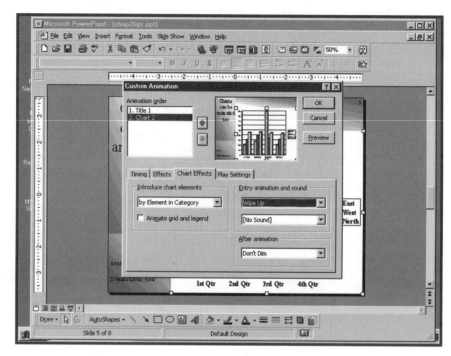

Figure 4.16

Charts can be animated in conjunction with other objects.

Wrapping Up

Congratulations! You have accomplished a great deal last night and today. You are almost a PowerPoint expert. You can now close the book and get a good night's sleep.

We'll get together again in the morning for two sessions to wrap everything together. Pleasant dreams!

How It Is Shown: Transitions and Interactivity

- ✿ Inserting transition effects and timings
- ✿ Creating hyperlinks
- ✿ Linking to other presentations, other programs or files, and Internet sites
- ✿ Planning interactive presentations

Welcome back. You will finish everything today in two easy but important sessions. They are broken into two sessions because they are different topics that require separate ways of thinking about the presentation. The morning session covers two topics: how to finish the presentation by adding transitions between the slides and how to build in interactivity to specific slides so that you can access what you need in non-sequential order.

Adding transitions between slides should be a simple topic because you have learned the basics already in the sessions yesterday. The issue of interactivity can be much more complex because you can do so many things with the interactive features in PowerPoint.

I think you probably know the best examples of interactivity and non-sequential presentation of material: for example, you present the fact that although third-quarter sales results are strong (+10%) for the company, the company president questions why Division 5 is -29%. To be interactive, and more importantly, to keep your job, you would want to address that issue right now and not wait until you've explained the sales results by each division. But there are other ways you can use the interactive potential of PowerPoint.

For example, you might simply want to show a demonstration of some simple custom VBA routines you have created in Excel. Or you may want to immediately jump to an Excel Pivot Table to interactively show various breakdowns of sales by region and division with a chart that updates on the fly, depending on the data you choose in the Pivot Table. Or you may even want to demonstrate your own custom software that connects to your own mainframe back at headquarters. Maybe you want a sales prospect at a trade show to be able to touch a computer screen and be led through a series of trouble-shooting questions to find exactly the right answer for a particular situation—all without your trade show staff having to know everything.

The whole point of interactivity is that no matter how well you think you are prepared for your audience, you may not be. Another one of Reilly's laws is that you can never anticipate everything. Creating an interactive presentation will help you jump to information that you have that you didn't plan to present. This morning's session will illustrate a wide variety of interactive presentations and show you how easy they are to achieve.

The second session covers getting the presentation out the door and into the location where it will be shown. Basically, the underlying word is *publish*. Publishing the presentation is the whole point of the creating the presentation. You should consider the term *publishing* interchangeable with the word *presenting*. That brings you full circle to the end, which is where you started on Friday evening.

So, if you have had your second cup of coffee and at least the first bite of breakfast, it's time to get started. I want you to have time to do something else this weekend, whether it's watching the sports broadcast of the day or doing the laundry. After all, PowerPoint should not be your entire life. It should just be another tool in your toolbox that you know how to use.

Slide Transitions

Slide transitions are special effects that smooth the transition from one page to the next. We have all been in the typical meeting given on overhead projectors in which the presenter fumbles with the next page while taking the last page off the overhead projector. I think of those situations as the base level of transitions. Everything that is a little smoother can only be better than the base level. PowerPoint and virtually all presentation

packages have made smoothing these potentially embarrassing transitions easier with a host of prerecorded transition effects.

You should already be used to many of the effects; you see them every time you watch the evening news. The broadcast cuts from one story to another, or dissolves into another subject in the same story, or fades to a commercial. If you pay attention to these transitions in television, or movies, for that matter, you will see that each of these transitions does prepare you for the next piece of film. You would probably never see a fade or a dissolve used when cutting from one person talking to another person in a very intense conversation. Why? Because the fade and dissolve transitions carry with them a connotation of the elapse of time. An intense conversation, on the other hand, is immediate. You would use direct cuts from one face yelling at the other, to the other face yelling back. Note that the transition is immediate and does not suggest the elapse of more than a millisecond.

In summary, transitions are now just pretty effects between two images on the screen. Transitions carry meaning. It's the same thing with transitions between slides in PowerPoint. Many of the same kinds of transitions that you are accustomed to from television are available in PowerPoint—not every last one, but certainly more than the basic transitions. The trick is to learn how to apply them, which is quite simple. You also need to know when to apply one, and which one to use.

Transition Effects

Slide transition effects are very similar to animation effects. In fact, many have the same name and look identical. The biggest difference is that the effect applies to the entire page and not to any individual object on the page. As with animation effects, you can set the transition to occur either on a mouse click or by a predetermined amount of time. A slide transition can also be accompanied by a sound just as with animation effects. The biggest difference between transition effects and animation effects is that transition effects can be set to happen at three different speeds—slow, medium, and fast. Slide Transitions are set using the menu command Slide Show, Slide Transition (see Figure 5.1). You then see the Slide Transition dialog box, in which you actually set the transitions, as shown in Figure 5.2.

The Slide Transition dialog box has a preview window, which automatically shows you what the transition effect will look like as you select an effect. Taking a minute and stepping through each of the transitions to see what they look like in the preview at the Slow and the Fast speed is a good idea.

You can apply slide transitions in two different views in PowerPoint. The first way, which I have just shown, is done in Slide view. Slide view gives you the choice of applying a single transition, either to one slide only or the entire presentation. To apply a transition to just the current slide, click on Apply. For the latter choice, use Apply to All.

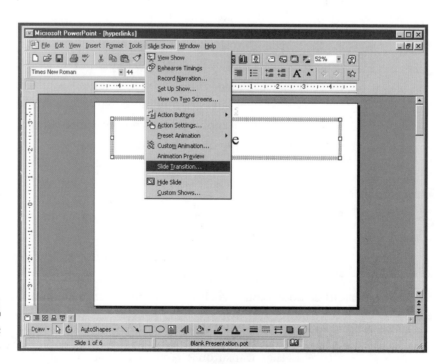

Figure 5.1

Transitions are
easy to set.

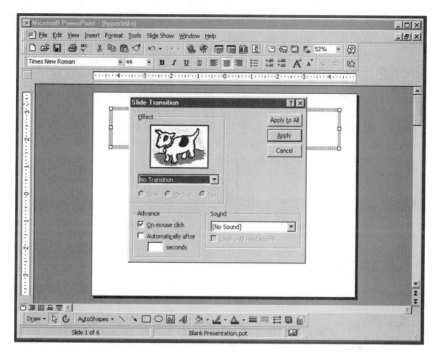

Figure 5.2

Slide transitions
are much like
animation settings.

The other way to apply slide transitions is to switch to Slide Sorter view and select multiple slides by holding down the Shift key and clicking on the slides that you want to select. Then you can apply a specific transition to multiple, even noncontiguous slides, simultaneously. See Figure 5.3 to identify the icons for setting transitions while in Slide Sorter view.

Transition Timings

You have the option of setting three different timings to slide transitions: slow, medium, and fast. Generally, using fast timings for most of the presentation is best. You really want the audience to focus on the content, not on the effects.

You can use the slow transition timings, however, to serve as a subtle clue that the next point is either a different subject or a very important subject.

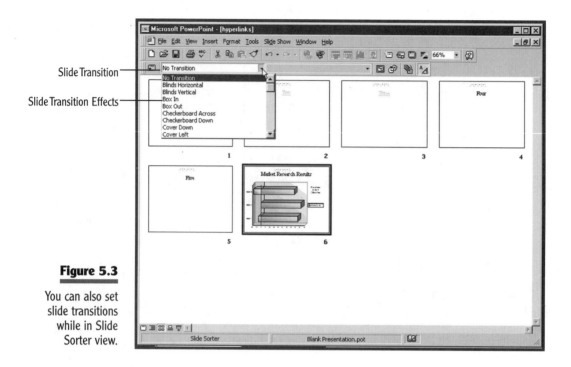

Figure 5.3

You can also set slide transitions while in Slide Sorter view.

To set the transition timing for a specific transition, make sure you are in the Slide Transition dialog box, as shown previously in Figure 5.2.

TIP

A good technique is to use one transition, such as wipe right or wipe down, for almost every transition and set the transition speed to fast. This technique keeps the audience focused on the content. When you change subjects in the presentation, you should use a completely different transition, such as dissolve, and set it to slow. This subtly lets your audience know that something different is coming.

Advancing Slides by Preset Times

You already know how to set timings on slide transitions because it is exactly the same as setting timings with animation objects. To keep your presentations interesting, and especially to get complex thoughts across in a simple way, you should consider mixing automatic slide advances with manual advances. For example, when you change subjects within a presentation, you might string several slides together with automatic advances every second to give a little preview of the kinds of things that the audience might expect in the next part of the presentation.

For example, say that you were giving a presentation on the contents of PowerPoint's clip art. You would probably divide this presentation into different sections. Each section would then cover in detail each piece of clip art in the section. In this case, when you want to stop talking about the animal category and start talking about the people category, you might string a series of slides together with automatic timings and show all of the contents of the people category before starting in and discussing each one in detail.

Although setting the timings for slide transitions is very much the same as setting timings for animations, let me run through the steps again just in case you skipped that section.

1. Choose Slide Show, Slide Transition.

2. In the Slide Transition dialog box, select an effect in the Effect group box, and then click on Slow, Medium, or Fast depending on the speed of the transition you want to apply.

3. In the Advance group box, you should set how you want to be able to advance the slide. You can advance either On mouse click or Automatically after x seconds. The x represents the number of seconds you need to specify, which can be any number of seconds greater than 0 and less than 9999. For the record, if you wanted to know some PowerPoint trivia, 9999 seconds is two hours, forty-six minutes, and thirty-nine seconds.

4. In the Sound group box you can apply a sound. If you do apply a sound, the check box next to Loop until next sound is activated for checking or not. Check it if you want the sound to loop until a sound is activated on the next slide automatically. In addition to

the standard choices of pre-recorded sounds to apply to slide transitions, you can also apply Other sound. See the session on Saturday afternoon concerning animation effects about inserting or recording your own custom sound effects.

This Slide Transition dialog box is available either from the Slide View mode or from the Slide Sorter View mode, and there is no difference in the transition effects or timings that you can set. The availability of the dialog box just gives you two different ways to accomplish exactly the same thing.

Interactive Presentations

Interactivity is the word of the moment. It not only applies to the Internet, but it is even bigger than the Internet. Interactivity also applies to electronic presentations given in any electronic environment.

Table 5.1 shows a few real world examples of interactivity:

TABLE 5.1 EXAMPLES OF INTERACTIVITY	
ATMs (Automated Teller Machines)	Who could live without a withdrawal on a Saturday night at 1 am. Or any other time, for that matter. Just stop at the machine.
Voicemail systems	Press 1 to leave a message for me. Press 2 to leave a message for my boss. Press 0 to talk to the Operator who isn't here right now.
Looking for this book in the bookstore's computer	Please ask them what shelf it is on.
Programming a VCR	That may be too tough for most of us.
A reception desk lookup screen to find a company or person in a building	A hypertext lookup system at its simplest.

Who could live without these simple interactive environments? The electronic presentation world is not only no different but potentially much more powerful than any of these simple little programs. And that is what these examples are: simple little computer programs that basically jump you from one place to another without having to get there sequentially.

Take the ATM situation. You have the option of withdrawing cash, depositing cash (hopefully sometimes), paying bills, transferring money to your cash advance line, and so on. You wouldn't want to step through each of these choices with all of the options available to make your one transaction. And you certainly wouldn't want to see all of the information available. For example, you don't need to see what your remaining balance is and what checks have already been cashed if all you need is $100 cash for the evening. If you didn't get the $100 dollars on the first try, you might be very interested in more detail about how much your current balance really is, whether your rent check had already cleared, or whether that check won't clear.

That's real world interactivity. Presentation world interactivity isn't much different. And it can be much more powerful without you having to really learn all of the underlying programming code to make it happen.

One of the most valuable capabilities of PowerPoint presentations is the ability to create completely interactive presentations so that you can present your story in a non-sequential order. You can jump, at the click of the mouse, not only to another slide in the same presentation but also to another presentation altogether. But that's not all. Two other valuable interactive capabilities are built into PowerPoint. You can even jump to a Web site or launch another application, whether it be an Excel worksheet to see all of the details about particular expense items or to your own computer back in your office in another state to look up a particular client's orders and accounts payable status.

You can make any of these jumps right from within PowerPoint without closing the slide show or closing PowerPoint. When you are done checking on the other information, you can be right back in the same location in your presentation if you wish to be.

Face it, PowerPoint assembles and presents information very well, but it is a terrible spreadsheet and a worse database manager. And PowerPoint wouldn't have the slightest clue about understanding your accounting system. But PowerPoint knows how to let you jump to each and every one of those applications and is polite enough to let you run those applications right from within the PowerPoint presentation.

All this means is that you can have your cake and eat it, too. Well, sort of. Hyperlinks are wonderful things; they will take you just about anywhere you want to go, as long as you plan ahead.

How do hyperlinks work? They are really just *Jump To* commands that jump you from where you are to the target. That target can be any of the following:

- ❂ another slide in the same presentation—even hidden slides
- ❂ the first slide in another presentation
- ❂ any slide in another presentation
- ❂ any other program (a program with an .exe extension)
- ❂ any other file
- ❂ a specific location in some other files, for example, a named range or a bookmark
- ❂ a specific URL on the Internet

I think you can see the power of using interactive links to get at any information you wish to access during a PowerPoint presentation. Seems to be the premise for the Microsoft advertising campaign, "Where do you want to go today?"

Creating Hyperlinks

There are two different interfaces you can use to create hyperlinks. Both ways perform the same activity when you run the slide show and click on a hyperlink. The two interfaces are really just that: two different interfaces.

Shortly, you will learn about both interfaces. First there is one last fundamental concept to be sure that you understand about hyperlinks. You can attach hyperlinks to any object on a page; also, and this is important, they can be attached to any object on a Slide Master page. Now you'll create a few simple hyperlinks to see how to set them and identify some of the issues concerning how they work. Because this exercise does not concern graphics but rather focuses on hyperlinks, you should quickly create a simple five-page presentation. To save time, just fill in the title of each page with a number from one to five so that you know which page you are on.

If you need the steps to follow, try this:

1. Choose File, New. Click on the General tab and double-click on Blank Presentation.

2. Double-click on the 11th AutoLayout (named Title Only).

3. Type **One** for a Title and press Ctrl+M for a new slide. Press Enter because the AutoLayout defaults to the last one chosen.

4. Type **Two** for a Title; then, press Ctrl+M and Enter again.

5. Add pages for **Three, Four,** and **Five.**

Now you will create a few hyperlinks in this presentation using an interface available under the Slide Show, Action Settings commands on the menu. You will add your first hyperlink to jump from page two to page four.

1. Save the file. It is recommended that you always save files before creating hyperlinks because the link is path and filename specific.

2. In Slide view, press PgUp until you get to Slide 2 in your presentation.

3. Select the Title placeholder, Choose Slide Show, Action Settings. If Action Settings is grayed out in your menu, you haven't selected anything.

Now you will actually set the hyperlink to Slide 4, which has the Title Four.

4. You set the hyperlinks in the Action Settings dialog box. Click on Hyperlink To, and then set the link in the drop-down list immediately below that.

5. In this case, click on Slide as shown in Figure 5.4. Doing so opens another dialog box showing a list of the titles of all of the available slides in this presentation.

6. In the Slide Title list, click on Four. Notice that you get a small preview of Slide 4 in the preview window, as shown in Figure 5.5.

7. Click on OK to select that slide.

8. Click on OK on the Action Settings dialog box to return to Slide view.

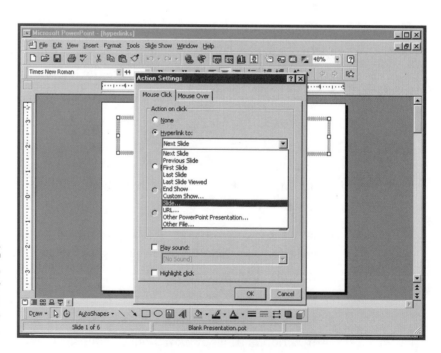

Figure 5.4

Set a hyperlink to another slide by choosing Slide in the Hyperlink To drop-down list.

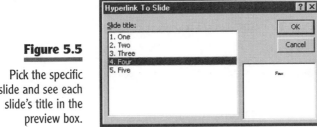

Figure 5.5

Pick the specific slide and see each slide's title in the preview box.

If you have not changed any of the defaults in the Color palette, you should see the Title <u>Two</u> in a different color and underlined to indicate that it is a hyperlink. Run the slide show now by backing up to Slide 1 (press PgUp) and clicking on the Slide Show icon at the bottom-left corner of the screen. You can click the mouse to advance from slide to slide. If you return to Slide 2 and place your mouse over the Title <u>Two</u>, you will see the mouse cursor change to the pointing hand, indicating that this object is a hyperlink. If you click the mouse on the hyperlink object in Slide Show view, you will jump immediately to the target, page Four.

Another issue concerning Action Settings is whether you want to have the action take place by a mouse click or set it to happen when the mouse just passes over the object. The same commands are available on the two separate dialog box tabs in the Action Settings dialog box. You can choose to set your action settings to one or the other, or both. These settings are available by choosing either the Mouse Click or the Mouse Over tabs in the Action Settings dialog box. If you have set your hyperlinks by using Insert, <u>H</u>yperlinks, the default setting will be for the hyperlink to be active only by mouse click.

The fundamentals of hyperlinks are that simple, but this little exercise does point out some planning problems. You are now at Slide 4 and have skipped Slide 3. You may want to do just that, or you may want to return to Slide 2 to continue from where you left off. Keep in mind that no automatic command exists to take you back to the location from which you jumped. You will have to assign another hyperlink to Slide 4 to decide where to jump to, unless you just want to continue on to page 5.

You have two different ways to do that. The first way is to place a variety of objects on a page and assign individual hyperlinks to each object. Doing so is appropriate when the locations that you might want to jump to will vary depending on where you currently are. In this case, you might want to be able to make a decision about where to go, either to Slide 2, *or* to yet another entirely different presentation to further explain the information on Slide 4. If you do that, you will need to have two different objects available on Slide 4 so that you can decide which way to proceed.

TIP

Keep in mind that you don't have to use a hyperlink to proceed; you can click the mouse or press Enter and proceed forward, just as you can from any page. Nothing special has happened to the underlying presentation. You have just *jumped to* this location. All other underlying properties, such as transitions and animation settings, are intact.

Another way to handle this transition, which is much more Web-like in feel, is to place the hyperlink targets on the Slide Master. If you do, they will be available on every page. You'll do that next; just keep in mind that this example uses pages with titles that correspond to page numbers. This example adds hyperlinks on the Slide Master to every page so that you can access any page from every page.

You may want to consider placing icons on the Slide Master page that will permit you to jump to various sections rather than every page. A good example of this type of icon placement is the aforementioned hypothetical presentation on all of the Clip Art categories in PowerPoint Clip Art. In that case, you could create small icons for each of the categories, such as animals, buildings, and so on. Because these hyperlinks would be incorporated into the Slide Master design, you could set the hyperlink for each of these to the appropriate first page of each section.

Go ahead and place hyperlinks to all pages on the Slide Master page. If you have this five-page presentation open, choose View, Master, Slide Master to get to the Slide Master page. Now add a Text Box to the very top of the page above the title and type 1 - 2 - 3 - 4 - 5 in the text box. Then, center the text box on the page, as shown in Figure 5.6.

To set the hyperlinks for each page, you (obviously) will attach a hyperlink to page one to the number 1 on the Slide Master, a hyperlink to page two to the number 2, and so on. You set these by doing the following steps:

1. Select just the 1 in the text box by dragging over that character with the mouse (see Figure 5.7).

2. Choose Slide Show, Action Settings to display the Action Settings dialog box.

3. Click on the option button for Hyperlink To.

4. Click on the drop-down arrow just below that and select Slide; then, click on One in the Slide Title list box (see Figure 5.8).

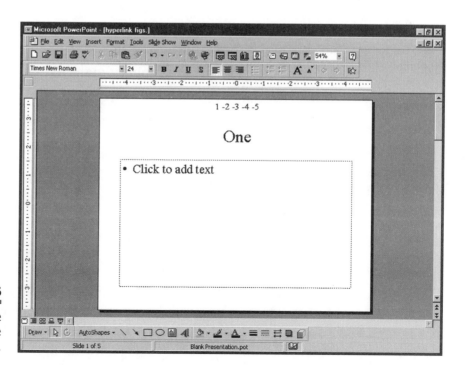

Figure 5.6

Place the hyperlinks on the Slide Master page.

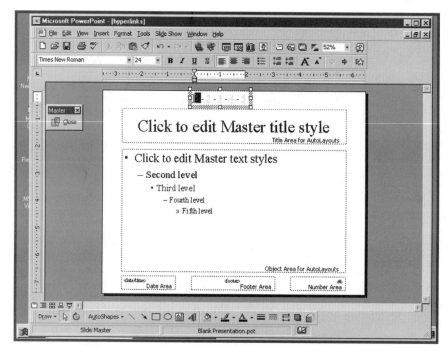

Figure 5.7

To attach the
hyperlink to a
selection of text,
drag over that text
with the mouse.

5. Click on OK twice to return to Slide view on the Slide Master.

6. Repeat these steps for each number in the text box and choose the appropriate slide to link to.

Now run the show by clicking on the Slide Show icon at the bottom-left corner of the page. You will be able to jump to any page from every page by clicking on one of the hyperlinks. Or, you can advance to the next slide in the presentation directly by clicking the mouse anywhere but on a hyperlink or by pressing Enter or PgDn. Press Esc to end the presentation from any slide.

TIP   This example uses simple page numbers so that you can keep track of what page you are jumping to, but you can easily design a graphically interesting background on the Slide Master and attach various hyperlinks to various graphics objects.

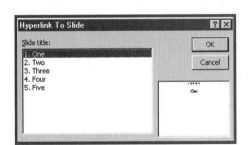

Figure 5.8

Select the slide
you want to link
to and click on OK.

That covers how to create hyperlinks to another page in the same presentation. But hyperlinks can do much more for you. Hyperlinks to several other options are also available. You can jump to another Power-Point Presentation, another file altogether—such as an Excel or Word file—a Web site, or even a completely different application. You will now walk through each of these possibilities, which will also show you the second interface for establishing and managing hyperlinks.

NOTE Interactive presentations can be a tremendous way to provide much flexibility to presentations. They truly take the constraints of linear thinking away from you and give you great power. But, hyperlinks do require planning so that you don't end up on a one way street with no return. See the section "Planning Interactive Presentations" later in this chapter.

Linking to Other Presentations

Changing the target of your hyperlink employs much the same method as opening any file. You just select the object to set as the hyperlink object, as you have already learned to do. Then, rather than choose another slide in the same presentation to link to, you choose:

1. Slide Show, Action Settings, and then click on Hyperlink To and select Other PowerPoint Presentation from the drop-down list, as shown in Figure 5.9.

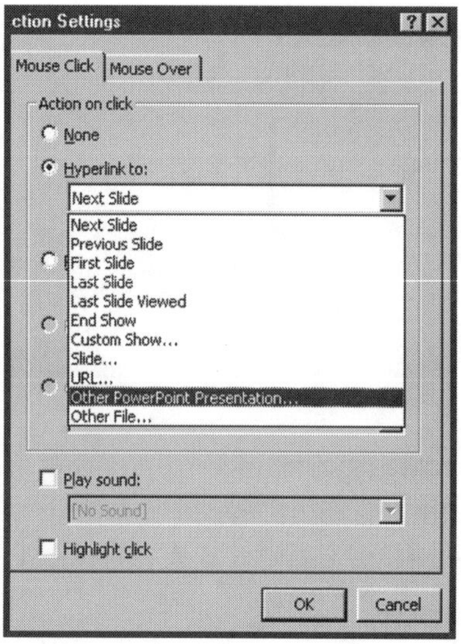

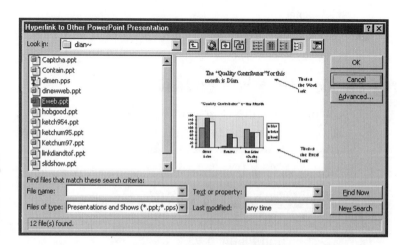

Figure 5.9

Select Other
PowerPoint
Presentation to link
to a completely
different
presentation.

2. A dialog box appears that will enable you to find and select the file to which to link. Using this dialog box, shown in Figure 5.10, find the correct file and click on OK.

3. A dialog box appears, as shown in Figure 5.11, from which you select the specific page to link to, and it will show you the page title text.

Figure 5.10

You can link to
any presentation
by finding it on
your drive.

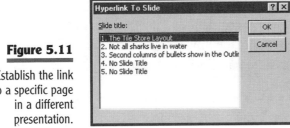

Figure 5.11

Establish the link to a specific page in a different presentation.

The look and feel is very much like the previous dialog box, which enabled you to link to a different page in the same presentation. The only real difference is that you have to tell PowerPoint the file to which to link.

Clearly, using hyperlinks to other presentations and to a specific page in a presentation can let you jump around like a frog on a hot sidewalk. But don't forget to leave some bread crumbs to find your way home. There are three ways to get back to the departure point: establish another hyperlink from that targeted presentation to go where you want to go, finish that presentation, or hit the Esc key.

What happens when you launch the hyperlink to another PowerPoint presentation is that you are launching a second copy of the Power-Point Slide Show on top of the current presentation. To demonstrate this to yourself, you can create a hyperlink to another presentation as outlined previously, and when you are in the second presentation press Alt+Tab to see the other programs that are open at this time. There will at least be one copy of PowerPoint (the underlying edit mode program), and two copies of PowerPoint Slide Show.

Linking to Other Programs or Files

Not all of your supporting data exists in PowerPoint files. You may need to show backup support of detailed expenses in an Excel spreadsheet or show a long list of employees earning bonuses in a table in a Word document. Just like you can create a hyperlink to another PowerPoint presentation, you can also create hyperlinks to other files such as Excel or Word files. And if you have used defined range names in Excel or bookmarks in Word, you can point the link right to that location just like you pointed the link to a specific page in PowerPoint.

CAUTION

The biggest difference to hyperlinking to a named range in Excel or a bookmark in Word is that you need to know the name of the range or bookmark. You cannot browse for the name like you can browse through the pages in a PowerPoint presentation.

The hyperlinking capabilities in PowerPoint are so powerful that you can even link to a completely different program or a specific file in some other program. For example, say that you are giving a market research presentation and the real source data is in an Excel file called Research_Results.xls. You can create a hyperlink that will actually open the Research Results.xls file in Excel so that you can show whatever detailed support you need. If you had created the hyperlink from this particular chart, when you then click on the hyperlink, you can open the Research Results.xls file directly on top of the existing screen show and run Excel in the foreground (see Figure 5.13). You can then move around in Excel and answer any detailed questions that your audience might ask by showing them the actual underlying data.

These steps will show you the second interface for creating hyperlinks in PowerPoint. This example will use an Excel file named Research Results with a named range called my_range, as shown in Figure 5.12. To create this hyperlink:

1. In PowerPoint, select the object you are going to use as the hyperlink object and the choose Insert, Hyperlink (or Ctrl+K).

2. You will see the Insert Hyperlink dialog box, which has two drop-down boxes and two Browse Buttons. Click on the first Browse button.

3. You will see the familiar Explorer-like interface for the Link to File

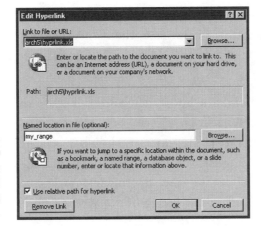

Figure 5.12

Browse for the
file to link to and
type in the
named range.

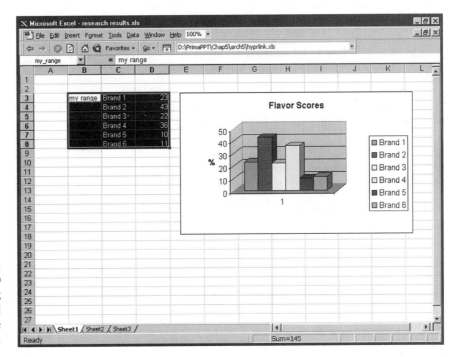

Figure 5.13

The hyperlink
opens Excel and
selects the
designated range.

dialog box. Select the correct folder and the correct file and click
on OK. The path and filename are recorded automatically in the
Link to file or URL drop-down box.

4. You can now link directly to the named range, although you cannot browse for it. In this case, the named range is my_range, so I will just type that in the <u>N</u>amed location in file (optional) text box. Then Click on OK.

Now if you were in Slide Show view and clicked on that Excel hyperlink object, you would launch Excel and automatically select the range my_range. When you are done with what you need in this Excel document, you can just minimize or close Excel, and you will return to the PowerPoint Slide Show where you left it. The Slide Show was left running maximized in the background, which you can check by using the Ctrl+Tab command to see what programs are still running in the background.

If you had not selected a named range for this Excel hyperlink, you would have just opened up the Excel document. The same procedure works for Word and Word bookmarks.

TIP

▪ ▪

If you have a tremendous amount of data to present along with charts of that data—such as interest rates for various periods for various countries—rather than creating each chart for each country, you could create a hyperlink in PowerPoint to a named range in Excel that contains a Pivot Table with a chart on the worksheet page that is sourced in that Pivot Table range. Then you could just use the Pivot Table to select which country or period to look at, and the chart would be instantly redrawn.

With a little knowledge of Visual Basic for Applications (VBA), You could even hide the Excel toolbars, menus, and even change the caption at the top of the sheet. Combining those steps with turning off gridlines in Excel and filling the visible cells with the same background color as PowerPoint will disguise that you are even running Excel.

▪ ▪

There are many uses for launching other programs from within PowerPoint. You can use hyperlinking in situations such as the one just mentioned to have endless amounts of additional backup support data at your fingertips, and only show what you need to at that moment. Another use of hyperlinking from PowerPoint to an outside file is that you can launch any other file or program on your computer from within PowerPoint, and then return seamlessly right back to PowerPoint when you are done.

This is a particularly useful tool for the following situations:

- Running demonstrations of custom proprietary applications, such as a special accounting package or database application
- Running existing Freelance Graphics or Harvard Graphics presentations without having to suffer through translating them into PowerPont
- Running high-end multimedia segments from a program such as Director

You can just point the hyperlink at that program file and let it start right up from within your PowerPoint presentation.

You don't need to exit any programs, especially if you might want to come back to the program later in the presentation. Just minimize the other program and continue your presentation. If you then use another hyperlink to jump back to that program, the hyperlink will maximize the program where you left it.

The simplest way to demonstrate this capability is to launch a simple program that I know you have on your computer. Calculator is a free-standing program and comes with windows and choices that will show you all of the steps you need to run anything. No matter what program you run, the steps are exactly the same—only the program name will change, probably to protect the innocent.

To run another program from a hyperlink in PowerPoint, select an object in your presentation to be the hyperlink object and choose Slide Show, Action Settings, and then follow these steps:

1. Click the option button for Run program.
2. The Browse button will become active. Browse to find the Calc.exe file. My copy is loaded in C:\Windows. Select Calc.exe and click

on OK. (You many not see the .exe in your dialog box depending on how your computer preferences are set.)

3. You will see the text box for Run program: on the Action Settings dialog box filled in with the path to that file and the name of the file. Click on OK.

When you run the PowerPoint Slide Show and click on the hyperlink to the Calculator program, the Calculator program is started in its own window in front of the PowerPoint Slide Show, which stays maximized in the background as shown in Figure 5.14.

Linking to Internet Sites

Who can talk about anything without wanting to link to the Internet these days? PowerPoint 97 will certainly let you do that as well. If you have a valid connection to the Internet loaded on your computer and

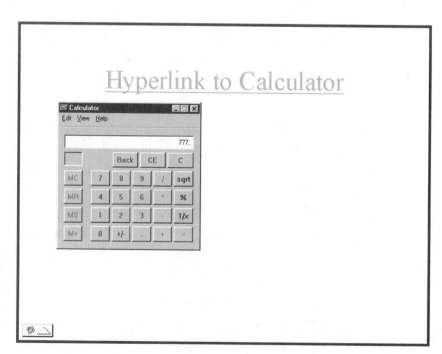

Figure 5.14

Calculator is started in its own window in front of the PowerPoint Slide Show.

you want to create a hyperlink to a specific Web site, just point your hyperlink to a URL address. You'll be surfing the Net from within your presentation as soon as you click on the hyperlink to a URL.

Well, maybe not just as soon as you click. Although you can launch hyperlinks to Web sites from a presentation given on your computer, the hyperlink has a lot of work to do before you actually see the site to which you have linked. The Internet connection has to be made. On my computer, a dialog box asks me to confirm that I do want to connect. If I click on Connect, it can take awhile to dial up my ISP and confirm my password, and then find the URL to which I am linked. Although you will get there most of the time, you may be in for some surprises due to busy phone lines and other variables out of the control of PowerPoint.

Additionally, if you are on POTS (Plain Old Telephone Service) phone lines, the connection will be slow. This may actually be devastating to the timing of a presentation. You should use this technique of linking from a computer presentation with caution. My feeling is the hyperlink to URL sites is much more appropriate for creating presentations for the Web, and then linking from your Web page to other Web sites. But you are the boss of your own presentations, so I'll show you the steps to establish hyperlinks from a PowerPoint presentation to a Web site. The steps are the same whether you are trying to establish the connection from the hyperlink on your own computer or from the same hyperlink on your Web site.

To establish a hyperlink to a Web site (URL), select the object to use as the hyperlink. Then, follow these steps:

1. Choose Insert, Hyperlink (or Ctrl+K) to view the Insert Hyperlink dialog box.
2. Pull down the Link to file or URL drop-down box.
3. Select a URL from the list that is the most recently visited Web sites or presentations viewed using your browser. If you do not find the correct site, just type in the URL address. Click OK.

That's all there is to adding a hyperlink to a URL in PowerPoint. That hyperlink will be active in Slide Show view when you run a slide show on your computer. It also will be active if you publish this slide show to your Web site either as HTML pages or as a PowerPoint Animation.

Planning Interactive Presentations

If you know where you want to go today, you will benefit by having a roadmap. Using hyperlinks will give you the opportunity to appear absolutely prepared for any possible outcome. You'll be able to have endless details merely a click or two away from any slide. You'll be able to switch seamlessly between applications and back to your presentation. You'll also be able to get yourself into trouble and freeze up your computer during the presentation if you are not careful. Here are a few final thoughts for planning interactive presentations to keep you out of trouble and keep you looking like a star.

Navigating

Before you start preparing the presentation, decide how interactive you need the presentation to be.

If you only need to be able to jump to another location or file infrequently, you can just keep track of likely places you want to jump from and create hyperlinks at those locations. Then, decide how you want to navigate from that hyperlinked location. If it's a hyperlink to another presentation, you realize that you can get back to the original location by pressing the Esc key or by finishing that presentation. But consider whether you will want to hyperlink from that second presentation to another location. If so, you may want to establish a hyperlink back to the first presentation, or else you will have to step back with the Esc key, going through every intermediate presentation.

If you do establish the hyperlink back, you need to recognize that you will now have four programs running at a minimum: PowerPoint, PowerPoint Slide Shows #1, #2, and #3. That's not so bad if you have a fairly good computer with adequate RAM and plenty of free disk space for virtual memory.

What if you now open up Excel and work with that? Should you minimize it so that it opens quickly with the next Excel hyperlink, or should you close it to conserve memory and accept that if you launch another hyperlink to Excel you will have to wait for Excel to be opened again?

What if you establish hyperlinks to URL sites to connect from your computer during a presentation? I already warned you about the connection times being potentially slow or the site being unavailable for some reason. If you still must (maybe you are a salesperson and the site is your company's homepage that you need to demonstrate), you should plan a short discussion to fill the dead air time while waiting for the connection. And a few jokes about the Internet and why it doesn't always work as planned might work well here. Forewarned is forearmed much of the time.

If you need to be able to jump almost anywhere from almost anywhere, you should build that flexibility into the design. In a case like that, you might add flexibility to the structure by designing one central simple presentation that has links to all of the other potential places you may need to go and automatically return there after each subject matter is completed. In fact, it's a good idea to place a hyperlink back to the central location on the Slide Master page of each separate presentation. You don't necessarily need to place any hyperlinks back in your Word or Excel documents or other files because you could just choose to minimize or close those applications directly.

If this last route seems to be what might work for you, you could also consider designing separate objects into the primary design of this core presentation and attaching the hyperlinks to the appropriate object. For example, you may be doing a presentation for an annual meeting and needed to cover the following areas:

- Sales Results
- Financial Results
- Forecast for the Future
- New Products
- Status of the Outstanding Product Recall

You might design a one-page presentation that had five objects, each hyperlinked to the appropriate presentation, spreadsheets, or Word documents. If you designed this well, you could clearly give more design emphasis and space to the first four issues and very little space to the Product Recall subject. When you get to the question and answer period, if you did get questions on the Product Recall, you could still get to that information easily because the hyperlink would be tied to one of the objects on the page.

The trick to interactive presentations is in the planning and in the design of how to get around easily. Good luck with the tool. It can be used in many imaginative ways and be very powerful.

Wrapping Up

Well done, you are almost there. You have just one section left to cover, and then you will be a first-class PowerPoint expert! The last section is easy, but it is extremely important. All of your brilliant work so far will be a failure if the presentation isn't shown correctly.

So, take a short break, and then you can finish.

How It Is Shown:
Finishing Touches
and Distribution

- ✿ Rehearsing slide timings and transitions
- ✿ Distributing your presentation
- ✿ Presenting to an audience at a meeting or on your Web site

Welcome back. You now have learned everything about how to design and create your own fabulous presentations in Power-Point. But you haven't done the most important thing yet—give the presentation. As I stated at the beginning of the book, the whole purpose of the presentation is the *effective* communication, not the *preparation*, of the content.

If you don't pull off the actual delivery of the presentation, everything will have been for naught!

You shouldn't have any problems with the final steps because PowerPoint is generally a well-behaved software package. But to make sure that you don't run into any problems, this chapter discusses the ins and outs of actually getting the presentation out the door, so to speak. So read on. You'll find a lot of tips on what to do and some troubleshooting tips for typical problems that you might run into.

As you read each of these issues, keep in mind that you will probably want to come back to this chapter in the future as you do different kinds of presentations. Many of the issues deal with specific problems rather than the general issues of showing all presentations.

How it is shown is the last step in the presentation cycle. But it was also the first thing that I discussed at the start of this book. You have now come full circle and are back to the end. These final steps are often the

most important steps in getting the presentation out the door and unfortunately almost always occur when there is not enough time to make significant changes when you encounter problems.

That is why I so strongly recommend that you always start at the end, before you make any mistakes that will create problems for you when you are almost done and under the pressure of the rapidly approaching deadline. If you have clearly defined the end result before you start creating a presentation, you will be able to test some of the more obvious issues that may come up and bite you at the last minute.

These may be issues such as the following: the fonts and bullets all changed on another computer; the sound won't play; the file won't fit onto one floppy disk; the text is covered by solid boxes when printing; the projector cuts off part of your screen; a specific slide takes too long to load. The list can be endless. If you have planned the presentation correctly, however, the list should be very short or nonexistent.

Now you'll explore how to finalize a presentation so that it will be successful.

Finalizing the Presentation

Great, all of your pages are done. You think you are finished. Almost, but not quite. Have you gone through every page to look for inconsistencies? Are all of the headlines consistent in style? Do the headings all use no punctuation, or have a few periods crept in without you noticing? Have you been consistent in your use of initial caps on words, or are you consistently using sentence style? Are all of the pages consistent in these areas? Have you run the spell-checker?

PowerPoint can help with some of these areas, but checking for these inconsistencies is really your responsibility.

If you do want some help from PowerPoint, you can use the Style Checker, but you should only do so after carefully setting the options that you want. Take a few minutes to examine the Style Checker, which

will help make your presentations consistent in a variety of areas if you choose to use it.

You can access the Style Checker any time that a presentation is open. You don't have to wait until you are finalizing the presentation. First, look at the options that you can select with the Style Checker. Choose Tools, Style Checker, as shown in Figure 6.1. Click on the Options button in the Style Checker dialog box (see Figure 6.2).

You are presented with two tabs in the Style Checker Options dialog box; the first tab is for Case and End Punctuation. On this sheet, you set the Case preferences for both the Slide Title Style and for the Body Text Style. There are five different settings for checking the Case of your text (see Figure 6.3).

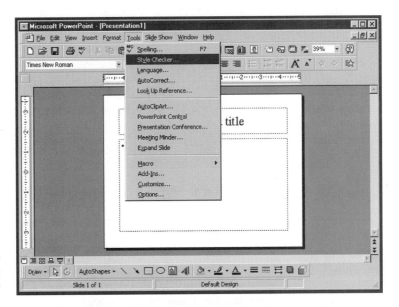

Figure 6.1

PowerPoint 97's
Style Checker

Figure 6.2

In addition to spelling, you can use the Style Checker to check for visual clarity, as well as case usage and end punctuation.

Figure 6.3

You can change the
Case settings on
the Case and End
Punctuation tab.

With End Punctuation, you have three options. You can choose to Remove, Add, or Ignore end punctuation altogether. Again, the End Punctuation settings can be set differently for both the Titles and the Body Text.

◆◆◆◆◆◆◆◆◆◆◆◆◆◆◆◆◆◆◆◆◆◆◆◆◆◆◆◆◆◆◆◆◆◆◆◆◆

CAUTION Text that is entered into a text box is not checked for style, but is checked for spelling. Text that is entered in a chart in Microsoft Graph is not checked for style, spelling, or punctuation.

◆◆◆◆◆◆◆◆◆◆◆◆◆◆◆◆◆◆◆◆◆◆◆◆◆◆◆◆◆◆◆◆◆◆◆◆◆

The other tab in the Style Checker Options dialog box is the Visual Clarity tab. This page contains another seven options for you to determine whether any pages in your presentation might be more complex, and therefore possibly unclear to your audience. Six of these settings can be increased or decreased in value by you. One of the settings can be set only to on or off. Table 6.1 shows the settings for Visual Clarity and their default settings.

After you have set the options to your own settings, click on OK to accept them. You can check the current presentation against these style settings

TABLE 6.1 — SETTINGS FOR VISUAL CLARITY AND THEIR DEFAULT SETTINGS

Visual Clarity Setting	Default Setting Number	Default Setting On/Off
Number of fonts should not exceed:	3	On
Title text size should be at least:	36	On
Body text size should be at least:	24	On
Number of bullets should not exceed:	6	On
Number of lines per title should not exceed:	2	On
Number of lines per bullet should not exceed:	2	On
Check for title and placeholder text off slide	N/A	On

immediately by clicking on the <u>S</u>tart button in the Style Checker dialog box. If you don't want to check the presentation right away, you can click on Cancel, and the settings for the Style Checker options will be saved. The check boxes for the Style Checker dialog box, Sp<u>e</u>lling, <u>V</u>isual Clarity, and <u>C</u>ase and end punctuation are always checked when you start Style Checker.

Any time in the future, you can check the style of the presentation using the saved settings by choosing <u>T</u>ools, St<u>y</u>le Checker, and then clicking on Start.

You have already seen that the Style Checker does not check everything. It does, however, change everything that does not fit the style. So be careful if you have anything that you might not want to change. If you have a presentation that may, for very valid reasons, have some inconsistencies in the style that you want to keep inconsistent, don't use the Style Checker. A good example is when you want to use sentence style and you include names that should be capitalized, such as the first and last name of people in the audience. The Style Checker would erroneously change those uppercase letters to lowercase (see Figure 6.4).

You should determine in the very first step of starting a presentation how the particular presentation is to be shown. How it is shown affects how it appears on the screen. You may choose a traditional screen show or choose to view it in a separate window, which will leave other programs available to the viewer. These settings are in the Set Up Show dialog box that appears when you choose Slide Show, Set Up Show, as shown in Figure 6.5.

Each of the settings in the Set Up Show dialog box is explained in Table 6.2.

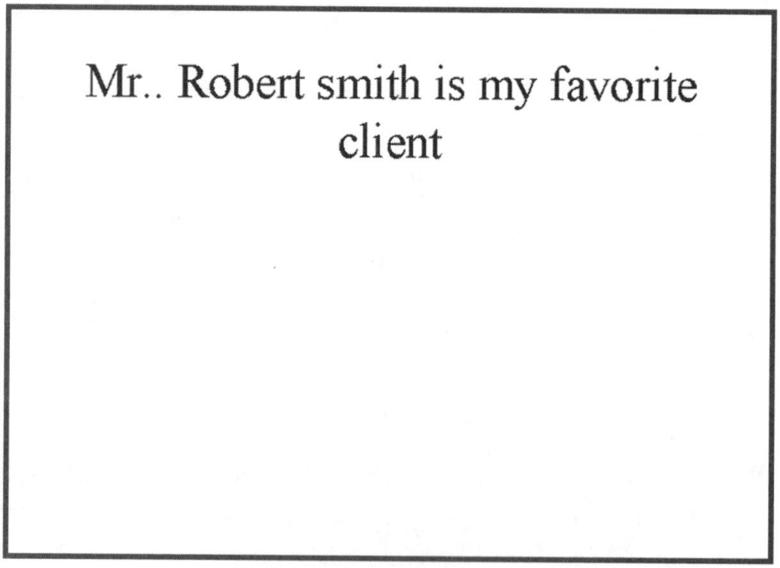

> Mr.. Robert smith is my favorite
> client

Figure 6.4

PowerPoint is never as smart as you are.

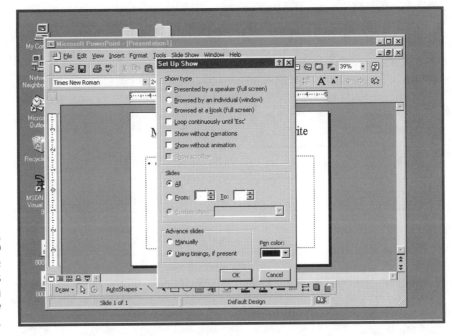

Figure 6.5

You can choose from different kinds of screen shows in the Set Up Show dialog box.

Option	Description
TABLE 6.2 OPTIONS IN THE SET UP SHOW DIALOG BOX	
Show Type Options	
Presented by a speaker (full screen)	The traditional slide show setting.
Browsed by an individual (window)	Shown in a less than full screen window. Users can switch from the slide show to any other window to access other programs as necessary. They can then switch back to the Show window at any time.
Browsed at a kiosk (full screen)	Similar to the traditional slide show, but it provides the ability to take away the user's ability to edit the show. A great tool for self-running demos at trade shows. You can specify that the show automatically restart if a page is idle for more than five minutes.

TABLE 6.2 OPTIONS IN THE SET UP SHOW DIALOG BOX (CONTINUED)

Option	Description
Loop continuously until 'Esc'	Runs a show continuously until the Esc key is pressed.
Show without narrations	Turns off any narrations added to specific slides.
Show without animation	Turns off any animations added to specific slides.
Show scroll bar	Available only for Browsing in a window.
Slides Options	
All	Shows all slides in a presentation.
From and To:	Enables you to set a range of slides to show.
Custom show	Enables you to select custom shows if you have set them up for a specific audience. See the online help in PowerPoint for information on custom shows.
Advanced Slides Options	
Manually	Advances the slides with either the mouse, the Enter key, or the PgUp and PgDn keys.
Using timings, if present	Advances slides based on preset timings if they have been set for a particular slide. Otherwise, the manual advance will advance the slides.
Pen color	Sets the color of the Pen for onscreen drawing during a show. Available only in Presented by a speaker mode. Can use any one of 16 million colors with the familiar Colors dialog box.

Rehearing Slide Timings and Transitions

Okay, I know that you learned how to set the animation settings perfectly on Saturday. But that doesn't mean that your slide show will actually run those animation settings at the speeds that you set. After all, you aren't trying to surprise your audience by running 30 different full-frame, True Color images to display at 0 seconds, are you? If you are, you will be in for a surprise when the presentation runs.

That is why you need to check what actually happens now when you try to run the presentation that you have created and saved. You will see exactly what happens, especially if you run the presentation in Slide Show view with the equipment on which you plan to actually distribute the presentation.

Depending on what you see and how long the next slide takes to load, you may need to make some modifications. You should always, always, always run through a presentation in Slide Show view to check the timings and transitions to be sure that what you think you are showing is actually what is being shown.

PowerPoint follows the timings that you set as well as it can. Some objects take longer to load than others, however, so you may not be able to scroll through a section of a screen show as quickly as you would like. For example, if you create a simple six-page presentation with only a single word on the first five pages, add a chart with gradations on the last page, and set the transition timings to be automatic and immediate (0 seconds), the chart page will take longer than the other pages to load. The result is that your apparently immediate transition to the chart page will not be immediate. And it doesn't matter which position in the slide show that complex chart page occupies. The complex chart page will still take longer than the other pages to load.

TIP
You can actually help PowerPoint run the show with quicker transitions by previewing the show once just before the actual presentation. PowerPoint Slide Show seems to have a memory for knowing what the next slide is going to be after it has been told this. But it won't remember this if the presentation is closed. So, have the presenter run through the show once before the real show if possible.

Rehearsing Timings on Selected Slides

In addition to setting your slide advance timings manually, you can also rehearse timings and have PowerPoint apply those rehearsed timings to your show. This is an extremely helpful feature if you do have some pages that take longer to load than others and would like to smooth out the transitions. When you rehearse timings, you see a separate rehearsal clock that lets you know as you are proceeding how long your total show is and how long you are spending on the current page (see Figure 6.6).

Rehearsal timer

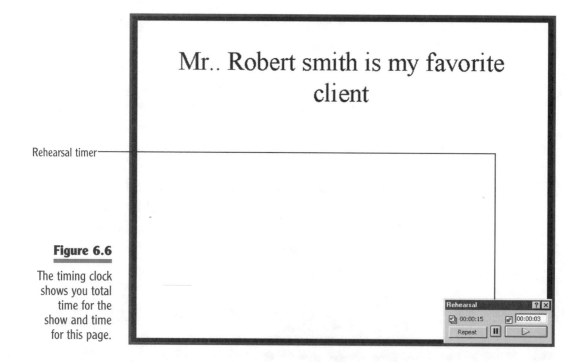

Figure 6.6

The timing clock shows you total time for the show and time for this page.

To rehearse timings of a slide show:

1. Choose Sli<u>d</u>e Show, <u>R</u>ehearse Timings. You will launch the presentation in Slide Show mode and see the Rehearsal timer. The left side of the timer keeps track of total elapsed time. The right side keeps track of elapsed time on this page.

2. Press Enter to move to the next slide (the mouse does not function while rehearsing timings unless you select the check box for Slide Transition Advance).

3. When you have finished the show, you will see a message box telling you the total time recorded for that rehearsal and giving you the option to save those timings. Click on <u>Y</u>es to save them or <u>N</u>o to discard them.

4. If you chose <u>Y</u>es, PowerPoint presents you with the option to view the timings in Slide Sorter view. Click on <u>Y</u>es to view them or <u>N</u>o to not enter Slide Sorter view.

What happens if you rehearsed all of your slides and are happy with most of them, but unhappy with a particular section of slides? Say that you clicked too quickly and would like to slow that section down a little. You have two choices. You could just go to Slide Sorter view and change the particular pages manually. Or you could rehearse the timings for just those pages and save the new settings for just those pages. To do that, you have to tell PowerPoint that you want to deal with just a range of pages. This is easy, but it is not quite obvious. You tell PowerPoint the range of slides to work with by choosing Sli<u>d</u>e Show, <u>S</u>et Up Show. In the Slides section of the Set Up Show dialog box, you can change the range of slides to work with by clicking on the <u>F</u>rom option and typing in the start and end pages in the range that you want to rehearse (see Figure 6.7).

CAUTION If you do change the Slide Show Setup range to only a selected range of pages, be sure to set it back to <u>A</u>ll before distributing the presentation. If you don't, the audience will see only that selected range of pages when the presentation is shown.

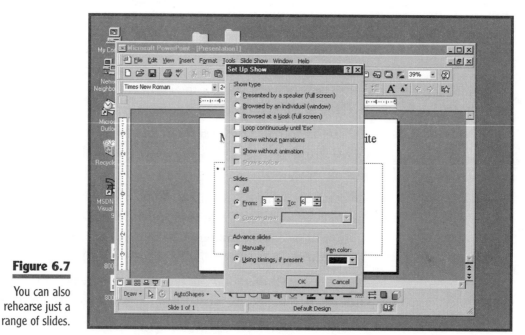

Figure 6.7

You can also rehearse just a range of slides.

Distributing the Presentation

How are you going to get the presentation from here to there? Frequently, presentations are created on one computer, maybe in the graphics department, but are shown from another computer, maybe the rented computer at the sales meeting out of town or on the salesperson's laptop. A host of ways are available to get it from one place to another. You can put it on floppy disks, you can put it on another form of movable media such as a Zip disk, you can transfer it by cable directly to another computer using a program such as Laplink or PC Anywhere, or you can send it by modem.

However you plan to distribute the presentation, you should be sure that the method to get the presentation off of your hard drive is compatible with the capabilities of the other computer to get the presentation onto its hard drive. The issues to consider depend on the method that you choose, as discussed in the following sections.

Moving the Presentation on Floppy Disks

One of the most common ways to move files from one place to another is to copy them to a floppy disk. How many times have you heard someone say, "Just give me the file on a disk"? Simply dragging the file from the hard drive to a floppy disk is something that you probably know how to do. But have you thought about whether the file is actually less than the 1.4MB capacity of a floppy disk? If you add a picture (or two or three) to the presentation, the file may not fit on a floppy disk. Have you thought about whether the laptop user in the field actually travels with the swappable floppy disk drive?

You can't do much with this option if the laptop user left the swappable floppy disk drive at home. But if you are sure you have a floppy disk drive on the target computer, there is a simple way to get a PowerPoint presentation onto a floppy or multiple floppy disks for distribution.

PowerPoint versions since PowerPoint 95 have come with the capability to save a compressed file to floppy disks, and you can automatically copy the file to more than one floppy disk if the presentation will not fit on a single disk. The Pack and Go feature provides this capability (choose File, Pack and Go).

Pack and Go is actually a six-step Wizard that enables you to make a few simple choices, and then it does all of the fancy footwork for you. After you have chosen File, Pack and Go, I walk through the six steps so that you can see just what choices you have to make at each step.

1. Start: Choose Next to proceed to Step 2 or Cancel to exit the Wizard. If you choose Finish, you will not be able to choose any of the settings within the Wizard. You may not get what you are after or may have trouble finding the finished, packed presentation.

2. Pick files to pack: You can choose the Active Presentation, which is usually the option you want. You can also select multiple presentations to be included in the same packed file. Click on Next.

3. Choose destination: You can choose to send the appropriate files to any drives available to your computer. After selecting your destination, click on Next.

4. Links: You now have the option of including any linked files, always a good option to check even if you don't remember any links. You also have the option to Embed TrueType fonts in your presentation. Click on Next after deciding on these two choices.

5. Viewer: You now have the choice of including the Viewer or not. Click on Next.

6. Finish: Click on Finish and let PowerPoint's Pack and Go do its work. If you choose to send the files to a floppy drive, you may be prompted to insert another disk into the drive if the disk in the drive is currently full.

That's all there is to the *packing* part of Pack and Go, but you are not done. You need to make sure that you have the files. Yes, there are two files—one named Pngsetup.exe, which is small (55K), and another named pres0.ppz. The second file is actually the compressed file that contains the presentation and all of the other related content that you may have chosen, such as linked files.

How do you *go* with the resulting files? You need both files. If you packed the presentations to floppy disks, you won't have any problem if you remember to send all of the disks. If you packed the presentations to a hard disk or some movable media drive, such as a Zip drive, you need to be sure that you move both files to the new computer. After you have done that, here's how to open the packed file on the new computer:

1. Make sure that both files are available on the new computer and are in the same folder, whether in the floppy disk drive, the hard drive, or a removable media drive.

2. Double-click on the file named Pngsetup.exe. You will be presented with another dialog box asking you where to place the unpacked

presentation files. Unfortunately, you must type the exact path; you can't browse and select a destination. The good news is that if you mistype a folder, PowerPoint prompts you that such a folder does not exist and gives you the option to create it.

3. Click on OK. You may be warned about overwriting files if the folder is not empty. It's up to you here to worry about your file management problems. Just be aware that you won't get any more nice warnings. Any file of the same name will be overwritten.

4. Click on <u>Y</u>es and the file is automatically uncompressed. Power-Point then presents you with another message box telling you that the file was correctly installed and giving you the option of running the show immediately or not. Click on <u>Y</u>es to immediately launch the show in Slide Show mode, or click <u>N</u>o to view it later.

Pack and Go is really a terrific feature in PowerPoint. It basically compresses the files that you select much the same as PKZip or WinZip would do. In fact, the results of the files that I have tested are essentially the same file size. The resulting file sizes using any of these programs will be about the same size. The big difference will be that Pack and Go does create its own installation program, giving users who do not have PKZip or WinZip the ability to install the presentation and Viewer, if you included it, on their own computers with no muss and no fuss.

TIP

One of the files that is saved to the target drive is Pngsetup.exe. That file is always exactly the same file every time you use Pack and Go. You can tell by noting the date on the file, which is 7/11/97 at 3:00 a.m. If you plan to receive Pack and Go files while you're on the road, you may want to carry a copy of this file with you in case someone forgets to send it to you along with the Pres0.ppz file, which is a common mistake. You can then just place both files in the same folder and save the day.

Pack and Go Issues

Pack and Go has always worked flawlessly for me, but not for everyone. Why? A not-very-obvious requirement of Pack and Go is that the Power-Point Viewer program be installed on the computer performing the Pack and Go. Another reason is that Pack and Go will hang before completing the packing. I can help you with both of these issues, which are easy to troubleshoot.

Why does Pack and Go need the Viewer to do its magic? I don't have a clue, but it is a fact of life: If no PowerPoint Viewer is installed, the Pack and Go Wizard will not work. End of story. Either go back and install the PowerPoint Viewer from the installation disks, or download it from the Microsoft Web site and install it from the downloaded file. That will fix the most likely problem. If you do know that the Viewer is installed, keep in mind that the PowerPoint Viewer (see Appendix A) is a completely different program from PowerPoint and is not what is running when you choose View, Slide Show from within PowerPoint itself.

If that is not the issue, you may have insufficient disk space to accommodate Pack and Go's requirements. Pack and Go creates a temporary file of the current presentation before writing it to the destination drive. Therefore, someone can easily have too little free disk space to which to write the temporary file, and Pack and Go will hang without telling you why. If Pack and Go is not working for you, check your file size on the files that you are trying to pack. Make sure that you have at least twice as much free disk space available in the single location where you write temp files, which is usually c:\windows\temp. You may be surprised by what is actually in that folder. You absolutely must have adequate space available for PowerPoint to store the temp file; Pack and Go will not work otherwise. Depending on what other programs you have running at the time, they may also use available temp file disk space. You need enough breathing room for Pack and Go to work. If you are having problems and the Viewer is actually installed, this is probably the most likely reason and you have to guess for yourself. The Pack and Go Wizard does not provide you with very good feedback on this error.

Moving the Presentation on Removable Media

You can easily move files from one computer to another using removable media. Zip drives and other similar brands are becoming more common today. If both machines have compatible drives, you can often move the files from one computer to another by copying the files—you may not need to use Pack and Go with these kinds of drives using disks that can hold 100MB of data or more.

But you do need to make sure that the target computer is capable of connecting to the same kind of removable media. Several brands of removable media drives are available, such as Zip, SyQuest, and so on. They are not necessarily, and probably aren't, compatible with each other. If you plan to use this technique, you absolutely need to make sure that the target computer is exactly compatible with the media you are using. If you are unsure, then don't assume. *Assume* is one of those words that doesn't exist in the vocabulary of presentation personnel, unless it is used in the sentence, "I assume that they can't read this media type." Then you'll be safe.

Moving the Presentation by Cable to Another Computer

Another way to move files between different computers is to connect the two with a cable and use a software program designed to copy the files. You are actually setting up a rudimentary network without needing network cards. Two programs (and there are several more) that have proven to be excellent values are PC Anywhere and Laplink. They cost around $100 and are very easy to use.

Basically, you plug the supplied cables into either the parallel or serial ports on the back of both machines, and start the software on one of the machines, which automatically locates the other machine. You then can select multiple files and just drag-and-drop them into the other machine. The transfers can go either way.

TIP

If you are taking your presentations to an out-of-town location, such as a hotel site, and will be working with multiple computers at that site, the cable connection is an excellent way to move files between the computers quickly and effortlessly.

Moving the Presentation by Modem

Yet another way to move files from one location to another is to transfer them by modem. This book was actually written in New York and edited in Indianapolis, and all files, text, and pictures, were transferred by modem.

Something peculiar happens with transferring PowerPoint files by modem that does not happen with many other software packages. Of course, I am passing on to you the way to avoid any problems with modems and PowerPoint files. For some reason, some complex Power-Point files get scrambled and corrupted when they are transferred by modem. Who knows why, but it has happened to many of us who receive PowerPoint files by modem.

Those of us who move PowerPoint files by modem on any regular basis always compress our files using a program such as PKZip or WinZip. This protects the file from corruption. Compression not only protects your files but also makes them transfer over the phone lines faster because they are smaller files. If you remember to zip your PowerPoint files before sending them, you can rest assured that they will be safely transmitted.

TIP

If you use a compression utility to compress the files, be sure that the recipients can uncompress them. If they don't have that ability, you should make sure that your compression software can make the file self-extracting. In fact, you could even use Pack and Go, which compresses the file and will protect it. Just remember to send the Pngsetup.exe file as well.

Starting a Presentation Automatically

Many people have expressed the desire to have a PowerPoint presentation start up automatically in Slide Show mode. You can do this in several ways using command line switches. The easiest way is just to change the filename to give it an extension of .pps, for PowerPoint Show. If you do that and double-click the file icon in Explorer, the show will start immediately on the first page in Slide Show mode.

Font Issues

Now that you have figured out the best way for you to move your finished presentation to the actual computer where it will be shown, you need to worry about one last thing, which has been covered many times in this book. But this is such a common cause of frustration that it cannot be emphasized too frequently. Check the fonts again. Make sure that the fonts that you used in creating the presentation are available on the final computer.

If they are not, you have two options left at this point: either load the necessary fonts so that you won't have to change anything else, or change the fonts that PowerPoint is using.

Replacing a missing font globally in the presentation is quite easy to do and, with luck, won't create many problems for you on the pages, especially if you choose a font that is very similar.

First, check what fonts have been used in the presentation. PowerPoint automatically keeps track of that for you. Choose File, Properties and click on the Contents tab. The fonts used will be shown at the top of this dialog box, as shown in Figure 6.8. If you have used fonts that are not embedded in the presentation or are not available on this computer, you can replace those fonts with other ones that are available.

Choose OK to close the Properties dialog box, and then choose Format, Replace Fonts. You will see the Replace Font dialog box, as shown in Figure 6.8. The Replace drop-down list shows only the fonts that have

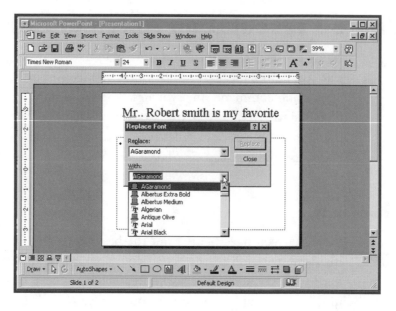

Figure 6.8

Replace any
unavailable fonts
with ones that
are available.

been used in this presentation. The <u>W</u>ith drop-down list shows what
fonts are available on this computer.

TIP

Figure 6.8 shows two different icons for fonts. The fonts that are preceded by the two Ts,
such as the Arial font, are TrueType fonts and may or may not be embeddable in a
PowerPoint presentation, depending on what company created that font. Not all True-
Type fonts can be embedded. The other icon, such as the one preceding the Agaramond
font, is for an Adobe Postscript font. These Adobe fonts cannot be embedded in presentations. They will have to be legally installed on every computer that will use them.

File Size Issues

What is the maximum file size for a PowerPoint presentation? That upper
boundary is determined by the capabilities of your computer, not by
PowerPoint. You should keep a few things in mind when thinking about
file size, however.

No matter how powerful your computer is, a tremendously large file of 100MB or more will take awhile to open and save. Why is this? First, PowerPoint loads the entire file from your hard drive into memory. It does not just load a few pages at a time. So, the file size that you are constrained by depends on the total available memory and your available virtual memory. But that still isn't the entire picture. PowerPoint, when it saves a file, creates a temporary file in addition to the actual file before saving the temporary file over the existing file. Therefore, a 100MB file would require the first 100MB of RAM plus virtual memory just to open the file, but you would need an additional 100MB of disk space free for PowerPoint to store the temporary file during the save operation.

If you see your presentations approaching tremendous file sizes, you should seriously consider breaking them up into several smaller presentations. After all, a 100MB presentation has to be an awful lot of pages if you followed the guidelines given in this book on scanning, and most meetings would need to schedule a break before you would show all of the pages. You could use the break time to quit one presentation and open another. If you do this and your system crashes during the presentation for some reason or another (such as someone tripping over the power cable), you will be able to reopen the existing file that much faster. Forewarned is forearmed.

Presenting to an Audience at a Meeting

Now that you have the presentation completed and moved to the actual room in which you will present it, you may want to consider some additional issues. If the meeting is a small one and the presentation is on a laptop, you just need to be sure your audience can actually see the laptop screen. Remember, you probably know what is in the presentation and don't need to see much of it to know what the content is. So, you shouldn't be the one sitting directly in front of the laptop. If you have hyperlinks built into the presentation that will operate from mouse clicks, you will also probably want to have a mouse available rather than have to rely on the laptop's clumsy built-in pointing device. This also enables your audience to grab the mouse and get involved with the presentation.

If you are presenting to a larger audience and using some sort of projector, you will also want to make sure that the computer screen is visible to the presenter so that he or she doesn't have to turn around and look at the screen.

For big meetings when you have an AV staff person working behind the scenes, and especially when the speakers are not highly PowerPoint presentation-literate, you should consider protecting these speakers from pressing the wrong keys during a presentation and doing something unexpected. Placing a remote monitor facing the speaker so that he or she can see the current slide without turning around is a good setup. Another possibility is to move the computer running the show away from the speaker so that a skilled operator can fix any surprises without the pressure of entertaining the audience at the same time.

TIP

Placing a mouse on the podium allows the speaker to choose when to advance and protects the speaker from pressing the Esc key unwittingly and jumping out of Slide Show mode. You might consider using a wireless mouse to do this. None of my professional show colleagues do this, however. Wireless mice can frequently be affected by cell phones and other wireless radio waves, creating unexpected havoc in a meeting. The other problem with a live mouse on the podium is that the speaker gets very confused with the forward and back buttons or hits the buttons twice by accident.

For more important meetings, hook up an old-fashioned wireless slide projector pickel to a 35mm slide projector. The speaker can use the pickel to signal an advance. When the speaker clicks on either the advance button or the reverse button, the 35mm slide projector, which doesn't have any slides loaded or even have the light turned on, will advance. The projector (which should be placed on the AV producers desk) will signal to the AV staff to advance the slide. If the speaker does want to back up, as inevitably happens, the speaker just needs to say something in their normal speech pattern and the projectionist staff can then back up one page. This system can help smooth out projection problems at shows and help keep the speakers focused on what they are saying, rather than worrying about equipment that they are not used to.

Creating Speaker Notes

Good speakers don't need notes. They are called rainmakers. Those of us who are not rainmakers, but merely the rained on, may need notes to glance at while we are speaking to remember all of the points to cover. Keep in mind that the public-speaking experience can be very unnerving even to the very intelligent. The real fear of speaking in front of an audience needs to be recognized and allayed with whatever techniques you can use. Taking the control of the computer show away from the speaker is one way. Another way is to provide the speaker with notes that are easy to read and show the speaker what the slides look like.

PowerPoint has a feature called Speaker Notes, which shows a half-page image of the slide page and leaves the other half of the page available for the speaker to write notes relevant to that slide. The Speaker Notes have their own Slide Master page just like slides follow the Slide Master page, as shown in Figure 6.9. And just like the Slide Master page, you can change the settings on the Notes Master page to follow different settings.

Figure 6.9

The Notes Master page is customizable just like the Slide Master page.

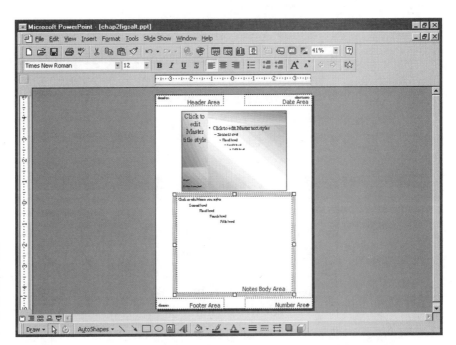

For example, you may want to increase the font size to make it easier for the speaker to see the notes. Here's a quick lesson in how to access the Speaker Notes and make a simple change to the font size:

1. With any presentation open, choose View, Master, Notes Master.

2. You will then see the Notes Master page, which will have a preview of the Slide Master page and a Click to edit Master text style placeholder. This area is for the speaker to use for notes, and settings for this placeholder apply only to the Notes pages. They will not affect the Slide or Slide Master page in any way. Change the font size by clicking the Click to edit Master text styles placeholder and choose Format, Font and change the Size from 12 to 20.

3. Click OK.

The speaker can create any notes that will help him or her on a particular page. The notes are attached to each individual slide just like any text is attached to an individual slide. To enter notes that can be printed later, select a specific page in a presentation while in Slide view and follow these easy steps:

1. Choose View, Speaker Notes.

2. You will see the Speaker Notes dialog box for that particular page. Just type the text you want to print on the Notes page for this particular slide. Figure 6.10 shows the input box for typing your speaker notes.

3. Click on Close.

Creating Handouts for the Audience

Handouts are always an issue. At many presentations that I produce, my clients insist on passing out handouts of the presentation so that the audience can follow along. In my opinion, this is absolutely the wrong thing to do. First, if the audience is looking at the notes page, they aren't paying attention to either the speaker or the screen. Second, any last-minute changes made to the show will probably not be reflected in the printouts, which will make the audience think that the speaker is not well organized.

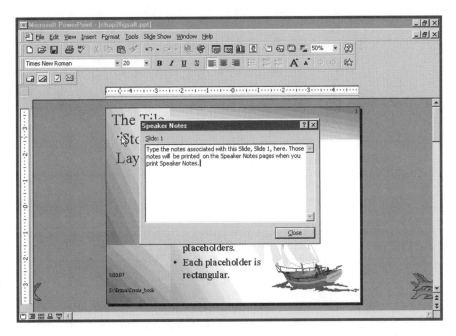

Figure 6.10

Type your notes into this input box.

TIP

Do you want to have your printed pages centered on a page? Some printers have a problem printing slides that are centered on the page. The reason is that there is an area at the bottom of the page that the printer cannot print on—what a colleague of mine calls the Twilight Zone of the printer world.

If you have this problem, you can use print Speaker Notes instead of Slides to work around the problem. Modify the Notes Master page to delete the notes text placeholder first. Then, make sure the orientation of the Notes page setup (File, Page Setup) is the same orientation as your slides (probably landscape). Then, measure one of your printouts of a slide page to find the no-print zone at the bottom of the page. Say it is 1" on an 8 1/2" × 11" page.

Make that margin of 1" apply to both the top and bottom of the page, and size the slide on the Notes Master page to be, in this case, 11" × 6 1/2" wide. This should generate printouts that are centered on the page, although it might take a little finagling to get the exact measurements correct. But, it is possible to end up with centered pages using this technique.

Both of these drawbacks to handouts that can happen during the show create less than effective communications. Don't do it!

If you are set on providing handouts of the presentation, do it after the presentation is complete. You can print handouts in PowerPoint in a variety of formats: two on a page, three on a page with lined rules for note taking, or six on a page.

To print handouts of your presentation:

1. Choose File, Print from the menu.
2. In the Print what section of the Print dialog box, click on the pull-down menu next to Print what and select the kind of layout for the Handouts you wish to print.
3. Click on OK to print the Handouts.

How about handing out electronic copies? Show your audience you live in the electronic world. Consider giving them the handouts on floppy disks and include the PowerPoint Viewer for those who don't have a complete copy of PowerPoint installed on their computers. Then, they can view the presentation and even see all of the animation effects you have put into the presentation. It is a very effective way to send your message back to colleagues of the audience who couldn't make the meeting.

Customizing Existing Presentations for Multiple Audiences

On frequent occasions, you will probably want to utilize the same core content of an existing presentation for multiple audiences. A good example of this is the Marketing Manager's presentation to the division president on the results of a new product introduction. This core presentation, which probably had a lot of thought put into it, is often a good candidate for being presented over and over again at various staff meetings. The likelihood is that you will not want to present all of the information contained in the original presentation, such as sensitive financial figures or inventory problems or whatever.

This situation has been around since Day One in the world of presentations. Many of us can remember sifting through 35mm slide trays the night before one of these presentations, taking slides out of the carousel that we didn't want to show. And then having to re-rack the entire show to eliminate the empty slots in the carousel. PowerPoint makes it a lot easier with a feature called Custom Shows. In essence, you create the name of a custom show, say New Prod. Employees then quickly pick the slides to add to the show. The original is never touched and the custom show is literally just a list of indexes to various slides in the original show. Actually, the list of the show's slides is really not an index in the sense of the third slide and the seventh slide, and so on. The Custom Show indexing method is actually a listing of slide names that stay attached to the slide even if you change the copy on a slide or change the order of the slides in the main presentation.

This feature is a variation on what some of us used to do in the recent past, which was to save the original file under a new name so that the template never changed. Then, in Slide Sorter View, we deleted the unwanted slides. The benefit of this is that you have a preview of the slide, and if you had a title that was the same on several sequential slides, you could probably guess which was the correct file to delete based on what the slide looked like. In Custom Shows, although you do not have a slide preview, you do see the title text of each slide, if there is any, and you never disturb the original. This way, you can always have only one master presentation that you can continue to update, and then add or remove slides as necessary from the Custom Shows. I guess the differences are purely a matter of choice.

If your choice is to create Custom Shows, here's how:

1. With your complete main presentation open, select Slide Show, Custom Shows.

2. You will then see the Custom Shows dialog box (these dialog boxes are getting quite familiar by now, I should bet). Click on New.

3. In the next dialog box (Define Custom Show), type the descriptive name of the show over the default of Custom Show 1. The default

name of the show is supplied because PowerPoint needs a reference to find the Custom Show again. See Figure 6.9, which also shows a few slides added to this Custom Show from the next step.

4. To add the specific slides to the Custom Show, use the two windows that are show in Figure 6.9. Select a slide, such as the title slide, and click on the <u>A</u>dd button.

5. Repeat step 4 to add the rest of the slides you wish to include in this Custom Show. If you would like to remove a slide that you have already added, just click on the <u>R</u>emove button.

6. Click the OK button, and at this point you should choose <u>S</u>how to see the Custom Show that you have created from your main presentation.

7. After viewing the Custom Show, if you have missed or added slides by mistake, you can choose Edit from the Custom Shows dialog box until you are satisfied. When you are satisfied with this Custom Show, click on <u>C</u>lose.

Multimedia Projectors

Multimedia projectors for computer presentations are, on the surface, not that much different than the 35mm projectors that everyone has used in the past. Multimedia projectors enable you to present your image on a bigger screen in front of different-sized audiences and are especially appropriate for meetings when the audience size is too large to see the presentation on a monitor. One might argue over exactly what size audience this is necessary, but it does make sense for any decent-sized conference room or larger.

These projectors have made a lot of progress in the past few years and have segmented into three different kinds of projectors. They all function with the computer in basically the same way; the key differences are in the quality of image, size, and weight of the projector. The first type of multimedia projector is the overhead panel, which is designed to be placed directly on an overhead projector. The second is a bigger unit, often 12–16 pounds, and is a complete projection system unto itself. It does not need an external light source, such as the overhead panel. At this weight, these projectors are quite portable. The third kind of unit is designed with better sound capabilities and is somewhat heavier because it is designed for a more permanent installation, such as a board room.

Next, take a closer look at each of these three different kinds of projectors and see what you might expect at each level.

LCD Overhead Panels

These are truly designed for the road warrior and weigh less than five pounds. They usually come in screen resolutions of 640×480, but panels capable of showing 16 million colors at 800×600 resolution are also available. They may even have the ability to support full motion video and play back sound through their internal speaker. They cost about $5,000.

Portable Projectors

These units weigh in at 12–16 pounds. They are very good quality and can give you a very bright, high quality screen image in 16 million colors at 800×600 screen resolution. The image is better than the LCD overhead panel because it is brighter and the image can still be seen in a room with more ambient light. Additionally, the sound quality is better because the speakers are better. As you might expect, they are somewhat more expensive and may cost around $7,000. If you need to display high-quality presentations in a nonpermanent installation, these are extremely good units.

Semi-Permanent Projectors

These are the best and the brightest of these projectors. They not only have brighter images (brighter is better), but also some additional features for zooming the image to exactly fit the screen and higher quality connections for connecting directly to more video sources. These are the state-of-the-art projectors and may cost between $8,000 and $10,000.

Renting vs. Purchasing Projectors

The good news is that if you have only occasional needs for a projector or need additional projectors for one meeting, you can rent them easily and at very reasonable prices of $250 to $500 per day.

Many local companies in most major cities rent projectors by the day or for a short period of time. You can probably find these companies in the Yellow Pages. Or if you are staying at a hotel, the Audio/Visual department will likely have a reliable source that it uses.

Or if you are truly a road warrior who knows the inside of far too many airports, you can contact one source who will use FedEx to have a projector waiting for you in the next city; then, when you are finished with it, you can ship it back by FedEx. This is the InFocus Systems company, which actually ships the projectors out of Memphis, Tennessee, the FedEx hub. You can place your order late in the day (as late as 9:00 p.m. Central Time and it will be at your location in the morning of the next day). You can reach InFocus at 800-294-6400 (Option 6).

Presenting on Your Web Site

You may actually not plan to be in front of your audience during your presentation. You may actually plan to make your presentation available on your Web site. PowerPoint presentations are easy to publish to a Web page and can even include all of the special effects that you get in PowerPoint with hyperlinks and even animation effects.

If you have a Web site and the software to load the files up to the Web site, PowerPoint takes care of the preparation of the files for you. The one caveat of publishing PowerPoint presentations to a Web site is that people trying to view the presentation in their Web browser must have the PowerPoint Animation player loaded in order to view the presentation. If they do not have it loaded, they are automatically prompted that they must install the PowerPoint Animation Viewer. After this prompt, they receive the option to be automatically hyperlinked to the Microsoft

Web page where they can quickly install the Viewer. They can then view your PowerPoint presentation, including all animation effects, live on the Web. It is a very nice feature.

FIND IT ON ▶ **THE WEB**   If you haven't seen any PowerPoint presentations with animation effects, you might want to take a quick look at an example at the following address: **http://ourworld .compuserve.com/homepages/Reilly_and_Associates/sld001.htm**

To save a PowerPoint presentation so that it is capable of being viewed on your Web site, you need to save the file in a different file format. This file format is in HTML, the hypertext markup language, which is how the Web does things. The process uses a wizard similar to the Pack and Go Wizard, so you have only a few choices to make.

To save a file as HTML, choose File, Save As HTML from an open presentation and follow the steps in the wizard:

1. Start: Click on Next.
2. Layout selection: This is where you save specific layouts for future re-use. Select New Layout and click on Next for an additional page style selection for this layout. Choose either layout and click on Next.
3. Graphic type: Choose any of three file formats—GIF, (only 256 colors), JPEG (can be 16 million colors), or PowerPoint Animation. Click on Next.
4. Graphic size: Choose the size of the actual images in the final graphics. Click on Next.
5. Information page: You can include specific information to be included about you, if you like, which will appear on the Index page. You also have two check boxes on this page. The first is to let the person viewing your page download a copy of the original presentation. The second is a bit of free advertising for Microsoft—a hyperlink to the Microsoft Web site for downloading the Internet Explorer program. If you check this box, the familiar logo "Best

Viewed with Internet Explorer" is placed on your Index page. Fill in the options as you see fit and click on Next.

6. Colors and buttons: You can use the default browser colors or create your own set of custom colors using the familiar PowerPoint Color dialog box. For today, click on Use Browser Colors, and click on Next to choose a button style for the page. Pick a style and click on Next.

7. Layout Options: You choose from four options for placing the navigation buttons on your page. Choose one option and click on Next. Another dialog box comes up for you to tell PowerPoint where to place your finished files. There will be a lot of files, but they will all be placed in a new folder that has the same name as the current presentation, so finding all of the files will be easy when you need to upload them to your Web site. Click on Next.

8. Finish: Click on Finish and you have the option to save these settings if you would like to use them again. After you have figured out which settings work for you, you should save the settings here for re-use. Click on Don't Save today, but fill in a descriptive name and click on Save to save the settings and proceed.

PowerPoint executes your commands, which may take a few minutes. When it is done, you will see a message box stating, "The presentation was successfully saved as HTML." Click on OK and the PowerPoint part of getting this presentation onto your Web site is done.

Before you load the files up to the Web to see what they look like, you can actually view the files right on your own computer using the browser that you have installed. The actual files that you want to view are the files in that folder that have the .htm extension. Double-click on one of those to launch your own browser and show you the file on the screen. Viewing the files onscreen will help you figure out what options to set for saving your files. Figure 6.11 was saved at 640×480 at full screen. Notice in this figure that the image is partially clipped when viewed in Internet Explorer 3.02 when the Address toolbar is on the second line. You should

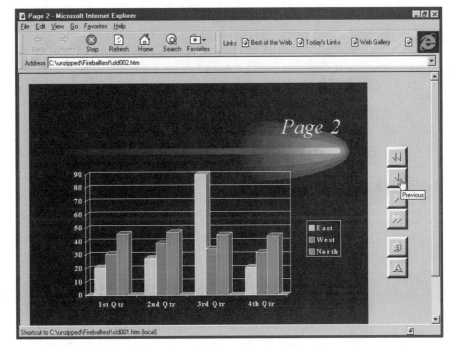

Figure 6.11

Preview your Web page in your browser before uploading it.

test various settings with various browsers to pick a size that works best for what you consider to be the likely screen resolution of your intended audience.

All of the appropriate files from your presentation are now located in the folder that you created. The rules for uploading them to your Web site will vary depending on what software you are using to upload the files. They are not uploaded with PowerPoint.

◆ ◆

CAUTION The PowerPoint Animation Viewer is still one version behind PowerPoint 97 and treats animation objects differently than PowerPoint 97 does. You should test your animations using the PowerPoint Animation Viewer, and you may want to make some modifications just for your Web site so that they play correctly.

◆ ◆

TIP You can make your finished presentations downloadable from the Web site by selecting the <u>D</u>ownload Original Presentation check box on the Information page of the Save as HTML Wizard. That will place an icon automatically on your Index page along with your name to make it easy for people viewing your page on the Web to download the original presentation to their own machine.

Wrapping Up

Congratulations, you made it through the weekend and have learned how to be an expert in PowerPoint. As easy as it should have been, there is an awful lot to remember.

Don't worry if you don't remember it all now. I've tried to give you the tools to think about PowerPoint in a fluid sort of way so that what you don't remember, you can figure out with the process you have learned. I certainly don't remember every detail. Just keep in mind the reality of life that applies to both money and computer software knowledge: "As much as you have, someone has more."

And please stop by in the Microsoft PowerPoint newsgroup or the CompuServe MSDesktop forum and say "Hello." I'll be happy to hear from you.

Get out there and make some terrific presentations. You now know enough to create and present PowerPoint presentations better than 99% of the people out there, and probably even better than I can. Go pump those pixels!

"Show time!"

PowerPoint Viewer Issues

After you've created a PowerPoint presentation, you may want to distribute the presentation to people who do not have PowerPoint installed on their computers. To get around this potential problem, you can send them a copy of the PowerPoint Viewer, which enables them to view the presentation on their own computer. The PowerPoint Viewer is a self-contained program that can view PowerPoint presentations. You are free to distribute the PowerPoint Viewer without any license restrictions. This program cannot edit the presentation; you need the PowerPoint application to do that.

Differences Between the Three Available Viewers

Several issues with the PowerPoint Viewer can confuse some people. For example, three different viewers are now available. Two of the viewers are 32-bit programs and require Windows 95 or Windows NT in order to run. The third viewer is a 16-bit program and will run on Windows 3.x, Windows 95, or Windows NT. These three viewers are summarized in Table A.1

These files are actually the installation files that you use to install the particular Viewer that you want. The actual Viewer expands to many files, including .DLL (dynamic link library) files that take up more room on the hard drive than the actual installation file. This raises several issues when considering shipping the Viewer to potential customers for them to view a presentation on their computer.

If you plan to use floppy disks, neither the Viewer for PowerPoint 95 or PowerPoint 97 will fit on a single floppy disk. In the case of the Viewer

TABLE A.1 THE THREE VIEWERS

Filename	File Size	Comments
PPView97.exe	2.8Mb	Opens any version of a PowerPoint file up to and including PowerPoint 97. Requires Windows 95 or Windows NT.
PPTView32.exe	1.6Mb	Originally shipped with PowerPoint 97, but opens PowerPoint files only up to and including PowerPoint 95. Opens a PowerPoint 97 file saved as PowerPoint 95 or PowerPoint 95-97 format. Requires Windows 95 or Windows NT.
PPTView16.exe	1.1Mb	Opens PowerPoint presentations for version 4. Works with Windows 3.x, Windows 95, or Windows NT.

for PowerPoint version 4, you are limited to a presentation size that cannot exceed about 300K if you want to fit both the presentation and the Viewer on a single floppy disk. That pretty much limits you to not adding any scanned photos to your presentation, or certainly not many.

The good news is that both PowerPoint 95 and PowerPoint 97 have added a feature called Pack and Go, which compresses a PowerPoint presentation and packs the Viewer on as many floppy disks as are needed. When one disk is full, Pack and Go prompts you for an additional disk.

Potential Problems with the PowerPoint Viewers

Although the PowerPoint Viewers are generally very good programs, there is often a difference between the user's expectations and what the Viewer actually delivers. The Viewer is not just the Slide Show part of the PowerPoint program; it is actually a separate program. Due to file size considerations, the Viewer doesn't perform exactly as the Slide Show in PowerPoint does. So, although you may obtain fairly good results using the Viewer, you will not be able to do everything that you can do with the complete version of PowerPoint. Additionally, you may be in for some surprises if the computer system on which you install the Viewer is not as good as the system on which you prepared the presentation. The following sections itemize a few points that you should consider when preparing a presentation for distribution with the Viewer.

Fonts and Bullets May Change

If you haven't embedded the fonts into the presentation that you are distributing, they may not be available on the system on which the Viewer will be installed. If this is the case, the fonts will change and you may end up with letters for your bullets, or a completely different font that not only looks bad but also doesn't fit on the page.

You could just embed the fonts if you are using Microsoft's TrueType fonts (which are embeddable). But if you have installed someone else's TrueType fonts that are not licensed to be embedded, you may not be able to embed them in the presentation. Additionally, each font that you embed takes up about 150K of disk space. If you are really squeezed for space, you may not want to embed the fonts.

The only two fonts that are always installed on a machine that runs Window 3.x or later are Arial and Times New Roman. Therefore, you may want to consider using one of these two fonts and the asterisk (*) or the minus sign (-) as a bullet. Or, you may choose to not use any bullets. If you are willing to put up with the extra editing necessary, you can use a shape such as a circle or a triangle filled with a color to look like a bullet. It won't actually be a bullet but rather a separate drawing object for each time that you think you have a bullet. As I said, it creates a lot of extra work, but it will show on any machine running the Viewer, which is the objective.

Special Effects May Not Work

Depending on which version of PowerPoint that you used to create the presentation, and which version of the Viewer you choose to show it with, some of the effects that you used in the presentation may not actually show up on the screen correctly. For example, slide transitions, objects that have textured fills, builds for bullets, and some interactive settings may change from what you expect to show and what actually shows under the Viewer. You may get objects that you thought were textured show up as solid colors. Or slide transitions may get remapped from one effect to an another effect.

This is not to say that the Viewer is unpredictable. It will always show the same thing consistently; however, what appears onscreen may not be what you are expecting. The solution is to always test your presentation by reviewing it on the Viewer that you are shipping with the presentation.

Visual Basic Code Won't Run

You cannot distribute the new PowerPoint 97 Viewer with an interactive presentation that uses Visual Basic for Applications (VBA) code to get information from the audience. No VBA code of any kind will work with the Viewer. The explanation from Microsoft is that adding VBA to the Viewer will result in a file size that far exceeds the current 2.8MB file size.

You can distribute interactive presentations, however, because hyperlinks are quite functional under the PowerPoint 97 viewer.

Installing the PowerPoint Viewer

If you use the Pack and Go feature in PowerPoint to include the Viewer with a presentation, installation of the Viewer is automatic. The Pack and Go Wizard creates two files when the file is packed. The first is an executable file with the extension .EXE, and is relatively small (about 55K). The second contains the actual presentation and the Viewer setup file. If you distribute both files, you should include instructions for the intended user to double-click on the smaller file with the .EXE extension. This will automatically launch the installation process, which will let the user select where to place the files. It will also give the user the option to immediately view the presentation.

NOTE When installing PowerPoint 97 from floppy disks for the Professional Edition of Microsoft Office 97, the viewer file (Ppview32.exe) is not automatically installed. This applies only to the floppy disk installations for the Professional Edition only, and does not apply to the compact disks or to the Standard Edition of Office 97. The solution is to download the PowerPoint Viewer from the Microsoft Web site and install the viewer from that file.

FIND IT ON ▶   You can find a whole lot of extras to PowerPoint at the Microsoft Web site. The site
THE WEB   changes frequently and you might want to add it to your Favorites list. Typing / into your browser and pressing Enter may turn up some nifty things like this and maybe give you some new surprises that have been added to PowerPoint.

Launching a Presentation Automatically with the Viewer

A frequent question in the PowerPoint newsgroups and on the CompuServe forum is how to launch the Viewer directly from a file icon. It is a little-known trick, but perfectly effective, to just change the file extension from .PPT to .PPS. If you double-click on the file named FILE.PPS in Explorer, the presentation automatically launches in slide show mode.

Some new features have been added to the PowerPoint 97 Viewer that were not available in previous versions of the Viewer. You can now perform the following tasks with the PowerPoint 97 Viewer:

❂ Launch the show and choose to either use or ignore preset timings.

❂ Launch the show in a continuous loop until you press the Esc key.

Running the Viewer from a List File

You can create a list file with the .LST extension that will run several presentations in sequential order. You can do this by using a Text editor such as WordPad or Notepad. You cannot use a word processor such as Word. The procedure is quite easy, but you must follow a few very important rules that often cause a fair amount of confusion to many people.

Follow these steps to create the list file:

1. From the Start menu, choose <u>P</u>rograms, Accessories, Notepad.
2. Type the name of your files, one file per line, such as:

   myfile1.ppt

   myfile2.ppt

   myfile3.ppt

3. Save the file and use Explorer to change the extension to an .LST extension. The .LST file should be located in the same folder as the PowerPoint Viewer, or Viewer may not be able to find the files.

If you want to play files from multiple folders, you can just add the full path to the line, such as d:\budgets\myfile1.ppt. The Viewer will then know where to find the other presentations.

 TIP You can also use a list file to play other list files. Just type the name of the list file in WordPad or Notepad as you would any filename. The Viewer will read the file line by line just as the computer does to read any program and execute the file in a line-by-line sequence.

Messages Cannot Register Hlink.dll During PowerPoint Viewer Setup

During installation of the PowerPoint 97 Viewer, a few people will receive an error message that is similar to the following: Setup cannot register

Hlink.dll in the system registry because an older version is in use. Close all applications and try again.

This error occurs because PowerPoint Viewer 97 contains an updated version of this file. For an easy way to deal with this issue, follow these steps:

1. Press Ctrl+Alt+Del to display the Close Program dialog box and determine what other applications are still running. Close the applications that might be using this file.

 NOTE You will probably not know what application is using Hlink.dll and should follow the instructions for a clean install that are given in Appendix C.

2. When you have finished closing the open applications, click on the Cancel button in the Close Program dialog box and return to the Viewer installation program. Click on Retry.

Files Installed with the Various PowerPoint Viewers

If you distribute the PowerPoint Viewer to people who don't have the complete version of PowerPoint installed, your presentation may be more favorably received if you tell them exactly what files are loaded onto their computers. That way, people who are concerned about being able to remove the files after they have viewed the presentation may do so. The following sections list files that are installed with each of the three Viewers.

PowerPoint 97 Viewer (PPView97.exe)

The following files are installed with the PowerPoint 97 Viewer:

TABLE A.2 PPVIEW97.EXE		
Filename	**File Size (bytes)**	**Date**
Base.srg	4K	6/13/97
License.txt	5K	6/13/97
Msppt8vr.olb	6K	6/13/97
Ppintlv.dll	155K	6/13/97
Ppview32.exe	1,391K	6/13/97
Rappt.dll	32K	6/13/97
Readme.txt	22K	6/13/97
Selfreg.dll	32K	6/13/97
Servrdep.srg	14K	6/13/97
Servring.srg	1K	6/13/97
Sshow.srg	1K	6/13/97

PowerPoint Viewer for Windows 95 (PPView32.exe)

Six separate files are installed for this version of the Viewer:

TABLE A.3 PPVIEW32.EXE		
Filename	**File Size (bytes)**	**Date**
License.txt	4,915	12/18/95
Pp4x32.dll	547,840	12/18/95
Ppview32.exe	1,924,096	12/18/95
Ppvwread.txt	5,178	12/18/95
Pngsetup.dat	12	12/18/95
Pngsetup.ex_	55,456	12/18/95

16-bit PowerPoint Viewer (PPTView16.exe)

The following files install with the 16-bit PowerPoint Viewer:

TABLE A.4 PPTVIEW16.EXE		
Filename	**File Size (bytes)**	**Date**
Compobj.dl_	47,475	4/5/94
Ole2.dl_	144,252	4/5/94
Ole2.REG	24,598	4/5/94
Ole2conv.DL_	29,914	4/5/94
Ole2disp.DL_	44,927	4/5/94
Ole2nls.DL_	40,507	4/5/94
Ole2prox.DL_	17,642	4/5/94
Pptview.DL_	533,674	4/5/94
Pptview.EXE	8,520	4/5/94
Stdole.TL_	1,885	4/5/94
Storage.DL_	68,983	4/5/94
Ttembed.DL_	45,082	4/5/94
Ttembext.DL_	3,507	4/5/94
Typelib.DL_	78,623	4/5/94
Vsetup.EXE	86,982	4/5/94
Vshare.38_	7,241	4/4/94

Troubleshooting PowerPoint Tasks

Some of us wish that a few of the tasks in PowerPoint would be easier to accomplish, or take less time to complete. PowerPoint is extremely proficient at certain tasks and less-than proficient at others. This appendix identifies some of the more complex tasks and describes some workarounds to get those tasks accomplished in the PowerPoint environment.

Everyone has a wish list of what his or her favorite program(s) should do. You need to identify the key necessities of any program and figure out what is commonly known as workarounds to accomplish what an individual needs to be able to do for a particular assignment but doesn't have that capacity with the present software package. Combining that list with another list of what software packages you actually know will help you figure out a plan to get the most out of PowerPoint. PowerPoint can do a lot of things. You sometimes just need to know how to do them in a *slightly different way.*

This appendix covers issues that come up in the electronic forum about PowerPoint. These issues are not necessarily bugs, but rather a list of common requests for certain features, followed by my suggestions about some avenues to follow to accomplish those objectives. Consider this more of a food for thought kind of appendix.

FIND IT ON ▶ **THE WEB** The Microsoft Knowledge Base contains a list of known issues with Microsoft products. If you need additional help on solving a particular problem, the Knowledge Base is a good place to start. It is available online on both CompuServe (type **go mskb**) and also at Microsoft's own Web site at **http://register.microsoft.com/regwiz/forms/ form521.asp**. You will first be asked to register, but access is free.

The list of PowerPoint issues that crop up most frequently are as follows:

- Various printing problems
- Pack and Go problems
- Inability to open PowerPoint file message
- No password protection
- Not enough memory errors
- Slightly distorted screen captures

These topics are covered in the following sections.

Printing Problems

PowerPoint presentations involve several issues with printing, most of which can be easily resolved. A few of the most common printing issues, relating to slow printing and the color or printed shapes, are discussed in the following sections.

Slow Printing

Extremely slow printing is caused by printing the presentation in the background. The benefit of this setting, the default setting in both PowerPoint 95 and 97, is that you can resume working on your presentation sooner than if you print in the foreground. The drawback is that the time to print a presentation may seem like an eternity.

To change this setting in PowerPoint, choose Tools, Options and click on the Print tab. Then, deselect the Background Printing check box and click on OK.

You may also want to change the spooling settings that are part of the Windows settings for a printer. Doing so slows down PowerPoint a little while you are spooling the print job (spooling is just sending the information from PowerPoint to the printer), but you will finish printing sooner. To change the spooling settings in Windows, click on the Start button, and then choose Settings, Printers. Right-click on the appropriate printer icon in the Printers window, choose Properties, and click on the Details tab. Click on the Spool Settings button, and then select the option button to Spool Print Jobs So Program Finishes Printing Faster. Also click on the option button for Start Printing After First Page Is Spooled. Then, click on OK twice and close the Printers window.

Printed Shapes Are the Same Color as the Background

Most presentations are printed to black-and-white printers, but are created in color using color monitors. This disparity leads to many unpleasant surprises at the last minute when you're rushing to print to a black-and-white printer. You end up with ugly borders around shapes that you thought had no border. Your printed page may look like lots of black boxes. Don't panic—an easy way to solve this is available, as well as a better way to create your presentations so that you don't have to face this calamity again.

One solution is to make sure that the print settings are correct in the Print dialog box. Choose File, Print; then, deselect the Black & White check box. Now the presentation prints in grayscale, which is probably the setting that you want to use most of the time. PowerPoint doesn't print in grayscale by default, because any background that isn't pure white uses a lot of ink to print each page.

Now, here's a better way to prepare presentations in advance. When you plan to print them on a black-and-white printer, switch to Black and White view using the Black and White View toolbar button on the Standard Toolbar. There is also a special toolbar button, named Black and White Mode, that is very powerful but not well known. Figure B.1 shows both of these toolbar buttons after the Black and White Mode button has been added to the Formatting toolbar. The Black and White View

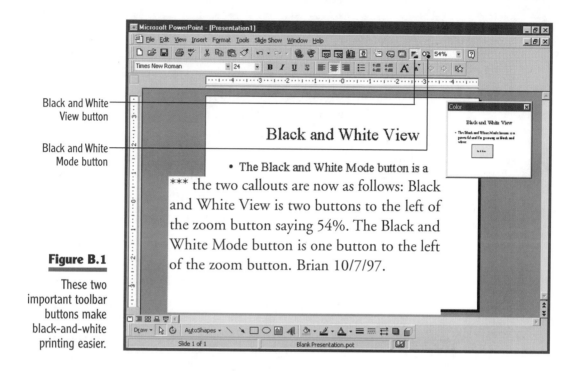

Black and White
View button

Black and White
Mode button

Figure B.1

These two
important toolbar
buttons make
black-and-white
printing easier.

toolbar button lets you toggle between Color and Black and White views. When in Black and White View, the Black and White Mode toolbar button gives you ten different ways to display a selected presentation while you are in Black and White view.

To add the Black and White Mode button to an existing toolbar, follow these steps:

1. With a presentation open, choose Tools, Customize; then, click on the Commands tab in the Customize dialog box.

2. Select View in the Categories list, and then scroll down the Commands window until you see Black and White Mode.

3. Drag the Black and White Mode icon next to the Black and White View button on the Standard toolbar at the top of the screen.

4. Click on Close to exit the Customize dialog box.

5. Click on the Black and White View icon on the Standard toolbar to switch from Color View to Black and White View. The main edit window switches to Black and White, and you also see a small color preview window that will continue to update as you edit.

6. Select an object on the page, and then click on the Black and White Mode icon to change the settings for this object. Select an option from the drop-down menu that appears, as shown in Figure B.2. Note that the <u>W</u>hite option turns the rectangle to white (which would be invisible on a white background).

You will now see onscreen how this object will look when you print it on a black-and-white printer. You have a lot of options here, so a little experimentation will get you exactly what you want and save a lot of trees.

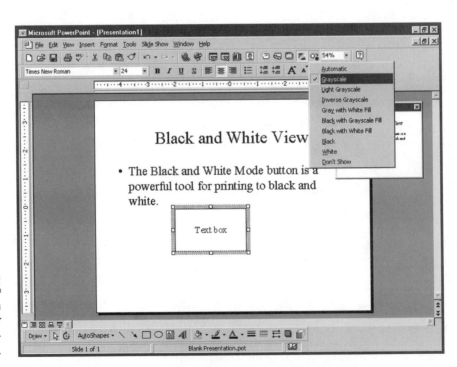

Figure B.2

PowerPoint has ten special settings for objects in black-and-white mode.

Pack and Go Problems

Pack and Go is a terrific addition to PowerPoint because it allows you to save files across multiple floppy disks in compressed format. You can even include the PowerPoint Viewer on the disks, if you want. Although Pack and Go works very well, the way it works is often misunderstood and creates problems for some users. Actually, Pack and Go is working, but it sometimes does not finish the task of packing the presentation, so users think it is a bug in the program. The error is not a bug, but the error does not tell you what the problem is that causes Pack and Go not to finish. The following will explain what is happening.

Understanding how Pack and Go works can eliminate those potential problems. Pack and Go actually works in several steps. The first step is to identify the files that you want to compress and then to set the options for what is to be included, such as the Viewer, fonts, linked files, and presentations. After you establish these elements, Pack and Go compresses all of the specified files into a temporary file. When the files have been completely compressed into one file, Pack and Go writes a copy of the temporary file to the target location. Then it deletes the temporary file.

This process can create a tremendous need for disk space. If you don't have an adequate amount of free disk space available, you won't be able to complete all of the steps, and Pack and Go will fail and not tell you why it failed. Because Pack and Go is creating a temporary file, you need to have free disk space greater than twice the file size of the files that you are packing.

The solution is to be aware of how much free disk space you have available and to make sure that your temporary file folder is empty, or relatively empty. The old saying about you can't have too much money or too much memory definitely applies to Pack and Go's capability to be successful.

TIP Generally, the Temp folder is located in C:\Windows\Temp. To check where your Temp folder is located, open PowerPoint and choose Help, About Microsoft PowerPoint; then click on System Info. Close the System Information window and click on OK. Make sure that your Temp folder is empty or nearly empty, and be sure to empty the Recycle Bin to free up disk space.

Cannot Open PowerPoint File

Although this error message doesn't occur often, it can ruin any day when it does. Why this message appears is not clear, so I won't give any advice on how to avoid the problem. With luck, if you are reasonably meticulous about managing your work, it won't ever happen to you. If it does, you can try several workarounds before you just give up and re-create everything from scratch.

These workarounds are nothing sophisticated like Dr. Watson or Norton Disk Doctor. They fall more into the arena of PowerPoint voodoo. And if none of them work, you will have spent only five minutes on them, at which time you are best off starting over from scratch.

Sometimes, if a PowerPoint file will not open using the File, Open command, it will open by double-clicking on the filename in Explorer. If that doesn't work, you can sometimes rescue some, if not all, of a presentation by opening a new blank presentation and inserting slides from the file that you cannot open. Follow these steps (you may get lucky):

1. Open a new presentation and choose Insert, Slides from Files.
2. Use the Browse button to find the file in question, and then click on Open.
3. Click on Display to see a thumbnail preview.
4. If you can see a preview of the individual pages in the thumbnail windows, select the first slide and click on Insert.

This Slide Finder interface is similar to Slide Sorter View in PowerPoint, but shows only three slides at a time. If you move the horizontal slider bar, you will be able to see previews of the entire set of pages.

5. Repeat step 4 to insert additional slides, until you have recovered as much of the presentation as you can.

6. When you are finished, click on Close to close the Slide Finder.

You could also try clicking on the Insert All button of the Slide Finder, but the reason the file wouldn't open in the first place is probably that an image on one of the pages is corrupt. This corruption may or may not prevent you from inserting every page into a new presentation. If neither of these methods works, get busy and immediately start from scratch—and remember to keep backup copies of everything in the future.

No Password Protection

One can only wonder why Microsoft Excel has a password-protection feature and PowerPoint does not. In any case, PowerPoint does not have any way of internally protecting a file from being changed if someone knows how to use PowerPoint. You can get around this limitation, however, if you need to protect a PowerPoint file from being edited. You can actually do this entirely with PowerPoint, although it does require a bit more work. The extra work involves just a few additional steps.

After you've created a PowerPoint presentation, follow these steps to protect the presentation:

1. When the presentation is in its final form, choose File, Save As. After naming the file, in the Save as Type drop-down list, select JPEG Interchange File Format (*.jpg).

2. After clicking on Save you see a message box asking you if you want to save all of the pages or just that page. Choose the option to Save All. This will convert every page in the presentation into an

individual .JPG (picture) file, which is a bitmap image. As a result, every individual piece of information that could be edited, such as the title or tables, will be converted into a picture (a collection of pixels).

Each of the pages will be saved as a new filename in sequential order, such as Slide1.jpg, Slide2.jpg, and so on. This order makes going back and creating a new presentation, and then inserting each page as a picture, easy (using Insert, Picture, as you learned earlier in this book).

Not Enough Memory Errors

Those who use Microsoft Organization Chart sometimes report this type of error. They usually say, "But I have lots of RAM and plenty of hard disk space available." The whole issue appears quite perplexing on the surface. The real issue, however, is that the error message does not describe the true problem.

The real problem, in virtually every one of these situations, has always been identified with too many fonts loaded in the computer. For some reason, PowerPoint and many other programs can function just fine with hundreds and hundreds of fonts installed. Microsoft Organization Chart cannot. Microsoft Organization Chart is a separate program that operates inside PowerPoint and, for some reason, chokes when you have too many fonts installed on the computer.

How many fonts is too many? To a well-disciplined graphics company, probably no more than two to six fonts would be used in any one document. But a well-disciplined graphics company certainly has many more than six fonts installed on its computers. Microsoft Organization Chart doesn't seem to have any problems until the number of fonts installed exceeds 500–600 fonts.

You can avoid this problem by trimming your list of fonts, which will probably increase your computer's speed of changing fonts.

NOTE If you actually need to use many fonts for different clients or different projects, you can keep your life manageable by grouping fonts into different folders and adding or deleting them from the C:\Windows\Fonts folder (or wherever you have installed them). Try creating a separate folder such as C:\Windows\Fonts\Client1 and change the fonts whenever you need to change projects that require new fonts.

Screen Captures Distort Slightly

Many people use screen captures to illustrate manuals. In fact, this book uses a great deal of them. A wide variety of programs are available to record screen images. The simplest way to record an image is to use the Print Screen key to capture the image to the Clipboard, and then paste it into either PowerPoint or another program.

Whether you use a special screen capture program or the Print Screen technique, PowerPoint will display the image with a slight, but noticeable, distortion. It is not the end of the world, but it is distracting because the distortion doesn't show up in any other program.

The distortion occurs because PowerPoint anti-aliases all pictures. *Anti-aliasing* is a way of attempting to smooth out the rough edges of objects by interpolating the pixel colors. The result usually is a better-looking picture. In the case of screen captures, however, a poorer-quality picture usually results. At the moment, you can do nothing to change this.

APPENDIX C

Installation Issues

Although most installations of Office 97 or PowerPoint 97 run just fine, there are still many instances when the installation does not work perfectly. This appendix serves as a reference for some of those issues. It also guides you through a perfect installation and helps you decide what parts of Office 97 or PowerPoint 97 you want to install.

You may not want to use all of the programs in Office 97, or you may not have enough available disk space for a complete installation. This appendix helps you make some informed decisions about how and what to install. You'll also be able to troubleshoot your installation if it failed in the first place, and you'll learn how to run multiple versions of PowerPoint on the same computer.

How to Prepare for a Clean Install

Having other applications open at the time of installation is a major cause of problem installations for any program in the Windows environment. Windows uses a lot of shared files and needs to be able to access certain files during an installation to determine whether that file exists in the first place, or whether the installation process needs to update an existing file with a later version. Another application, even if the application is minimized, may actually be using a specific file and creating confusion for the installation program. This can sometimes result in an incorrect installation.

"But I don't have anything else running; I installed from a fresh boot" is often said by someone complaining about a bad installation. The standard question to ask then is, "How about a virus-protection program?" Many virus-protection programs load automatically and run in the background, so you may not realize that one is running. If one is, it really should be closed before you start the installation program.

How can you tell whether you have any unwanted programs running before you run Setup? Press Ctrl+Alt+Del (hold all keys down simultaneously) to see whether any unwanted programs are running. In the Close Program dialog box that appears, you may see some programs open, such as Explorer, Findfast, Osa, and Systray. You can leave these running because they are either needed for the operation of the computer or they don't seem to interfere with installations (they certainly haven't on my system).

You might be surprised at what program is running on your computer that you are not aware of. For example, I just found Daemon32 on my computer, and I had no idea what this program was. Then I realized that it is the Microsoft Gaming Device that I loaded awhile ago to help with Microsoft FlightSim. I couldn't get the program running (probably because of a bad installation process), so I forgot about it. Maybe I'll follow my own instructions for a change and go back and install it correctly. I also just checked into the Microsoft Web site for some information on this issue, and then I left Internet Explorer and shut down my connection to my ISP. But when I checked again, I was still running Dialmon and Rnaapp, two programs that are connected with dialing into the Internet on my particular machine. I should close them before going back to install the Gaming device for FlightSim—oh wait, I have a book to finish. I'll have to postpone that because I just crash the planes, anyhow.

The main point here is that you may be running more than you think when you do an installation. Checking before you start, and shutting down everything that you can, are wise things to do.

Another good practice, which I have often ignored myself ("Heck, I just bought new software, I wanna run it—what do you mean I should behave and install it correctly!"), is to run ScanDisk and Disk Defragmenter before each major install. In fact, you should be doing that at least once a week, or certainly once a month, anyway. These programs fix disk errors and re-sort the files on your hard drive(s) back into nice, neat clusters. To run ScanDisk, click on the Start menu, choose Run, and type **scandisk** in the Open box. After you run ScanDisk, repeat the same steps for Disk Defragmenter, substituting **defrag** in the Open box. If you have run these programs before, their names will be available when you click on the down arrow beside the Open box to display the drop-down list.

NOTE Note that running ScanDisk before you run Defrag is important. ScanDisk cleans the disk space and Defrag puts files back together in nice, neat clusters. Running them in order is sort of comparable to separating the clean from the dirty laundry before putting your clothes away.

Installation—Step By Step

If you have not already installed Office 97 or PowerPoint 97, you can do so by following these steps:

1. From the Start menu, choose Settings, Control Panel and double-click on the Add/Remove Programs icon.

2. In the Add/Remove Programs Properties dialog box, shown in Figure C.1, click on Install (on the Install/Uninstall tab). Then, click on Next. Windows searches your available drives for a program named Setup.exe. When you are sure that it has found the correct copy of Setup (it should be the one in your CD-ROM drive, unless you are installing Office 97 or PowerPoint 97 from floppy disks), click on Finish.

3. At the Microsoft Welcome screen, type your name and your organization if appropriate (a name is required in order to proceed). Confirm your name and the product ID by clicking on OK on the next two screens.

4. Setup searches your hard drive(s) for installed components and suggests installing the new version to the C:\Program Files\Microsoft Office folder. Or, Setup gives you the option to change the folder so that Office can be installed in another location.

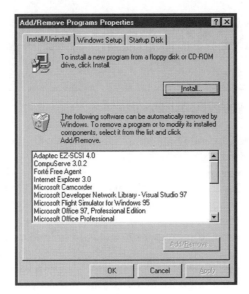

Figure C.1

Click Install to start the installation.

5. After setting the folder to which you want to install the program, click on OK. Setup presents you with three options on the installation: Typical, Custom, or Run from CD-ROM. I recommend always choosing a Custom installation because you will be able to choose exactly what is installed. This will eliminate a lot of problems that may occur with a Typical install; for example, the Typical install does not install some graphics file filters that you are very likely going to need.

6. This next screen is one of the most important screens to get to know and understand. It tells you exactly what programs and files are being installed, and lets you select options to add more items or deselect them to exclude them. Everything that you need to create PowerPoint presentations is listed in the options under PowerPoint. Refer to Table C.1 for an explanation of these options; then, make the desired selections.

7. Click on OK. Office 97 will continue the installation process and warn you if it is going to replace any files that are older than an existing file. Usually, you want to keep the newest version of a file.

TABLE C.1 POWERPOINT CUSTOM INSTALLATION OPTIONS

Option	Description
PowerPoint Options	
Content Templates for additional Templates	Gives you additional templates for use with the AutoContent Wizard
Special help for VBA macros	VBA is new to PowerPoint 97 and the help file for VBA is separate from the regular help file
Animation Effects Sounds	Lets you add prerecorded sounds to animation effects
Various Presentation Translators	Although the translators don't always work well because of significant differences in file formats, they may be useful to some people
A Link to Genigraphics	A direct link to the national slide imaging center for Genigraphics
Office Tools Options	
MS Office Shortcut Bar	Places a shortcut bar to the other Office apps on your desktop
Office Assistant	Here's where to turn off the Paper Clip guy if he bothers you
Spelling Checker	Supplies a common dictionary for all Office apps
Organizational Chart	The separate program for creating Org Charts
Microsoft Graph	Actually, MS Graph gets loaded automatically if you choose to install PowerPoint
Equation Editor	Allows special characters for scientific equations
Microsoft Photo Editor	A handy program if you don't have another photo editing program already installed

TABLE C.1 POWERPOINT CUSTOM INSTALLATION OPTIONS

Option	Description
Office Tools Options	
MS Info	A troubleshooting tool to look at information about your system. A useful program to install
Popular Clipart	The basic collection of clip art
Clip Gallery	Lets you manage clip collections: clip art, pictures, sounds, and video
Microsoft TrueType fonts	These additional fonts can be embedded into and distributed with PowerPoint presentations. Good fonts if you are going to distribute your presentations to non-PowerPoint users.
Lotus VIM Mail Support	Allows you to use Lotus Notes
Find All Word Forms	Needed if you use AutoSummarize feature, which creates a summary of documents
Text Converters	
Word for Windows 2.0 Converter	Converts from this version
Word for Macintosh 4.0-5.1 Converter	Converts from this version
Microsoft Excel Converter	Converts previous versions of Excel file formats
Word 6.0/95 Export Converter	Can create an RTF file
Word 97 for Windows/Macintosh	Converts from Word 97 to Windows or Macintosh readable files

TABLE C.1 POWERPOINT CUSTOM INSTALLATION OPTIONS

Option	Description
Text Converters	
Word 6.0/95 Export Converter	Converts documents into Word 6.0 format
WordPerfect 6.x Converter	WordPerfect 6 for DOS and Windows
WordPerfect 5.x Converter	WordPerfect 5 for DOS and Windows
Lotus 1-2-3 Converter	Converts 1-2-3 documents from versions 2.x, 3.x, and 4.0 to Word 97
Works for Windows 3.0	Converts to/from Works 3.0 for Windows
Works for Windows 4.0	Converts to/from Works 4.0
Recover Text Converter	Recovers text from files that have been saved prior to shutdown
HTML Converter	Converts documents to/from HTML
Converter for use with Lotus Notes	Allows reading Word and Excel files in Lotus Notes 3.x and 4.x
Graphics Filters	
A separate choice from Text Converters	Only 2MB in file size; any serious PowerPoint user will probably install most if not all the graphics filters to save having to go back and reinstall the one or two missed at installation time
Tag Image File Format Import	Imports most .TIF files

TABLE C.1 POWERPOINT CUSTOM INSTALLATION OPTIONS

Option	Description
Graphic Converters	
Encapsulated Postscript Import	Imports .EPS files
Windows Bitmap Import	Imports .BMP files
Enhanced Metafile Import	Imports .EMF files
Truevision Targa Import	Imports .TGA files
AutoCAD DXF Import	Imports .DXF files
Micrografix Designer/Draw Import	Imports .DRW files
CorelDRAW Import	Imports .CDR from versions 3, 4, 5, and 6 of CorelDRAW
Computer Graphics Metafile Import	Imports .CGM files
PC Paintbrush PCX Import	Imports .PCX files
WordPerfect Graphic Import	Imports .WPG versions 1.0, 1.0e, and 2.0 files
WordPerfect Graphics Export	Exports graphics to the .WPG format
Macintosh PICT Import	Imports Macintosh PICT formats but not QuickTime PICT files
Windows Metafile Import	Imports .WMF files

TABLE C.1 POWERPOINT CUSTOM INSTALLATION OPTIONS	
Option	**Description**
Graphic Converters	
GIF (Graphics Interchange Format)	Imports .GIF files
Kodak Photo CD Import	Imports Kodak Photo CD files
JPEG File Interchange Format Import	Imports .JPG files
PNG File Format Import	Imports Portable Network Graphics files
Other Options	
Web Page Authoring (HTML)	The tools to let you export PowerPoint presentations as Web-ready documents
Getting Results Book	Accesses the Online version of Getting Results with Microsoft Office from the CD; places a shortcut on the Office Shortcut Bar

NOTE   Depending on how much you interact with other versions of word processors or spreadsheets, or how many graphics file formats you may choose to use, the text converters and graphics filters are an absolutely critical item and are often overlooked during an installation.

It is a good idea to leave a reasonable amount of time between installations of different new software packages to make sure that each one is working correctly. Otherwise, you won't ever really know which package caused the problem, and you may spend hours or days trying to fix a problem with one software package that was in fact caused by another piece of unrelated software.

TIP If you plan to install multiple versions of Office, you should choose a separate folder and name it something descriptive, such as Office97. Many of us need to run multiple versions, and the ability to keep track of each version is helpful because the file formats change between versions. You'll find a separate section later in this appendix on running multiple versions of PowerPoint on the same computer.

Troubleshooting a Failed Installation

If you carefully followed the installation instructions in the previous section, you shouldn't ever have to read this section—unless, of course, you are asked by others to troubleshoot their bad installations. This happens to me all the time. I generally resort to one of the following two approaches.

The Sledgehammer Approach

Remember one of Reilly's Rules: Assume the worst and you'll never be disappointed. Generally, a failed installation occurs because the user did not take the precautions discussed earlier in this appendix. Not always—but usually. Chances are that the installer won't realize that another program was open. So, assume the worst and uninstall the bad installation. Don't erase it, uninstall it.

At Step 2 of the earlier procedure (in the "Installation—Step By Step" section), select Microsoft Office 97 in the list box, and then click on Add/<u>R</u>emove. Make sure that you leave the selections just as you set them in the installation process.

This should remove all (well, actually, most) of the files that were installed from the failed installation. It will leave any shared files that are needed by other programs—for example, certain .DLL's and so on—that actually are shared by multiple programs.

Then go back and follow the guidelines and installation instructions as stated previously, paying specific attention to closing all open programs. Following the directions will fix things 90 percent of the time. This still makes me wonder why we, myself included, don't just follow the rules. Probably because we are human!

The Subtle Approach

Okay, so in a few cases, following the rules doesn't work. Are you sure that no other programs were running when you installed the program? If you are, you can try some other things.

Frankly, most problem installations result from a few basic sources that none of us can control, such as the following:

- Other programs that overwrite files you really need to use
- Wrong versions of files that were installed by other programs
- Vague instructions on installation procedures
- The fullness of the moon (the only time I have bad installs!)

Other Programs Overwrite Files That You Need

No program in Windows lives in its own space. That means that Windows programs use other little programs to do a lot of things. And these little programs are shared by a host of other programs. These little programs are called Dynamic Link Libraries, or DLLs, and show up in your folders as .DLL extensions. You will never see the underlying code to these .DLLs. You may not even know that you have these .DLLs loaded into your computer.

For example, if you look under the folder that you have for MS Office and check for .DLLs, you may not find any. In fact, they are generally installed in various Windows folders where you may not even see them. But they are there. The purpose of the .DLL file is to share routine commands that many programs handle, such as Copy to Clipboard. A .DLL handles each of these commands so that you don't have to have that little bit of code handled in every program. Whatever program you are in under Windows just calls the little program (the .DLL) to copy the selected object to the clipboard. The idea is efficiency.

Unfortunately, some programs add new .DLLs to your system without asking you for permission. Very rude! Sometimes, those new .DLLs interfere with your existing programs because they make up a common group of underlying code that runs when told to run. Hence the subtle problems of new installations.

If you install programs and test them for a reasonable length of time, you will probably be able to identify the new program that you just loaded that has messed up your existing .DLLs. But that means running every program for a fair amount of time after you install a new program. Not likely, I know; I don't even do that. In fact, to make you feel a little better, not even my friends who are even more meticulous than I am about these things are completely guilt-free on this issue.

So, what do you do? Do your best to spread out the installations of new software. Don't be shy about doing a complete uninstall of a program, and then a completely new install to help reset the program's registrations. And never, ever, install a new program during a full moon.

Server Application Cannot Be Found

This is one of the most common sources of confusion with Office programs. The most common misunderstanding is phrased something like, "I get this message and I'm not on a network"; Why are they looking for the server? The error message "Server Application Cannot Be Found" happens when you are trying to edit an embedded object that was created with another application, such as Microsoft Graph, Microsoft Org

Chart, Excel, or Microsoft Word. The meaning of the message is always the same and usually has nothing to do with a network server, especially if you are not running on a network.

The error generally occurs for one of three reasons:

- The presentation was originally created in a later version of Power-Point than you are running. Now you are trying to edit the object in a server program (that is, one that reports to PowerPoint). Remember my discussion about tables really being created in Word, or graphs/charts really being created in Microsoft Graph? If the version that someone created the object in is not available on the computer you are working on now, you can have problems. When you double-click on the object, the program will try to fire up the version (the server) of the program that the object was created in. If that version, for example Word 97 or Graph 97, is not available on that computer, the object cannot open the server application.

- The original path to the file is no longer located in the exact same position. A good example of this is if you added or deleted a drive from your computer after the original installation, rendering the path that the program is looking for invalid. The program displays an error message, even though you know that the program is still available.

- You installed various versions of Office in nonchronological order, which can re-set the default registries of a program. You may think that PowerPoint is PowerPoint, but Windows 95 knows the difference between PowerPoint 97 and PowerPoint 95. Windows 95 doesn't really do a very good job at guessing which application you want to open, though, if you try to open the file by double-clicking on the file icon.

In this case, most often the program, that is, PowerPoint, is looking for the server program, that is, Microsoft Graph (or a similar program that created the original object, such as a graph), and cannot find it for some reason.

Microsoft Graph Issues

Progress is a wonderful thing. It creates chaos for the nonprogressive. It is inevitable that progress in software requires new file formats. Or, as most of us believe, new file formats are designed to make old file formats obsolete, which requires software upgrades.

Whatever the truth about that is, the truth about Microsoft Graph in Office 97 is that it is a new file format that creates chaos for those who try to edit the Microsoft Graph objects in previous versions of Power-Point (that is, in previous versions of Microsoft Graph, because it is actually a separate program). The problem is not that the graphs are not viewable when files are saved as previous versions of PowerPoint; rather, the problem is that the graphs are not editable in previous versions of Microsoft Graph.

If you have installed multiple versions of PowerPoint on a single computer, you will not notice this problem until you move the file to a computer in which Office 97 has not been installed. Then you will realize that you just can't edit the graph on that computer. The funny thing is that many of the new drawing effects of Microsoft Graph 97, such as the gradations, show just fine. The problem is that you cannot change the numbers in the underlying data.

The obvious solution would be to not install Microsoft Graph 97 when installing Office 97; however, even though the option appears to be available during the installation process, in reality, Microsoft Graph 97 is automatically installed with PowerPoint 97, and the new version of Microsoft Graph overwrites the previous one. All new graphs created on that machine using Microsoft Graph will, of course, use the Microsoft Graph 97 program.

The release of an update from Microsoft has alleviated this problem. The SR-1 version of Office 97 now allows you to save your graphs as Graph 5 objects, which will then be editable in earlier versions of PowerPoint.

You will lose the new features of Graph 97, however, such as the ability to build chart objects by each series during slide shows and changing the series colors using gradated colors.

FIND IT ON ▶
THE WEB

The Service Release 1 for Office 97 is available for download at the Microsoft Web site at **http://www.microsoft.com/office/office97/servicerelease/**. In the U.S., you can also get a new CD by calling the Microsoft order desk at 800-360-7561. They will ship an updated CD for a minor shipping charge.

The only options appear to be to go back to the first premise that this book started with: Start at the end. Everything is determined by the end result. If your charts need to be editable by people who use only Power-Point 95, you will have some real headaches if you create your charts in Microsoft Graph 97. The problem stems from the fact that Microsoft Graph will be installed if you install PowerPoint 97 on a given machine.

If you are faced with this situation, you probably just can't use Microsoft Graph to create your charts. You might consider using Excel 95 instead. You can copy and paste the charts into PowerPoint. They will not only display in PowerPoint shows but also will be editable by double-clicking in any version of Excel that is running on that particular machine.

Running Multiple Versions of PowerPoint on the Same Computer

Many of us work in more than one version of PowerPoint. Perhaps the entire workforce has not upgraded to the latest version simultaneously, or you have clients who have not upgraded to PowerPoint 97 yet. Therefore, you may want to install multiple versions of PowerPoint on one computer.

The normal installation process for Office 97 looks at all of your drives, even Zip drives, for installations of previous versions of Office. The installation program then gives you a choice of removing the old version(s) without touching any data files or folders that you've created. If that is what you want to do, you can make the decision to let the installation program remove any old versions. If you want to leave them intact, however, you should instruct the installation program not to remove your old versions. You also should have chosen to install the new version to a different folder from a previous dialog box.

If you chose to install Office 97 to a new folder during the installation procedure, the program will create a new folder for you (if one does not already exist) and perform the installation there, while leaving *most* of your previous installation of PowerPoint intact. I say *most* because there is no way to have two versions of Microsoft Graph installed on the same computer.

When you install PowerPoint 97, Microsoft Graph 97 is automatically installed, in spite of what you tell the installation program. That's it, end of story, no way around it. When you open an earlier version of Power-Point, such as PowerPoint 4, and insert a graph with Microsoft Graph, it will be a Graph 97 object. That Graph 97 object will have to be saved as a Graph 5 object for it to be editable in previous versions of PowerPoint.

APPENDIX D

Other
Resources

You should always have as many options at your disposal as possible so that you can meet almost any challenge easily. Sometimes you may need to convert a graphics file to a different file format that can be inserted into the PowerPoint program. Or you may have a very special charting problem that can be solved easily in Excel, but would be a terribly time-consuming job in Microsoft Graph. Sometimes you will know how to do something but realize that there is probably an easier way. I know these situations happen because they happen to me all of the time.

This appendix provides you with some outside resources that may prove to be useful at times when you need to find specific help *right now*. These resources are divided into several different categories: getting answers to questions, Microsoft Web sites, additional software, and examples of special applications.

Getting Answers to Your Questions

Several sets of resources are available for getting answers to specific questions about PowerPoint. These include the following:

☼ *Microsoft newsgroups*—These are peer-supported newsgroups that are specifically supported by a collection of Microsoft MVP's (Most Valuable Professionals). These are not Microsoft employees. They are individuals who have been recognized by Microsoft as being very knowledgeable in specific applications and contributing unselfishly to the support of the Microsoft newsgroups. You will also receive support from others who frequent the newsgroups. The

PowerPoint newsgroup is a very friendly place, and there is no such thing as a bad question. To access the PowerPoint newsgroup, point your favorite newsreader at:

microsoft.public.powerpoint.

- *CompuServe*—Stream sponsors a forum on CompuServe supporting PowerPoint. It is supported by several CompuServe Service Partners (CSPs) who volunteer their services. This group also is open and friendly. If you have a CompuServe account, you can access this group by using **GO DESKTOP** and selecting the PowerPoint forum.

- *Microsoft Standard Support*—Microsoft PowerPoint—(425) 635-7145—Microsoft offers support for usability questions for two incidents for purchasers of Microsoft Office Standard Edition and for two additional incidents, for a total of four, for purchasers of Microsoft Office Professional Edition. The cost of the phone call is extra because it is a toll call.

- *Microsoft Priority Support*—Microsoft offers unlimited calls for PowerPoint support at $35 per incident. Charges are billed to your American Express card, Master Card, or VISA card. Call 1-900-555-2200. Because this is a 900 number, there is also a charge for the phone call. Microsoft also provides an 800 number, but the per-incident charge is $45. Call 1-800-936-5700.

Microsoft Web Sites

Microsoft Knowledge Base (MSKB) is the first place look for technical answers to your questions. The MSKB has 2,000 articles that deal with issues in PowerPoint and a strong search engine to help you find just what you need. Point your browser at:

http://register.microsoft.com/regwiz/forms/form521

PowerPoint home page provides new templates, the Viewers, and several new add-ins. Point your browser at:

> http://www.microsoft.com/powerpoint/default.htm

See the Microsoft site to report bugs or requests for new products. Point your browser at:

> http://www.microsoft.com/regwiz/regwiz.asp

Additional Software

Many sources of additional software exist that can help you prepare files for use in PowerPoint. The following is a short list of some of them. They are timed trial versions so that you can try them out before purchasing the package.

○ *Paint Shop Pro*—This is an excellent photo editor if you do not already have Corel Draw or Photoshop. You can find a 30-day trial copy of Paint Shop Pro at **http://www.jasc.com**. Created by Jasc, Inc.

○ *Pixel 3D*—This is a very good 3-D rendering program to create 3-D images. The 15-session trial copy of Pixel 3D is available at **http://www.jasc.com**. This program was created by Forward Design and is distributed by Jasc, Inc.

If you want to purchase either of the preceding two programs, you can order them from Jasc, Inc., by payment with check or credit card (Master Card or Visa). The numbers for ordering are as follows: 1-800-622-2793; Voice: 612-930-9800; FAX: 612-930-9172. You also can place your order directly from the company's secured Web server: **http://www.jasc.com**.

○ *Ikon Editor - Neosoftware*—This is an excellent tool to create custom icons for use in custom toolbars. The 30-day trial version is available at **http://www.neosoftware.com/** (click on Products).

Examples of Applications

Many times, you might be looking for a specific example of how to perform a certain task in Excel or Word that you might need for a PowerPoint presentation, or for your own needs in Excel or Word. Several Web sites provide very helpful information. Some of these are listed next.

PowerPoint

http://www.rdpslides.com/—Steve Rindsberg is a Microsoft MVP and runs a service bureau in Cincinnati, OH. Steve's site has many useful articles, including how to go about converting presentation files between programs such as PowerPoint, Freelance Graphics, and Harvard Graphics.

http://www.slide-express.ca/—Tony Cook is also a Microsoft MVP and runs a service bureau in Toronto, Canada. Tony's site has some very good advice for preparing your slides for 35mm slide output.

http://ourworld.compuserve.com/homepages/Reilly_and_Associates/—This is my site and covers a variety of topics, including samples of PowerPoint animations and code examples using Visual Basic for Applications (VBA) to accelerate the production process in PowerPoint.

Excel

http://ourworld.compuserve.com/homepages/Stephen_Bullen/—Stephen Bullen is one of the world's leading Excel experts and has many examples, available for download, of unique applications using Excel.

http://www.lacher.com/—John Lacher is a CPA and a leading Excel expert. His site contains some very good simple examples of how to use VBA in some common applications to make your spreadsheets more powerful tools.

http://www.baarns.com—The Baarns Group is a consulting firm that has many useful utilities available at its Web site.

Word

http://ourworld.compuserve.com/homepages/Dian_Chesney/—Dian is a Microsoft MVP and has many examples of how to manage various tasks in Word.

Cross-Platform Issues

With the introduction of a new file format for PowerPoint 97, users who need to move files back and forth across the Macintosh and Windows platforms face some new challenges. This appendix addresses many of the major issues of moving files back and forth across platforms and identifies an underlying strategy for doing this.

The most recent release of PowerPoint for the Macintosh is Version 4, which is comparable to PowerPoint Version 4 for Windows. Files saved in PowerPoint Version 4 for Windows are readable on the Mac. Mac files are readable in PowerPoint Version 4 or higher. PowerPoint for Windows 95 files can be read on the Mac only if a special file converter is installed. Files saved in PowerPoint 97 format are not currently readable on the Mac. Microsoft has announced that it is busy developing a new version of Office for the Mac that will very likely be able to read all versions of PowerPoint files.

Working with PowerPoint files in both the Windows and Mac platforms is relatively simple, but you need to follow a few guidelines to help make this as effortless as possible. Essentially, the issues fall into the following areas, each of which are addressed in this appendix:

- Moving the files between the platforms
- Opening the file on the other platform
- File differences between platforms, specifically as they relate to graphics

Moving PowerPoint Files Between Platforms

Sometimes the hardest part about getting files moved to the other platform is the actual task of physically moving the file. If the Mac and the PC are on a network, this is not a problem. Simply copy, by dragging, the file to the appropriate drive.

If the two platforms are not networked, some additional issues may come up. If the file is smaller than 1.4MB (the size that one floppy disk will hold), copy the PowerPoint file to a floppy disk that has been formatted in PC rather than Mac format. Most Mac disk drives can read from and write to a PC-formatted disk; the PC disk drive cannot read from or write to a Mac-formatted disk, however.

If you are not lucky enough to have a PC-formatted disk handy and you have to open a Mac PowerPoint file from a Mac-formatted disk, you need to use a special software program to copy the file from the Mac disk onto the hard drive. A host of programs are available to do this for you. These programs, such as Mac-In-Dos and MacOpener, cost approximately $50–$100 and are available at most computer stores or through mail order.

Another way to move PowerPoint files from one platform to another is to move them via removable disks such as a Zip or SyQuest disk. If you do use one of these removable disks, however, you have to be sure that the units are compatible with one another on both platforms. You will also most likely need to have a software program that is mentioned in the previous paragraph.

If your file does not fit on a single floppy disk or you do not have a removable disk drive that is compatible on both platforms, you may be able to compress the file using a compression tool such as WinZip or Stuffit. Both of these programs will compress the file and expand it again later, so you may be able to fit the file on a single disk or several floppy disks.

WinZip is available from Nico Mak Computing and compresses files in the popular .ZIP format. Stuffit Expander, from Aladdin Systems, is a Windows program that expands files from many popular compression formats including the popular Stuffit (.SIT) format, which is a common Mac format, as well as the self-extracting .SEA and .EXE formats.

FIND IT ON ▶
THE WEB

You can download Stuffit Expander from Aladdin Systems' Web site at **http://www.aladdinsys.com/** and unstuff to your heart's content. You can download WinZip and evaluate it before you purchase it. An evaluation copy is available at **http://www.winzip.com/info.htm/** and you can decide if you'd like to purchase it.

■ ■

TIP

Anyone using graphics files should be using a file compression program such as Stuffit or WinZip. Compression not only makes transmission faster but also protects the file format from corruption, which can frequently occur when files are transmitted via modem in uncompressed format.

■ ■

Sending the file via modem is another way to get files from one platform to the other. If both locations have e-mail connections, the file can be sent as a binary file from one location to the other. Checking your e-mail program to make sure that you are sending the file as a *binary* file and not as an ASCII file is important. As mentioned in the preceding tip, you should also be sure to compress the file to protect the file from corruption. This may not be absolutely necessary, but uncompressed Power-Point files becoming corrupted during modem transmission is a common problem.

I hope that one of these methods will work for you. When the file is actually located on the hard drive of the other platform, it is time to open the file.

Opening the File on the Other Platform

The first thing to do when the file is located on the other drive is to look at the name of the file and change it if necessary. If the file came from the PC and was moved to the Mac, you can just open the file using the File, Open command from the main menu in PowerPoint. If the file came from the Mac, you have to be sure that it has a .PPT extension so that the PowerPoint for Windows program can see the filename when you choose File, Open. On the PC, use Windows Explorer to view the filename and be sure it has the extension .PPT.

When you choose File, Open from the PowerPoint menu, PowerPoint begins translating the file into a file format that can be shown on the platform on which you are operating. While PowerPoint is translating the file from the Mac to the Windows platform, a message box appears, stating that you are updating a file from a previous version (see Figure E.1).

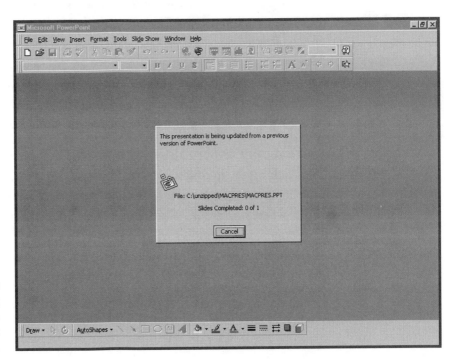

Figure E.1

A message box appears as PowerPoint translates the file.

When PowerPoint 97 has finished translating the file, it opens the file as a read-only file. PowerPoint 95 also opens the file as a read-only file, but that file must be saved using a different name.

When you open a Windows PowerPoint file that has been saved as version 4 of PowerPoint on the Mac, you see a message box that tells you that you are opening a Windows file.

PowerPoint 95 and 97 no longer warn you that you are opening a Mac file; PowerPoint 95 will open the file as read-only, and if you want to save it, you will have to use Save As and choose a new filename. PowerPoint 97 gives you the choice of saving the file using the same filename, but you are warned about which file format you want to use, such as PowerPoint 4, PowerPoint 95, or PowerPoint 97. Note that if you save the file in Power-Point 95 or 97 format, you may have some issues about what is readable on the Mac if you need to move the file back to the Mac.

TIP When you are moving PowerPoint files back and forth between the PC and the Mac, use the lowest common denominator principle to decide what enhancements you should add. Until PowerPoint 98 for the Mac is available, if you are planning to move files back and forth and be able to edit them, you should leave everything in PowerPoint 4 file format. It's really not that hard to do, after you get used to saving the file in the version 4 format.

You may also try to open the PowerPoint file on the other platform by double-clicking on the filename. In this case, however, the file may not contain adequate information to actually open the file in PowerPoint. For example, when you are in Windows, if you did not rename the file with a .PPT extension, Windows will not know how to open the file. On the Mac, the information about the file type is kept separately from the actual file, so you may also have problems opening the file this way.

Whichever platform you are on, always open the PowerPoint program first. Then choose File, Open from the menu, select the file that you want to open, and click on OK. This should work every time.

File Differences Between Platforms

Now that you have saved and opened the PowerPoint file on the other platform, you may think that you are home free. Almost, but not quite. A few things work on the Mac that don't translate to the PC. Likewise, the Windows versions of PowerPoint have a few differences from the Mac versions. Some things that work on the PC will not necessarily translate to the Mac.

Three areas that may cause problems when you move PowerPoint files across platforms are as follows:

✿ Fonts

✿ Non rectangular art

✿ Version specific effects

The following sections address these issues and identify how you can solve potential problems related to them.

Fonts

The fonts used on a Mac may have slightly different names from the fonts used on the PC. When you open a presentation, PowerPoint looks at the fonts that are being used. If the computer does not have an exact match for that font name, PowerPoint substitutes another font. Normally, this is not a big deal. For instance, Arial is substituted for Helvetica. Only a true font expert will see the difference in the two fonts. But if the presentation used a special font such as Bodoni, PowerPoint may not know the best substitute for this font. The results can sometimes be quite surprising. For instance, PowerPoint may display letters in place of bullets. Text may run off the page. But don't panic—PowerPoint makes it very easy to globally change all the fonts used in a presentation.

To change the fonts in a presentation, follow these steps:

1. Open the presentation in PowerPoint, and then choose Format, Replace Fonts.

2. In the Replace drop-down list, select the font that you want to replace.

3. In the With drop-down list, select the font that you want to use.

4. Click on Replace, and then Close to close the Replace Font dialog box.

The fonts will globally change in the presentation. At this point, you should check each page in the presentation to make sure that the text spacing looks acceptable. Usually, it will look fine, but in some cases you may want to make some minor changes.

TIP

One way to avoid font problems when moving files around to various computers is to make sure that you are using Microsoft's TrueType fonts. These fonts are likely to be available on either a PC or a Mac if PowerPoint is installed. Using Adobe PostScript fonts on either platform will mean not only that the fonts cannot be embedded, but also that Adobe Type Manager must be installed on any computer that uses these fonts. So, if you plan to distribute the presentation to different computers, keep in mind the end user's setup.

Nonrectangular Art

The use of nonrectangular art has always been a troublesome issue with PowerPoint and cross-platform presentations. The typical example is a logo that is created in Adobe Illustrator and is not a rectangle and does not show up as a rectangle when shown in Slide Show view. The trouble stems from the fact that PowerPoint for Windows does not handle Adobe Illustrator files well. PowerPoint prints these images to a PostScript printer perfectly, but what is displayed onscreen is generally a white rectangle with file information (see Figure E.2).

This has been very frustrating to Mac users because they have been able to use this kind of file on the Mac with no problems. Then, when they

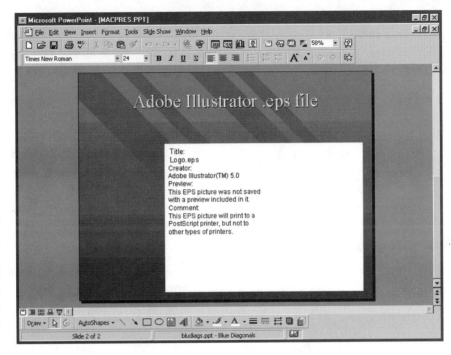

Figure E.2

Although
PowerPoint for
Windows cannot
display Adobe
Illustrator files
onscreen, you can
print them to a
PostScript printer.

port the presentation to the PC version of PowerPoint, they can't figure out what they are doing wrong.

The underlying issue is how PowerPoint for Windows deals with vector files. A vector file is the only way to get nonrectangular pictures.

PowerPoint handles vector files very differently than PowerPoint on the Mac. PowerPoint for Windows handles vector files that are .WMF files quite well. It does not do well with some kinds of .EPS files, whether created on the Mac or in Windows, if you want a transparent background. Adobe Illustrator .EPS files will print perfectly to any postscript printer in PowerPoint Windows but will show on the screen as a rectangular box. What you really need to do with Adobe Illustrator .EPS files is to translate them to Windows metafiles and the Windows metafile will print perfectly and show on the screen as a nonrectangular shape.

■■

TIP It is quite easy to convert an Adobe Illustrator .EPS (vector) file to a .WMF file, and then use the .WMF file in PowerPoint for Windows. To do this, save the Illustrator file as an .EPS file in a previous version, such as version 5. Then open the .EPS file in CorelDraw, and then save the file in Windows Metafile format (using the File, Save As command). You can then view and print the file in PowerPoint for Windows. If you don't have Corel-Draw and you don't want to purchase the program, you might consider renting computer time at a retail outlet that provides CorelDraw on computer workstations. Converting several files and saving them to floppy disks would not take long.

■■

Version-Specific Effects

Another frequent cause of unexpected results when moving presentations across platforms is special effects used, such as some transitions or bullet builds that don't translate because they aren't available in the Mac version of PowerPoint. For instance, in PowerPoint 97, you can apply builds to two columns of bullets. In PowerPoint on the Mac, however, this same presentation will build only the first column of bullets.

In summary, the safest thing to do when you plan to move PowerPoint presentations across platforms is to view the presentation on both platforms before distributing the final presentation. If that is not an option, just try to keep things simple by avoiding the use of special effects, complex graphics, or unusual fonts. Many presentations have been moved successfully from the Mac to the PC and vice versa, so don't be afraid to attempt this procedure. Just follow the guidelines given here, and the conversion should go smoothly!

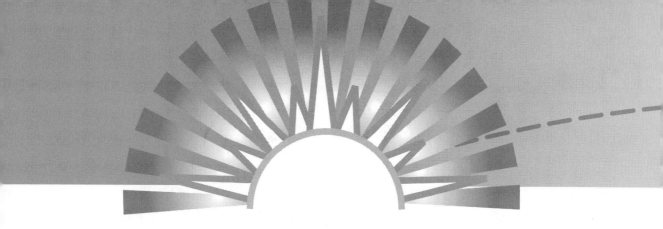

INDEX

Send Us
YOUR COMMENTS

Dear Reader:

Thank you for buying this book. In order to offer you more quality books on the topics *you* would like to see, we need your input. At Prima Publishing, we pride ourselves on timely responsiveness to our readers needs. If you'll complete and return this brief questionnaire, *we will listen!*

Name: (first) _____ (M.I.) _____ (last) _____

Company: _____ Type of business: _____

Address: _____ City: _____ State: _____ Zip: _____

Phone: _____ Fax: _____ E-mail address: _____

May we contact you for research purposes? ❑ Yes ❑ No

(If you participate in a research project, we will supply you with your choice of a book from Prima CPD)

❶ How would you rate this book, overall?

❑ Excellent ❑ Fair
❑ Very Good ❑ Below Average
❑ Good ❑ Poor

❷ Why did you buy this book?

❑ Price of book ❑ Content
❑ Author's reputation ❑ Prima's reputation
❑ CD-ROM/disk included with book
❑ Information highlighted on cover
❑ Other (Please specify): _____

❸ How did you discover this book?

❑ Found it on bookstore shelf
❑ Saw it in Prima Publishing catalog
❑ Recommended by store personnel
❑ Recommended by friend or colleague
❑ Saw an advertisement in: _____
❑ Read book review in: _____
❑ Saw it on Web site: _____
❑ Other (Please specify): _____

❹ Where did you buy this book?

❑ Bookstore (name)_____
❑ Computer Store (name) _____
❑ Electronics Store (name) _____
❑ Wholesale Club (name) _____
❑ Mail Order (name) _____
❑ Direct from Prima Publishing
❑ Other (please specify): _____

❺ Which computer periodicals do you read regularly? _____

_____

_____

_____

❻ Would you like to see your name in print?

May we use your name and quote you in future Prima Publishing books or promotional materials?

❑ Yes ❑ No

❼ Comments & Suggestions: _____

_____

_____

Visit our Web Site at: **http://www.primapublishing.com**
and simply fill in one of our online Response Forms

SAVE A STAMP

⑨ How do you rate your level of computer skills?

☐ Beginner
☐ Advanced
☐ Intermediate

⑪ I would be interested in computer books on these topics

☐ Word Processing   ☐ Database:
☐ Networking   ☐ Spreadsheets
☐ Desktop Publishing   ☐ Web site design
Other

⑧ Where do you use your computer?

Work ☐ 100% ☐ 75% ☐ 50% ☐ 25%
Home ☐ 100% ☐ 75% ☐ 50% ☐ 25%
School ☐ 100% ☐ 75% ☐ 50% ☐ 25%
Other

⑩ What is your age?

☐ Under 18
☐ 18-24   ☐ 40-49
☐ 25-29   ☐ 50-59
☐ 30-39   ☐ 60-over

PLEASE
PLACE
STAMP
HERE

PRIMA PUBLISHING

Computer Products Division
3875 Atherton Road
Rocklin, CA 95765

OTHER BOOKS
FROM PRIMA PUBLISHING
Computer Products Division

ISBN	Title	Price
0-7615-1175-X	ACT! 3.0 Fast & Easy	$16.99
0-7615-0680-2	America Online Complete Handbook and Membership Kit	$24.99
0-7615-0417-6	CompuServe Complete Handbook and Membership Kit	$24.95
0-7615-0692-6	Create Your First Web Page In a Weekend	$29.99
0-7615-0743-4	Create FrontPage Web Pages In a Weekend	$29.99
0-7615-0428-1	The Essential Excel 97 Book	$27.99
0-7615-0733-7	The Essential Netscape Communicator Book	$24.99
0-7615-0969-0	The Essential Office 97 Book	$27.99
0-7615-0695-0	The Essential Photoshop Book	$35.00
0-7615-1182-2	The Essential PowerPoint 97 Book	$24.99
0-7615-1136-9	The Essential Publisher 97 Book	$24.99
0-7615-0752-3	The Essential Windows NT 4 Book	$27.99
0-7615-0427-3	The Essential Word 97 Book	$27.99
0-7615-0425-7	The Essential WordPerfect 8 Book	$24.99
0-7615-1008-7	Excel 97 Fast & Easy	$16.99
0-7615-1194-6	Increase Your Web Traffic In a Weekend	$19.99

ISBN	Title	Price
0-7615-1191-1	Internet Explorer 4.0 Fast & Easy	$16.99
0-7615-1137-7	Jazz Up Your Web Site In a Weekend	$24.99
0-7615-1293-4	Learn HTML In a Weekend	$24.99
0-7615-1217-9	Learn Publisher 97 In a Weekend	$19.99
0-7615-1251-9	Learn Word 97 In a Weekend	$19.99
0-7615-1193-8	Lotus 1-2-3 Fast & Easy	$16.99
0-7615-0852-X	Netscape Navigator 3 Complete Handbook	$24.99
0-7615-1162-8	Office 97 Fast & Easy	$16.99
0-7615-0759-0	Professional Web Design	$40.00
0-7615-0063-4	Researching on the Internet	$29.95
0-7615-0686-1	Researching on the World Wide Web	$24.99
0-7615-1192-X	SmartSuite 97 Fast & Easy	$16.99
0-7615-1007-9	Word 97 Fast & Easy	$16.99
0-7615-1083-4	WordPerfect 8 Fast & Easy	$16.99
0-7615-1188-1	WordPerfect Suite 8 Fast & Easy	$16.99

TO ORDER BOOKS

Please send me the following items:

Quantity	Title	Unit Price	Total
_____	_____	$_____	$_____
_____	_____	$_____	$_____
_____	_____	$_____	$_____
_____	_____	$_____	$_____
_____	_____	$_____	$_____

Subtotal	$_____
Deduct 10% when ordering 3–5 books	$_____
7.25% Sales Tax (CA only)	$_____
8.25% Sales Tax (TN only)	$_____
5.0% Sales Tax (MD and IN only)	$_____
Shipping and Handling*	$_____
TOTAL ORDER	$_____

Shipping and Handling depend on Subtotal.

Subtotal	Shipping/Handling
$0.00–$14.99	$3.00
$15.00–29.99	$4.00
$30.00–49.99	$6.00
$50.00–99.99	$10.00
$100.00–199.99	$13.00
$200.00+	call for quote

Foreign and all Priority Request orders:
Call Order Entry department for price quote at 1-916-632-4400

This chart represents the total retail price of books only (before applicable discounts are taken).

By telephone: With Visa or MC, call 1-800-632-8676. Mon.–Fri. 8:30–4:00 PST.

By Internet e-mail: sales@primapub.com

By mail: Just fill out the information below and send with your remittance to:

PRIMA PUBLISHING

P.O. Box 1260BK

Rocklin, CA 95677-1260

http://www.primapublishing.com

Name_____ Daytime Telephone_____

Address _____

City _____ State _____ Zip _____

Visa /MC# _____Exp. _____

Check/Money Order enclosed for $_____ Payable to Prima Publishing

Signature _____

Prima's *fast & easy*™ Series

Relax, learning new software is now a breeze. You are looking at a series of books dedicated to one idea: To help you learn to use software as quickly and as easily as possible. No need to wade through boring pages of endless text. With Prima's FAST & EASY series, you simply look and learn.

Microsoft® Office 97
0-7615-1162-8
$16.99 (Can. $23.95)

Microsoft® Word 97
0-7615-1007-9
$16.99 (Can. $23.95)

Microsoft® Excel 97
0-7615-1008-7
$16.99 (Can. $23.95)

Internet Explorer 4.0
0-7615-1191-1
$16.99 (Can. $23.95)

ACT!™ 3.0
0-7615-1175-X
$16.99 (Can. $23.95)

Lotus® 1-2-3® 97
0-7615-1193-8
$16.99 (Can. $23.95)

SmartSuite® 97
0-7615-1192-X
$16.99 (Can. $23.95)

Windows® 95
1-55958-738-5
$19.95 (Can. $27.95)

Also Available

WordPerfect® 6.1 for Windows
0-7615-0091-X
$16.99 (Can. $23.95)

WordPerfect® 8
0-7615-1083-4
$16.99 (Can. $23.95)

WordPerfect Suite® 8
0-7615-1188-1
$16.99 (Can. $23.95)

Coming Soon

Access 97
0-7615-1363-9
$16.99 (Can. $23.95)

Windows® 98
0-7615-1006-0
$16.99 (Can. $23.95)

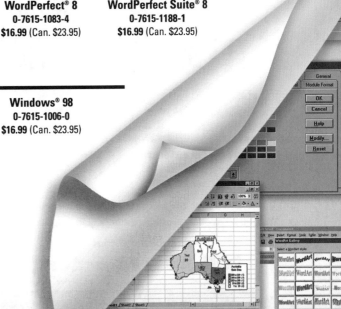

P PRIMA

www.primapublishing.com

Call now to order
(800)632-8676, ext. 4444

Prima Publishing, Visual Learning Guide, and Fast & Easy are trademarks of Prima Communications, Inc. All other product and company names are trademarks of their respective companies.

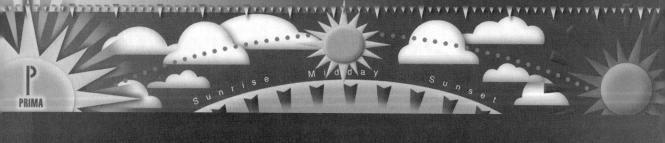

Prima's In a Weekend™ Series

Create Your First Web Page In a Weekend
0-7615-0692-6 • CD-ROM
$24.99 (Can. $34.95)

Jazz Up Your Web Site In a Weekend
0-7615-1137-7 • CD-ROM
$24.99 (Can. $34.95)

Learn Publisher 97 In a Weekend
0-7615-1217-9
$19.99 (Can. $27.95)

Learn HTML In a Weekend
0-7615-1293-4 • CD-ROM
$24.99 (Can. $34.95)

Increase Your Web Traffic In a Weekend
0-7615-1194-6
$19.99 (Can. $27.95)

Also Available
- **Create FrontPage Web Pages In a Weekend**
  0-7615-0743-4 • CD-ROM
  $29.99 (Can. $41.95)
- **Learn Word 97 In a Weekend**
  0-7615-1251-9
  $19.99 (Can. $27.95)

Coming Soon
- Learn Access 97 In a Weekend
- Learn the Internet In a Weekend
- Learn Windows 98 In a Weekend
- Organize Your Finances In a Weekend with Quicken Deluxe 98
- Upgrade Your PC In a Weekend

GOOD NEWS! You can master the skills you need to achieve your goals in just a weekend! Prima Publishing's unique IN A WEEKEND series offers practical fast-track guides dedicated to showing you how to complete your projects in a weekend or less!

www.primapublishing.com

Call now to order (800) 632-8676, ext. 4444

Prima Publishing and In a Weekend are trademarks of Prima Communications, Inc. All other product and company names are trademarks of their respective companies.